Faces of Despotism

Faces of Despotism

ERIC CARLTON

Published by
SCOLAR PRESS
Gower House
Croft Road
Aldershot
Hants GU11 3HR
England

Ashgate Publishing Company
Old Post Road
Brookfield
Vermont 05036
USA

British Library Cataloguing in Publication Data

Carlton, Eric
    Faces of Despotism
    I. Title
    303.3409
    ISBN 1–85928–045–5

Library of Congress Cataloging-in-Publication Data

Carlton, Eric.
    Faces of despotism/Eric Carlton.
        p.   cm.
    Includes bibliographical references and index.
    ISBN 1–85928–045–5
    1. Despotism. 2. Despotism–History. I. Title.
JC375.C37   1995
321'.6–dc20   94–31293 CIP

ISBN 1 85928 045 5

Typeset in 10pt Sabon by Poole Typesetting (Wessex) Ltd, Bournemouth and printed in Great Britain by Hartnolls Ltd, Bodmin

To my wife, who readily concedes that I am
the only despot with whom she
is personally acquainted.

Contents

CHAPTER ONE

Leadership and Autocracy

In an exercise of this kind it is always as well to begin by defining one's terms. Despotism connotes autocracy, and with autocracy, the rule of the one, we are really thinking about the exercise of power. That much seems clear. But what does this imply, and how can such a complex activity be analysed? Power mainly consists of influencing the thinking and/or actions of other people. It is the ability to get others to do what you want despite their possible opposition. Broadly speaking, this may be done either by coercion or persuasion. More subtly, it is the ability to get others to *want to do* what you want them to, hence the incalculable importance of ideology as an instrument of persuasion. It is necessary, of course, to make a distinction between the *agencies* of power – the autocrat, the judicial system, the army the police, and so on – and the actual *modes* whereby this power is effectively exercised. And this, in turn, must be distinguished from the *focus* of that exercise of power, because this may well condition the ways and forms in which it is used.

Usually the exercise of power is relative to particular situations. For example, what does an autocrat do when he is experiencing opposition to his policies and practices? Presumably he invokes sanctions of some kind, but he has to be very careful how this is done. He must decide just how much hostility there is and who exactly is responsible because by an injudicious use of force he could actually make the situation worse. It is therefore important for him to be clear about the mode or method of implementing the sanctions, the point at which they are introduced and – very importantly – the intensity with which they are applied, because too much or too little could prove counter-productive. Furthermore, this exercise of power must be depicted as *legitimate*, especially to the outside world, because authority (legitimized power) can often be much more effective when its operation is also convincing.

Autocrats come to power in a number of ways. Some come through inheritance, as in the case of some of the Roman emperors we shall be discussing such as Caligula and Nero, or through seizing power which is later legitimized, as was the case with their predecessor Augustus (although in this instance there was a power vacuum, and several contenders were vying for position). On the other hand, autocrats may come to power through revolution involving violence and bloodshed. A revolution may be seen as a successful revolt, whereas a rebellion is more of an *intended* revolution that does not succeed. Revolutions can range from palace coups d'état, a common experience for example in Achmaeinid Persia and Ottoman Turkey, to those upheavals which bring a near total transformation of society – the sort of thing we find in modern times in Nazi Germany and Soviet Russia. The autocracies which result from such revolutions may give rise to relatively long-lasting dynasties, as in ancient China, or they may be of disquietingly brief duration because they are followed by further and yet more violent revolutions, as in modern Latin America. So much depends on the nature of the autocrats in question and particularly on the situations which facilitated their bids for power. Much depends too on the nature of the claims of the revolutionary leader; they *have* to be legitimized on some basis or another. Sheer force of arms is not usually enough. There may be some vague and tenuous claim to ancestral rights and inheritance as with the none-too-convincing appeals of Henry Tudor (later Henry VII) in his attempts to secure the English throne. Alternatively, leadership may be based on rather spurious claims to divine ordination and/or charismatic gifts. This has been all too evident where the bid for power was supported by religious validations of a *traditionalist* nature, as with Alexander the Great who claimed a special relationship with Zeus, the greatest of the gods. Or the validations may be of a revolutionary nature such as those made by the militant prophet Mohammed, the founder of Islam.

The incidence of revolution is itself a rather interesting phenomenon, and with it the appearance of the revolutionary leader. Revolutions can be entirely predictable in given sets of circumstances, although sometimes when one would expect them nothing is forthcoming, as in South Africa until the last 30 years or so. In other circumstances they may occur when they are not expected, as in the case of the Suez emergency in 1956 and the advent of the enigmatic Colonel Nasser as the 'strong man' (= despot?) in Egypt. It should also be pointed out that such factors as race, class and gender are not issues here. Autocrats can – and often have – emanated from the so-called lower classes; furthermore, no theoretical distinctions can be made on the basis of race or colour. Even gender is not a disqualifying factor; women can be seen to have been just as ruthless as men when in positions of power. Admittedly, this has not been that often but one has only to think of, say, Olympias of Macedon, or Messalina, the wife of the Roman emperor Claudius, or Aggripina, the mother of Nero, or – perhaps better still – some of the Ptolemaic queens of Egypt to see how unscrupulous some women can be when they have the opportunity. The truth is that all humans can be violent and aggressive in given circumstances.

What then can we say about leadership and the leadership principle? For all practical purposes we can define leadership as the exercise of authority in initiating, directing or controlling the behaviour or attitudes of others.

Whether this is with or without their consent is a moot point. Leadership also implies those qualities of personality (often indefinable) and possibly of training which make that control of others successful. Among animal groups, hierarchies form, usually with the dominant males monopolizing control of the females and their young, and maintaining order among other rival – and perhaps younger – males. Where conflicts over dominance are resolved on a submission basis, the challenger may be 'banished' from the group. Among humans, we find that similar patterns are evident, though in this case much depends upon the *scale* of the groups involved. For instance, among traditional Bushmen groups, the leader, if, indeed, one can meaningfully use that term in this context, was little more than first among equals. Bushmen bands rarely numbered more than 30 or 40, perhaps half of which were children. They wandered from waterhole to waterhole on their periodic itineraries, and the 'chief' or leader was mainly responsible for the ritual tasks involved in directing these migrations. There were no institutions of social control as such, only customs to which the band traditionally adhered. After all, it doesn't take that much to keep a small, struggling group together. This could be contrasted with centralized, tribal societies such as those of the traditional southern Bantu where chieftainship was a widely recognized institution, and the chief had executive authority within the group. Scale required the appropriate institutions whereby authority was sustained and order maintained.

This apparent naturalness of leadership and its ubiquity among humans and higher mammals, begs a number of important questions:

Are leaders born or bred? The customary view was that some people by their very natures are leaders and others are followers. Born leaders were often associated with a particular *class*, as with the old British aristocracy (literally the rule of the best people, from the Greek *aristoi*); or with a special *caste*, as with, say, the Brahmins in traditional Indian society. The view was that such people were somehow uniquely qualified, either by birth and blood or by racial or spiritual endowments, to take control of the lives of others. A related view is that some people possess certain personality traits which again fit them for the role of leaders.

Such ideas are now seriously questioned because:

1. No universal leadership qualities have so far been discovered. All sorts of things have been suggested: intelligence, initiative, an extrovert nature, and so on, but quite apart from the difficulty of defining these terms, studies have shown that although certain *clusters* of characteristics tend to be exhibited by leaders, no single quality can be found that is common to all. Even if we persist in using that much abused term, charisma, we have problems: Hitler had a totally different personality from that of Mahatma Gandhi yet both possessed qualities

that attracted disciples. Charisma is thus often used to 'explain' that which we do not really understand. Similar puzzles relate to the 'relationship' between charisma and modernity. Specifically, we are thinking of charisma and the role of the media, an issue that was naturally not anticipated by Max Weber when he popularized the term. To what extent can charisma be contrived? Are the media instrumental in misleading the public? Are they culpable of creating images simply to be idolized? We know only too well how attraction even to false and fictitious personalities can be manufactured. And what of some of our modern cult heroes? Fame seems to be the primary product of our age. It is created and exploited with all the precision of an exact science. This quite remarkable phenomenon is thus forming everything it touches, and is used to promote everything from political personalities to perfume. What persuades Pepsi-Cola to spend $20 million buying the entertainer Michael Jackson's name – when he doesn't even drink the stuff? And why should Coca-Cola respond by seeking the endorsement of tennis star Boris Becker? The image has become all-important. Personalities have become *endowed* with charisma. Indeed, charisma is now a product – the most valuable and perishable of commodities (Sudic, 1989).

None of this, of course, becomes possible without the gullibility of the public. Thus we can say that:

2. Leaders only emerge in interaction with others. It is self-evident that there can be no leaders without followers. Others make it possible for potential leaders to achieve prominence, either by weakness and submission or by indifference, or – not infrequently – by an unthinking consensus which is only too willing to abide by precedent or the opinions of other people.

3. Leaders are largely 'made' by particular situations. Thus a singular politico-economic situation in Uganda 'produced' Idi Amin, originally a lowly member of the armed forces, who promoted himself to general and went on to make his own terrible reputation as yet another 'father of the people'. The situation needed the man, and the man needed the situation. It is reasonably conclusive from leadership studies carried out in all kinds of social contexts, management, sport, the arts, as well as in politics, that this 'contingency theory' of leadership (Fiedler, 1967), makes a great deal of sense. Similar scenarios are evident in all sorts of other social contexts. Just how leaders acquire or develop these qualities which attract, inspire, mesmerize or simply cow others is not all that easy to explain, but it is invariably true that they can only be manifested in particular situations. How else, for example, can we begin to make sense of the People's Temple Sect led by the would-be modern messiah Jim Jones? He was suspected by the US

authorities of what might be broadly termed incitement to subversion, so he led about a thousand of his people from California to Guyana to found an agricultural commune. His politico-religious rhetoric had attracted the impoverished classes – mainly black and Hispanic families – who regarded him as a dedicated and well-nigh infallible leader whose every edict was inspired. In 1978, when the law was closing in and the end of their utopian aspirations was threatened, the followers obeyed his last command to commit mass suicide. Men, women and children drank a lethal concoction of orange juice and poison, and virtually everyone in the commune died, including Jones himself. All their hopes for a new life away from what they regarded as persecution had now been dashed and they could apparently think of nothing else but to follow their leader in a final, despairing act of sacrifice.

One of the main problems with systems based on charismatic leadership is that of succession (Johnson, 1964: 337). If the movement in question is a new movement and is regarded as a 'cause' or mission, as with, say, early Islam, it will then be characterized by a dynamic ideology, although the details of its actual programme may not have been carefully worked out all the time the leader/founder is present. His vision and inspiration are usually enough. But with the leader's death, his chief lieutenants will have to decide on future arrangements; in particular they will have to codify the 'message', the new truth, and clarify their own statuses in relation to the rank and file of the movement. This sometimes leads to a struggle for power by rival claimants who all feel that they are the rightful successors. Alternatively, there could be some kind of charismatic competition with some candidates claiming to be more worthy than others. In this case it may be thought that there are 'signs' which mark out the appropriate candidate. Suitability may be based on the priestly interpretation of portents and oracles, although it was not unknown for these magical procedures to be 'influenced', as with the famous Greek oracle at Delphi, so that they might conveniently reflect the divine will in favour of an already fancied candidate.

In order to avoid such problems, it has been common for leaders – particularly in established systems – to designate successors, often from their own families, a procedure which validates the succession and, ostensibly, legitimizes the position of the claimant. This at least is the theory. The actuality is often very different, as can easily be seen in the history of the English monarchy, especially during the late Middle Ages when ambitious rivals resorted to war in order to justify their particular claims to the throne. The stakes were high and the risks were great. In the Wars of the Roses, for instance, execution was frequently the price one paid for backing the wrong side.

Before we leave the matter of leaders and their followers, perhaps we should consider the matter of whether or not obedience to leaders should ever be unquestioning. Understandably most would probably respond negatively. We feel instinctively that obedience should not be unquestioning, and that we should always have a chance to consider what it is that we are being asked to do. But is it quite as simple as this? Experience and experiments have shown that it all depends very much on three factors. The first is *who gives the command*. Is their authority regarded as legitimate? Is it an authority that demands respect? In the now well-known Milgram experiments, in which subjects were being tested on their obedience to authority by giving what they believed were electric shocks to unseen 'victims' (Milgram, 1974), commands were given initially by the professor to his students, who felt it was part of their education to act as instructed by their tutor. Second, there is the question of the ostensible *cause or purpose for which the command is given*. In the Milgram experiments commands were ostensibly given in the interests of science; as far as the subjects were aware it was to advance the cause of scientific knowledge. This legitimized procedures which seemed to some to present serious ethical problems. And third, and not least, there are the *circumstances in which the command is given*. The context is all important. With Milgram it was the laboratory which added reinforcement to the idea that these were scientific experiments. This tended to assuage any moral doubts that most students might have about obeying instructions. One can see how such knowledge is particularly valuable to agencies, which by their very nature operate systems that entail a reversal of values – espionage where deception, theft and even assassination are all permissible by the rules of the game. For instance, during the Cold War, the Americans and the Russians frantically sought intelligence about each other's intentions, and when an American U.2 spy-plane was brought down, the pilot, Gary Powers, was put on trial by the Russians. At one point, the prosecutor asked the defendant if he realized that such an incident might have started a war, to which he replied that such considerations were not his responsibility but the responsibility of his superiors. Normal moral attitudes were ruled out by national defence requirements.

So in considering what makes an effective leader, we must ask how he derives his authority and what that authority actually means. Normally, as we have seen, a leader's authority derives from a recognized hereditary principle, from appointment, or from some kind of consensus, possibly by means of an election system. But there are other aspects to leadership which have to be borne in mind by would-be tyrants and despots. A leader's authority need not simply derive from *position*. Being elected or appointed, or whatever, may not be enough; there has to be some kind of vindication. Positions usually involve clear tasks and responsibilities. They connote having to take the blame as well as the credit. And positions can be very precarious where results are at a premium. Lack of success, especially where expectations are high, can be a sure precursor to a not always bloodless takeover, as we shall see when we look at some Latin American dictatorships.

Does a leader's authority derive from the *power to reward and punish*? Our study will show that this was very much the case in a number of traditional African tribal systems where usually only the chief/king had the power to pronounce judgment, particularly in capital cases. Of course to have authority does not necessarily mean to be authoritarian. In fact particularly effective leadership is often found where the power to punish exists but is only used with considerable restraint. This judicious use of power – tempering justice with mercy – is sometimes seen as the hallmark of really great leaders. Julius Caesar prided himself that he possessed such qualities, but when one considers his campaigns in Gaul and Germany and the mass slaughter that they entailed, it would hardly be unjust to say that he was self-deluded.

Sometimes a leader's effectiveness derives from some *special knowledge or expertise*, which can be anything from athletic prowess to military achievement to believed ritual powers. The possession or manifestation of such 'gifts' may be held to signify a certain singularity of status which entitles this particular individual to a considerable degree of respect. So, for example, the special regard given to Mao Tse-tung derived largely from the fact that he was one of the early protagonists of the communist cause, and that he had endured the formidable Long March along with his people – a kind of Marxist Moses who had led his followers to eventual 'freedom'. This 'great man' theory of leadership has had many notable advocates, from Thomas Carlyle to Frederick Adams Wood who, writing earlier in the century about Western leaders from 1000 to 1789 (the French Revolution), maintained that there was a positive correlation between 'strong, mediocre and weak monarchs ... and strong, mediocre and weak periods' (Adams, 1960: 246). He studied some 386 rulers who enjoyed something approaching absolute power in their respective states, and although his argument is persuasive, it is by no means conclusive. The 'great man' argument certainly has some cogency but, as we have noted, the zeitgeist – or spirit of the times – argument that social forces determine the nature of leadership also has strong advocates. Obviously there is something to be said for both sides. In a much more recent study by Suedfeld and Rank on revolutionary leaders (1976), it was found that in the initial phase of the struggle for power, leaders with a single-minded approach to the overthrow of the existing regime could be particularly effective. But once in power, much depended on their ability to accommodate the disparate and sometimes conflicting aspirations of their followers. This hypothesis is supported by much historical evidence (for example, in the case of Mugabe in Zimbabwe), but the opposite could be argued for Stalin, who began his career by being opportunistically flexible in his approach and became more intolerant and indifferent to public opinion as time went on.

According to one set of theories, leadership is best looked at in terms of its functions. The US Army proposed 11 principles of leadership which were reduced to seven possible 'behaviours': performing professional/ technical specialities; knowing subordinates and showing them considera- tion; keeping channels of communication open; accepting personal responsibility and thus setting an example; initiating and directing action; training people as a team; and making decisions (C. Gibb, 1969: 228). Another study, this time of presidential tasks and perceived effectiveness in the US came to what amounts to basically similar conclusions (Wrightsman, 1984). This and other studies (Deaux and Wrightsman, 1984: 389ff) also give general support to the idea of fairness, openness, and so on. Obviously good leaders must be competent and – ideally – must have mastered the skills of their subordinates, or at least possess equivalent skills that can be respected. In other words, they should be able to lead from the front. It is argued that good leaders should *want* to lead, and display the necessary confidence in their abilities to command others. Confidence can be infectious; it requires confidence in order to inspire confidence. Followers need the conviction that achievement is possible. In this way, good leaders are able to motivate others. So many politicians, for example, seem incapable of doing this. It is interesting that Wrightsman (1984) found that modern US presidents were invariably thought less of at the end of their term of office than they had been at the beginning. This is understandable for it could be argued that to want to lead others is really a kind of arrogance, and that people are right to distrust those who presume to act as their moral and political superiors.

Political leaders tend to be of three main types (Sigmund, 1967: 7–8):

1. The *conservative* who wants to preserve the existing order, something that was not too difficult in traditional societies, although even here leaders might sometimes be called upon by the public to make certain reforms. There is the notable and not entirely uncommon case of Solon the law-giver in sixth-century Athens whose social reforms were primarily aimed at reducing tension between the classes. In the end he pleased no one, including those he was most trying to help. In more recent times, the conservative is typically the kind of leader that clings to the status quo despite a growing clamour for change. This he may justify in terms of stability and order, or of religion, or simply by an appeal to old-fashioned nationalism.

2. The *radical* who wants to institute revolutionary change. This change may begin with an actual or simulated crisis which is inflated to justify a takeover. It is then usually 'explained' by stressing the inadequacy of the old order to meet the needs of the people and mediated in terms of a new or revitalized ideology. In extreme cases, the changes are only accomplished by violence and the proscriptions of political enemies, as in Russia under Lenin, or by mass executions of the potentially subversive intelligentsia, as with the Khmer Rouge in Cambodia under Pol Pot.

3. The *progressive* who wants to stop short of any radical trans-formation. This kind of moderate is represented by many 'new nation' leaders, of whom Nehru in India and Mugabe in Zimbabwe would be fairly typical examples. These try – with varying success – to reconcile the need for change with the desire to preserve important cultural values.

But how does all this apply to despotism? How many autocratic rulers have recognized these ideals? By its very nature despotism is without constraint and tends to ignore such principles and ideal functions, and even when they are taken into consideration they are applied selectively and arbitrarily. Despots are not open; they do not normally share decision-making, nor are they likely to have very much consideration for others. They are often all too competent in their own ways and, in many cases, are able to inspire hope and confidence in others. This may even extend to their close followers who – contrary to common expectation – are often the most difficult to convince. Complementarily, there have been regimes where the leader has assumed a near-messianic persona and is trusted by the people even though his associates are the objects of some suspicion, as with the continued public adulation of Hitler when Germany was in serious difficulties in World War II. It was a form of cognitive dissonance; the people persuaded themselves that regardless of the failings of others, the Führer could do no wrong, even when the war was as good as lost.

Leadership and despotism are therefore obviously not the same thing. Leadership is the more inclusive term, and can encompass a range of behaviours of which despotism is but one type. But it complicates matters when we find that there are different kinds of despotism, as we shall see from the following discussion. The situation becomes even more blurred when we think of non-despotic leaders who decline into despotism like Oliver Cromwell, and potentially despotic leaders who initially do not display their despotism, such as Caligula in Rome, and compare these with the more unusual cases of despots who become respectable, such as the Roman emperor Augustus. But before we consider these different types of despotism, we must look briefly at despotism per se.

CHAPTER TWO

Despotism, Tyranny and Totalitarianism

Despotism has to be distinguished from other terms with which it is often used synonymously in everyday speech. Autocracy is the umbrella term which covers despotism, tyranny and in some cases totalitarianism, can be roughly equated with our modern term dictatorship. Despot (Greek *despotēs*) relates to someone who resorts to arbitrary rule; despotism therefore denotes a *style* or *mode* of leadership. Tyranny (tyrant = Greek *tyrannos*) on the other hand, concerns the process of seizing and holding power unconstitutionally. It is a term that especially relates to the ancient Greek city-states (*poleis*) where populist leaders often appropriated power and ruled without formal sanctions. This might well involve violence and dictatorial government, but this was not necessarily the case even though it is implied in our modern use of the word. Totalitarianism, on the other hand, relates to the type of polity, and implies that no other parties or political loyalties will be tolerated. It is arguable, as we shall see, whether the term totalitarian can be strictly applied to societies other than modern technological societies as only they have the means to make true totalitarianism possible (Friedrich and Brzezinski, 1965). This is somewhat like the complementary thesis which contends that democracy too flourishes where there is a high level of economic development. In advanced, literate societies, people expect to be able to participate in the political process because these societies usually have the degree of political stability that makes such participation possible and probably also a large, commercially active middle class that has a substantial stake in the system and is reluctant to endure political upheavals of any kind. Interestingly, it was just this class that provided the primary support for the Nazi regime in Germany in the 1930s. Totalitarianism is obviously best served where there are few institutional curbs on the power of the state and where there is no strong tradition of dissent. It also thrives where there is little access to information and where there is strict media control. Any kind of diffusion of power or unrestrained exchange of ideas is patently anathema to autocratic systems.

Having briefly defined our terms, we shall now look in more detail at the bases and agencies of autocratic power, and then consider the contrasting cases of dictatorship in Stalinist Russia and Nazi Germany.

The means whereby any individual gains ascendancy over others is seemingly simple. He may use force or some other slightly more subtle form of coercion such as bribery. Or he may trick others into compliance by convincing them that their interests and his are basically the same and that they can only gain by acceding to his rule. What is not so simple is just how he is able to muster sufficient force in the first place, or how he manages to con others against what may soon be their better judgment. Usually it is the bold and conscienceless who succeed, but it is not invariably the strong that govern the weak or the dishonest who exploit the honest. As we have noted, much will depend upon a combination of factors, not least of which is the particular context in which this kind of all-too-frequent drama is played out (Lapiere, 1954: 387). Furthermore, the would-be autocrat must have some means whereby he can maintain surveillance over those he controls or at least ensure that he is continually appraised of their actions. And perhaps most important of all, having gained power he must determine just how he is going to *keep* it and possibly pass it on to his appointed successors. Like military conquerors, autocrats take what they can get, but only keep what they can hold. Intimidation of one kind or another often has a limited effect in that it gradually generates a seething resentment on the part of the oppressed who will come to value their rights even more, no matter how limited those rights may be. The autocrat who relies exclusively on force will naturally only survive as long as he has the military and/or the police on his side, and this really means as long as he has the wherewithal to pay them. When these desert him, as with the late Shah of Persia (Iran), there is little to do but flee, or face the firing squad as with the Ceaucescus of Romania.

The military and the police, then, are the main agencies of intimidation. Despots rely on extensive networks of agents to provide invaluable intelligence about dissent and subversion. A special 'security police', such as the KGB and its predecessors in Russia and the SD/Gestapo in Germany, are required to inspire the requisite degree of terror and where necessary to punish the offenders. It pays enormous dividends if the security police are ideologically committed to the regime, but if there are residual doubts the intimidators can themselves be intimidated and even liquidated as in Stalinist Russia. As agencies of intimidation, the military and the police are dependent for their continued existence on a political sponsor or sponsors, usually the autocrat. In the East German Communist regime, it was Erich Honecker, although unlike the East German case where the autocrat is deposed, these agencies may survive to serve a new master. Such highly bureaucratized systems of state security are often characterized by subtle degrees of venality which tend to impair their efficiency because organizational goals become vitiated by the temptation for personal gain. Corruption of various kinds is endemic to the system and not unknown even where there is strong ideological commitment.

Autocratic requirements are typically transmitted by a system of administrative fiat. Orders are given with the expectation of unquestioning
obedience and because these orders are enforceable there is generated in the
subordinates a habit of uncritical compliance, indeed one of submission and
servility. Servants of the system take this as normal, and carry out
instructions without serious reflection. Thus the purpose of such orders,
say, the carrying out of executions of innocent hostages – so common with
oppressive regimes in wartime – come to be accepted as necessary, even
routine. It is the ends not the means that matter. This habituation to
unthinking obedience is particularly evident where the autocrat is regarded
as irreplaceable or, better still, if he is endowed with a superhuman degree
of infallibility, as with the divine rulers of ancient China and Japan, for
instance. But where these ideological supports barely exist, there is usually
the power available to demoralize and to crush resistance.

But in no case does power last indefinitely, and where there is a waning
of authority there will also be some dilution of autocratic orders as they
are passed down from echelon to echelon in the command structure. Or
there may be a process of attrition in which the orders may be 'redirected'
or actually disregarded. This happened in Germany in the very last days of
the Third Reich when Albert Speer ignored Hitler's order to destroy the
country's industrial resources before the advancing Allies could capture
them. He knew that somehow Germany must survive even if the Third
Reich didn't. As a last resort, the needs of the system or organization may
require the termination of the despot, as was attempted by the German
generals in the bomb plot of July 1944. Hitler survived this attempt on his
life, as we know too well, and wreaked a terrible revenge on the perpetrators. But even if he had been killed there is no guarantee that things
would have changed that much. Not unusually in such circumstances they
continue in a slightly different guise; someone from the old hierarchy takes
over. In this particular case, we have no reason to suppose that the intention of the generals was to transform Germany into a radical democracy
overnight, rather it was to rid themselves of a particularly obnoxious and
destructive dictator – and hopefully save themselves in the process.

If we can safely assume that survival is the main goal of the vast
majority of people, we can probably make the further assumption that the
power to take life is the most effective form of intimidation. There will
always be exceptions, of course, but people usually respond to force, so the
ability to bestow life or death, often inconsistently, must constitute one of
the principal bases of an effective despotism. When the ruler is the ultimate
arbiter, the final court of appeal, autocracy is complete. No state willingly
allows independent forces to operate within its borders, and certainly no
despot is going to tolerate any rival sources of power. Force, or the threat
of force, is one foundation of sovereignty. As Thomas Hobbes put it,

'Covenants without swords are but words' (quoted by Lenski, 1966: 50). And where such systems are overthrown, as we shall see, they are often replaced by other systems which are frequently even more repressive. This change of mandate will either be formally institutionalized under an impersonal bureaucracy or focused on a new leader. The rule of might has become transformed into the rule of right (Lenski, 1966: 56–58).

In order to illustrate just how these conflicting forces manifest themselves in historical systems, we could compare their theoretical components with their operation in actual societies. First of all, however, we should note that there are four main ways (with variants) in which comparisons can be made:

1. By analysing a particular phenomenon in a single unit of society, that is by breaking down the phenomenon in question by intra-social analysis. For instance, in studies of crime or some specific form of crime, the incidence could be looked at in terms of region, class/age/race of the victim(s)/suspect(s), and so on. This method is similar in many ways to that used by Emile Durkheim in his famous work on suicide.

2. By analysing a particular phenomenon which exists in various forms in societies of a *similar* nature. What is broadly called fascism could be examined in its different guises in Spain/Italy/Germany in the 1930s. Or by analysing a phenomenon which does *not* exist in similar societies, or perhaps is very imperfectly developed in those societies, say totalitarianism in the 1930s. Why, for example, did it flourish in Italy and Spain, but did not really get underway in England and France?

3. By analysing specific institutions and/or practices in different situations in

    (i)   separate societies of different types, say witchcraft in nineteenth-century Africa and seventeenth-century Europe, and
    (ii) in the same societies at different periods, say religious beliefs and practices in Britain in medieval and modern times.

4. By analysing the ubiquitous facts of social existence such as marriage and the family, economic organization, and so on, and correlating these with their various forms in different social circumstances.

Useful as these guidelines are, there are a number of qualifications that can be made regarding the comparative method, and these should be borne in mind as we look at various kinds of despotism in more detail. To begin with, *classification* presents problems because we are not always sure just how to categorize the phenomena in question. When, for instance, is a society to be designated 'pre-industrial' when certain forms of rudimentary industry existed in early societies – for example, shield-making factories in ancient Athens? When is a society to be seen as medieval when scholars are in dispute as to when the 'middle ages' – whatever is meant by that term – really began? Or again, when is a society to be labelled 'capitalist'? Can we say that it is when there is capital accumulation, banking and investment, and so on, when these are also to be found in some traditional, theoretically *non*-capitalist systems? All this raises the related question of *terminology*. What terms are the most precise, or better still appropriate, for our purposes? Structure, function and differentiation do not always mean the same things to professionals and aficionados. So they can certainly be a source of confusion to the layman. Similarly, there is the not inconsequential matter of *contextual definitions*. Such terms as 'Underclass', 'deprivation' and the like, for instance, vary with social situations. The actual historical circumstances are critical for the understanding of any situation. For example, it is imprecise to designate societies other than traditional India as 'caste' societies. They may have rigid class divisions, but the term 'caste' has a very strict, historically limited meaning that should not be applied haphazardly. Important too is the appreciation of the relevant economic and political factors which are likely to influence the perspectives of any particular actor. *Operational concepts* may indeed be culture-bound and therefore affect the whole question of impartiality, although it is difficult to see how this can be completely avoided. *The units of study* also present problems. It is particularly vital not to confuse comparable and non-comparable, not to equate same with similar. For example, if we wished to examine slavery in classical society, it would be a mistake to think that slavery in Greece was the same as that in Rome. It was similar in time but not in type. Furthermore, are we to concentrate on structures, institutions, roles or practices? If we are ambitious and opt for macro studies, our conclusions are liable to be ultimately unsatisfactory because they may have to be pitched at such a high level of generality that specific meanings tend to get lost. It goes without saying that at the quantitative and qualitative levels research and the sources for research can be open to bias and misinterpretation. This means that we must also avoid the danger of choosing subjects or material that appear to confirm our preconceptions. It is better to take the weaker case and extrapolate to the stronger on an 'if A, how much more B' basis, than settle on the best case we can find.

There is a limit to the kinds of methods that social and political scientists can employ, especially in relation to historical materials. This is one reason why they have a particular preference for using models in their investigations. It can be quite instructive to compare a model which is really just a simplification of reality with the reality itself. Models are 'used' by comparing the mental construct with the actual courses of events.

Of course this sort of methodological device is open to all sorts of criticisms and qualifications, but it does help to indicate the difference between the 'pure type' (the model) and the actuality in the real world. Such pure types are not average types or representative types, and are certainly not basic or original types. In our study of despotism, we must not even confuse a pure type with an extreme instance of the case, say, Nazism as a form of fascism. A pure type is only pure in the sense that it corresponds to an idea and as such is simply a tool which may possibly help us in our analysis of social phenomena.

A particularly good example of the use of models can be found in a study of totalitarianism – something very close to our concerns – as exemplified by Soviet communism and German Nazism (Friedrich and Brezezinski, 1965). Here the typical characteristics of totalitarianism are identified as:

1. *An official ideology*: This is a body of doctrine to which all members of the society are supposed to adhere, passively if not actively. Non-belief or open rejection, however this is manifested, is a punishable offence. The ideology is characteristically focused towards some final (perfect?) end-state of mankind (the Thousand-Year Reich, the class-less society, or whatever), and is based upon a radical rejection of the existing society and the imposition of a new, totalizing regime. This chiliastic claim is utopian in emphasis, has strong quasi-religious, eschatological overtones, and is operationalized in quite specific ways. Not every totalizing system is totalitarian in this sense. Roman Catholicism has practised ideological thought control for much of its history, and various Protestant sects have been chiliastic in intention (for example, the Fifth Monarchists of the post-Reformation period). But these characteristics *taken alone* are not held to constitute totalitarianism.

2. *A single mass party*: This is typically led by an autocrat – the dictator – no matter what the formal arrangements are supposed to be for oligarchic control; for example, Stalin and the Supreme Soviet. A relatively small percentage of the population will actually be members of the Party (perhaps no more than 10 per cent), and these will con-stitute the ultimately dependable core of the system. The Party will be hierarchically organized, and may either be superior to or intertwined with the bureaucratic machine. For instance, in Nazi Germany the practice was to have a 'leaven' of Party members at every level of government organization. This Party interiorized bureaucracy is seen to have the technical advantages of economy, loyalty and precision. Impartial, objective considerations are said to give it an impersonal efficiency. But the more it succeeds in eliminating the personal,

emotional and irrational elements from official affairs, the more de-humanized it becomes.

3. *A system of terroristic police control:* Some form of state security force will exist to support and supervise the Party for its leaders. Its activities will be directed against demonstrable 'enemies' of the regime, including arbitrarily selected groups within the population: Jews, gypsies and communists particularly in Nazi Germany, and 'profiteers' and chosen categories within the intelligentsia in Stalinist Russia. In modern states, these security agencies will typically make use of up-to-date scientific methods in the pursuit of their goals, especially psychochemical techniques of interrogation.

4. *Communications control:* A technologically conditioned monopoly or near monopoly of control by the Party of all the mass media. It is notable that in many coups d'état, almost the first thing the insurgents do is to seize control of the mass media so that all intelligence that is communicated both within the state and to the outside world is that which accords with the interests of the new regime.

5. *Weapons control:* This entails a monopoly of all means of effective armed combat. Admittedly in a country such as the US weapons control is not complete; the Fourth Amendment gives every citizen the right to bear arms, something that is said to be symbolic of their freedom, so there is a proliferation of handguns, sporting rifles and the like for sale for ostensibly legitimate purposes. But understandably, it does not give citizens the right to bear tanks, warplanes and nuclear weapons. The citizen as an individual is defenceless against what must remain the overwhelming technological superiority of the state. The corollary of this is that Popular Front movements usually have to be supplied with weapons by outside powers if they are to be at all effective. This has been most evident where relatively small revolu-tionary groups have been armed by sympathetic governments, as with Iran and the Lebanese, the US and the Contra guerrillas, and China and the Khmer Rouge in Cambodia.

6. *Centralized economy:* This entails the control and direction of the entire economy through the bureaucratic machine. This control extends to most, if not all, other associations and groups (including unions) that might present any potential opposition or resistance to the regime.

Totalitarianism is said to develop in the context of mass democracy. This may sound strange, but the point is being made that totalitarian systems have claimed to be democratic, for instance National *Socialism* and the Union of Soviet *Socialist* Republics. Furthermore, they often arise out of democratic situations, that is, where there is a breakdown of democratic structures, as with the tyranny that often replaced democracy in many ancient Greek states.

Many of these model features can of course be found in non-totalitarian states, particularly weapons control and, with some qualifications, a centralized economy as well. Others, such as communications control, can be found in pre-industrial as well as industrialized societies, though again with serious qualifications. The governments of early societies could often control the dissemination of information, but they could also be the victims of poor communications networks; an insurrection could take place in outlying areas and it might be weeks before the central government even heard about it, let alone dealt with it – a situation which faced ancient Rome, Achmaenid Persia, and the Mongol empire.

Friedrich and Brezezinski argue that no historical autocracies exhibited this combination of features, and that totalitarianism, in the sense in which it is typified, is by definition rooted in modern technology as this alone facilitates *complete control* of the state. Only where every facet of the state and its economy are harnessed to the needs of the regime is there really total control.

Models are models, and any model is legitimate. It can be neither true nor false, only useful or not so useful as the case may be. And interesting as this model is, it does present some problems concerning totalitarianism *as a type*. Can there in fact, be a typical totalitarianism? As we shall see from our case studies, it is all too evident that totalitarianisms vary considerably in practice. Can we, for example, equate Mussolini's Italy with Franco's Spain? The circumstances of their inception and development and even character were quite different. Or what of Italy and its Axis partner Nazi Germany? Again, they are very different in many important respects. Their constitutions differed, the Italians retained a monarchy which had certain clearly defined powers, and also a powerful religious organization which exerted considerable influence over public opinion. In the actual practice of totalitarianism, they also differed significantly over the question of race. The Italians practised a form of racism in some of their African colonies (Mack Smith, 1979), but this was not the expression of some carefully worked out racial philosophy. Italy had no fanatical race theory, certainly not with regard to the Jews. There were no proscriptions until 1938 when the Nazi influence was beginning to bear fruit, and there were no actual deportations to the death camps until the Germans took over in Italy in 1943.

Whether any of these forms of fascist regime, particularly that of Nazi Germany, can be sensibly compared with that of Stalinist Russia remains problematic. To begin with, there is a difference in the *direction of the appeal*. The Nazis directed their message to all levels of society, but it had most appeal to the middle classes and the industrialists who felt most threatened by the volatile political and depressed economic situation that existed before the Nazis came to power. Hitler's promises of rearmament and a resuscitated Germany also had a considerable attraction for the professional military elite. In the aftermath of World War I, the military, though not necessarily thirsting for revenge, were still smarting from the humiliations of defeat and the impositions and restrictions of the Treaty of Versailles. By contrast, the communist appeal was directly to the proletariat. Not that Stalin personally went directly to the masses as Hitler did, he was more of a committee man who made his way by stealth and deviousness.

What we are really asking is, how are the people to be won? Is it to be an appeal to national or party tradition or is it to be a more cynical appeal to material benefits? And how is power to be maintained? By some kind of rapprochement with the army, with industry, with commercial interests, or religious organizations or by coercion? In autocracies, there is usually an appeal for loyalty to the leader and to his infallible judgment. Charisma is important, but it is mediated in different ways. The Stalin/Hitler image was mediated through a hierarchy of power, whereas the Mao/Castro image was mediated directly to the people, as a form of populism. When this is done, it makes usurpation more difficult, and certainly more difficult to justify. It is also argued that despots/dictators have to justify their policies and be able to mobilize support from both their immediate subordinates and the people in general (Eisenstadt, 1967). Obvious as this is, it too is subject to qualification. We shall see that Caligula (Gaius) who was Princeps (= emperor?) of Rome during the early Empire did not justify some of his most infamous acts. But then his reign was mercifully short – his own guard saw to that.

Furthermore, the *goal-orientation of each varied*. We can surely distinguish them on the basis of their long- and short-term objectives. Nazism was an elitist ideology which implied eventual global domination by conquest. (If the Axis powers had won World War II, it is interesting to conjecture whether Hitler could have lived with Japan's Hirohito in the long term. Could they have reconciled their interests; could they have shared the world to their mutual satisfaction?) By contrast, Russian communism had long-term revolutionary aims. Its intention was to exacerbate the contradictions of capitalism, to win by 'evangelism', infiltration, and the indirect advantages of local, Popular-Front wars to which it gave its support.

All totalitarianisms have the *problem of establishment and maintenance*. And on this point we should note that the conditions which facilitate the emergence of totalitarian systems may not be the same as those which aid the consolidation of power of those systems. This, in turn, raises the issue of the *degree* and the *extent* of control. In which terms is totalitarianism to be defined? If it is by extent, then it is worth bearing in mind that the larger the area to be controlled the greater the possibility of revolutionary and subversive action. When the Nazis reached their greatest extent of power in 1942, they had incalculable problems with partisans in Yugoslavia, Crete, Greece, Russia and so on, and this was accompanied by questionings among the German military hierarchy itself. This point has been made forcibly by Karl Wittfogel who has argued that there comes a stage in expansionist regimes when it becomes increasingly less profitable to conquer more and more. Wittfogel calls this the law of diminishing administrative returns (Wittfogel, 1957). The more you take, the more you have to hold, and the wider the expansion the more bad friends you make – something the Romans found to their cost (Carlton, 1992).

Alternatively we could define totalitarianism in terms not of extent but of degree of control. Here we again observe that scale is an important factor. Small-scale societies can experience greater *intensity* of control than their larger and more complex counterparts. This is especially notable in pre-industrial societies, though not exclusively so. For this we have only to look, say, at modern Haiti or Zanzibar, or – as we shall see from our studies – the totalizing nature of such organizations as the Mafia, where infringements of the basic values of the group can invoke the sanction of amorta. Much therefore turns on the question of definitions. Should one put the stress on the *phenomenological aspects* of totalitarianism, emphasizing its positive features, its technology, its arsenals and so on, or would it be better to concentrate on its *essential nature*, what it really is, its internal dynamic, its ideological imperatives? This is a central issue – perhaps *the* central issue. Is the ideology a dependent variable, subject to the politico-economic realities of actual situations, or is it an independent variable which may not determine situations but does interiorize affairs and actually influence what takes place? Does ideology shape the system, or does it merely provide a justification for goals which are sought for alternative reasons such as power, wealth and status?

The Friedrich and Brzezinski thesis is only partly supported by the later work of Maurice Latey (1972) who contends that 'totalitarian' should be reserved for any state that demands total service from its citizens. This would therefore apply to those relatively small societies where control can be more easily exercised. Such states, he admits, would not necessarily be governed by an 'absolute ruler' or despot (in his terms, a 'tyrant'). Using this kind of analysis, a democracy – if such it can be called – such as ancient Athens would have to be regarded as totalitarian, whereas its constitution and social policies actually defy any simple definition. Similarly Sparta too becomes 'the most totalitarian state of antiquity' but, here again, its constitution requires a much more careful analysis than this. Indeed, its longevity was almost certainly due not just to its formidable army, but also to the nature of its many-faceted constitution. For Latey, a despot ('tyrant') is someone who exercises arbitrary power beyond the scope permitted by the laws, customs and standards of his time. He maintains that this restricts the field by setting the 'tyrant' against some kind of constitutional background. Initially, this sounds plausible enough, but it presents us with four problems: firstly, what *are* the standards of any particular time? These often varied from state to state as in many ways they still do. Secondly, absolute rulers/despots/dictators or – if we prefer the term – tyrants, have a tendency to ignore rules they don't like or to change them *legally* if it suits their purposes, as Hitler did in Germany. Thirdly, it means that they can *only* be judged against the standards of their time. By de-limiting the boundaries in this way, we can legitimately excuse some of the worst offenders in history, a course that leads to uninhibited relativism.

Lastly, the use of the term 'absolute ruler' is a complicating factor. In Republican Rome, for example, it was not unusual to give the power of dictator (imperium) to one man in special circumstances, often times of national emergency. But technically it was a temporary affair, normally lasting only six months. In theory a person could be impeached for any abuse of power once his period in office was over, though, needless to say, there were abuses which had disastrous consequences especially in the last days of the Republic. A similar system existed in Britain during the Roman invasion of the first century, when the tribal leader Caratacus was given super-tribal authority to counter the Roman threat. This was a precedent set by other Celtic princes: Cassivellaunus against Caesar in the previous century, and Vercingetorix on a much greater scale in Gaul. The term 'absolute ruler' can therefore be misleading and relative to particular situations. It does denote a kind of despotism that may be exercised in a totalitarian way, but a despotism that was usually circumscribed by traditional safeguards.

Hannah Arendt (1958) has argued that totalitarianism is really a flight from reality. Is this so, or is it actually the imposition of a new reality? Totalitarian systems often claim to 'see' what the world is really like, perhaps as the conflict of Superior and Inferior with survival as a law of nature, or as the scene of an ongoing class struggle. What may be closer to the truth is that totalitarianism is the *re*-imposition of an old reality; an atavistic tendency to try to trace the roots back to certain desired origins, to primitive equality, or to Teutonic values. (It is interesting that the 50 departments of the Ahnenarbe, the SS research organization under SS Col. Seivers which was concerned with this very issue, cost more to run than the Allies' 'Manhattan Project', the construction of the first Atom bomb.) Putting the ideology into operation therefore becomes a mission, an historical task: to rid the world of Jews, or privilege or whatever. Thus the ends are seen to justify implementation by the most unthinkable means.

Alexander – One Man's Despotism

It really goes without saying that by definition despots are usually ruthless and often cruel. But we cannot dismiss them as simply as that. They are also enigmatic characters who are not easy to assess, with many-faceted personalities that are not simple to fathom. Contrary to popular impression, their policies and practices are not always characterized by overwhelming ambition to the exclusion of everything else. It might therefore be instructive to look at some of the common features of 'typical' despots and despotism to show something of their kaleidoscopic subtleties and variations. We can see this in the personality and experience of just one man – Alexander, commonly called the Great, though with occasional allusions to others, and cautiously extrapolate from this single example to despots and despotism in general.

In broad terms, we can say that despots tend:

1. *To be ruthlessly opportunistic.* This applies not only to the implementation of their plans for the maintenance of power, but all too frequently to the expansion of that power by military conquests. It can also mean the exploitation of relationships and situations for their own purposes. The evidence suggests that in seeking the throne Alexander was quick to take advantage of the unabated pique of a rejected homosexual lover of his father, Philip II of Macedon, and encouraged him to murder Philip in circumstances that would then ensure that the assassin was also killed by the king's bodyguard – a neat and tidy plot without any obviously incriminating loose ends. In this he was aided and abetted by his mother, Olympias, a particularly scheming and vindictive woman, who also helped her son to dispose of his closest rivals for the throne, even to the extent (not included in the original plan) of killing her unlamented husband's latest wife and her infant children in horrendous circumstances.

2. *To be inordinately revengeful.* Alexander never forgot a slight or an insult. He would nurse grievances for years, and pay back the culprit no matter how long it took. A case in point was that of one of his most able generals, Parmenio, who had also been one of his father's most reliable officers. Parmenio would often point out the young king's errors of judgment and hint at his political and military immaturity; for example, in the dispute over the correct military tactics to adopt at Granicus, the first great trial of strength with the Persian

army en route to Alexander's conquest of 'Asia'. The evidence, which is very ambiguous, suggests that against advice Alexander made an unwise and impetuous initial attack on the Persian forces which failed. The next day, however, he succeeded by following Parmenio's alternative plan. The actual accounts of the battle give every appearance of having been doctored and conflated so as to disguise the failure (Green, 1991: Appendix 489–512). After this Parmenio was given some of the most unpalatable military tasks in the campaign, and it is not entirely surprising to find that some time later both Parmenio and his son were executed, purportedly for plotting treason. One wonders if the king's vengefulness had found a welcome occasion to be rid of someone who had tainted his image.

3. *To be violently opposed to criticism.* This underpins our previous point. The despot becomes impatient with any form of obstacle or any kind of frustration. He may well be prepared to listen to advice, but will rarely entertain any kind of serious disagreement. Macedonian kings traditionally saw themselves as those who were first among equals. Their power derived not only from royal birth, but also from acceptance from their nobles and military 'companions'. Philip II had never really seen himself as any more than this. Alexander, on the other hand, after his notable conquests in Persia, began to harbour ideas of personal divinity. He was recognized as divine, a new pharaoh in Egypt, and even made special journeys to Libya (Siwah) and Gordion, the 'gateway to Asia', to confirm his suspicions. After his conquest of Persia he began to assume the manners and attire of the typical oriental despot, something completely alien to his once trusted subordinates. The ultimate indignity came when he insisted that they honour him by the practice of proskynesis, a Persian salutation that was akin to the obeisance of an inferior to a supreme, godlike monarch. This was too much, especially for his friends, and when during a drunken quarrel one of them, Cleitus (the Black) mocked Alexander's divine pretensions, the king grabbed a spear and killed him. It is true that when his fury had died down he was filled with remorse and reputedly hid himself away for three days. But regretful as he was that he had murdered a friend, that friend had been guilty of lese-majesty. His death could therefore be seen as just in the circumstances because technically the king could do not wrong.

4. *To regard expediency as more important than morality.* The will of the despot and the realization of his wishes are paramount. Alexander wanted to be recognized by the conquered Persian nobility as a worthy successor to the defeated Great King, but he waited in vain for official religious confirmation of his de facto overlordship. Subsequently, and hardly coincidentally, the Persian holy city of Persepolis was put to the

torch and its magnificent buildings burned and the treasuries ransacked. Alexander authorized his men to kill any adult males on sight (in fact, no prisoners were taken because they would fetch so little money). There were even incidents where the troops actually killed one another in their frenzy to grab as much of the loot as possible. Irreplaceable art treasures were either plundered or smashed as acts of wanton vandalism. The fire, in particular, has been largely excused by some writers as the tragic and accidental outcome of one of Alexander's drunken revels, but it may well have been a calculated act of revenge for his rejection by those who were by right of conquest now his own subjects. It is difficult to find any extenuating circumstances to justify the violence and the orgy of destruction wrought by these hordes of 'civilized' Greeks.

5. *To act in an arbitrary manner.* The actions of despots are frequently unpredictable. One of Alexander's great strengths as a military commander was that he often did the unexpected. Though not faultless, his tactics in battle, and especially his careful preparations *before* battle, often confounded his enemies, and have been the subject of study by military experts ever since. But this unpredictability showed itself in other ways as well. He could be both extremely cruel and unexpectedly magnanimous. When he captured the Great King's family, they were apparently given every courtesy. Even when after defeat the Great King himself was unceremoniously shackled and then murdered by his own subordinates, Alexander treated the body of his old adversary with considerable respect. Yet when as a preliminary to his final engagement with the Persians he decided to subdue their dependencies on the Lebanese-Palestine coast (largely to neutralize Persian-Phoenician naval power) it was a different matter. Sidon quickly surrendered, but those cities that tried to hold out, particularly Tyre and then Gaza, were absolutely devastated by Alexander's troops. In Tyre, a city that infuriated Alexander because it had taken so much time to capture, some 7,000 people were butchered and 30,000, mainly women and children, were sold into slavery. And just to show his respect for the troops that had resisted his efforts, he had 2,000 military age males taken and crucified. At Gaza it was a similar story. Here, instead of treating his main adversary, Batis, with some degree of clemency, he had him whipped, and then – possibly in imitation of his hero Achilles' treatment of Hector outside the city of Troy – had him lashed to a chariot and dragged round the walls of the city until he died. These were not just straightforward acts of military expediency, but terroristic acts of gratuitous cruelty.

6. *To be 'conveniently' self-deceived.* This does not contradict what has already been said. Despots often have perceptual blind-spots which, in their own way, contribute to their style of government. Alexander, for instance, was extremely discomforted when someone referred to him as a 'tyrant'. He obviously did not see himself that way at all. He regarded himself as a leader, a unifier of the Greeks, a supreme military commander, and finally as an oriental monarch. And, in different ways, he was all of these things. But, more questionably, he also saw himself as a devout servant of the gods, as a patron of the arts and a promoter of popular culture, though others might argue that he was little more than a gifted and opportunistic philistine.

7. *To be most dangerous to their immediate subordinates.* This is generally true – witness the cases of Stalin and, to a much lesser extent, Hitler. Subordinates are much more likely to detect the weaknesses of a despot and exploit them, and they are also in a much better position to effect a successful coup if required. But by the same token they are so close to the despot that their machinations are more likely to be detected or betrayed. If they become persona non grata for whatever reason, the ruler can more easily engineer plots against them, as was perhaps the case with Parmenio and his son, Philotas. Subordinates too are usually people with considerable responsibility and can therefore always be conveniently blamed for 'failure', not least for the failures of the despot himself – a not uncommon feature of Hitler and his generals.

The despot's entourage, then, was not always safe, but this is by no means always the case. Some despots maintain a quite remarkable devotion to those who are loyal to them (note Hitler's almost untiring support for an increasingly dissolute and inefficient Goering). By and large, it is still the ordinary people who suffer most at the hands of despots. Alexander could sometimes be moved by suffering, but the lives of his troops and certainly the lives of the conquered really meant little to him in the pursuit of his imperialist goals.

8. *To have keenly focused ambitions.* This follows from the previous point. Despots often have a furrowed mentality that concentrates on some specific goal or purpose. In Alexander's case it was not just the subjugation of the Greek states or even the conquest of the Persian empire with all its fabled riches. Alexander does not seem to have wanted wealth for its own sake. The wealth that he pillaged from the Persians was simply useful to finance further operations. It paid for new levies of troops, for new equipment, and, not least, for generous bribes to those who had to be kept sweet – at least for the time being. His real ambition was to conquer – perhaps even to conquer the world, the world that he didn't know but about which he had an

abiding curiosity. Thus he cajoled his troops to venture beyond Persia's outermost eastern satrapies (administrative districts) and on into India, where despite some success he had to turn back for fear of a mutiny among his forces. It wasn't that he was braver than his troops. He shared their privations and at times displayed an almost foolhardy courage in battle. It was that his motivation was very different from theirs. He was gripped by the obsession that the Greeks called *pothos*, a kind of insatiable yearning that remained permanently unsatisfied. He was never contented for long. Shortly before he died, it is said that he had plans to move west, perhaps to challenge the burgeoning power of Carthage on the North African coast.

In view of his record it is probably a mercy that Alexander died when he did. As it was, his conquered territories were divided up into barely manageable sub-empires by his almost equally ambitious generals. They squabbled and fought among themselves, though unlike Alexander they hardly pined for new worlds to conquer. They had enough trouble holding on to what they'd got.

9. *To tend to generate contradictory re-evaluations*. How are we to assess the contributions that despots have made to history? As a very general rule, as we shall see, they end up with a disastrous debit balance. What precisely do we make of them? (And are we all potential despots given the right situation and the right opportunity?)

How, for example, can we 'explain' Alexander? So many interpretations have been given, of both a revisionist and anti-revisionist kind. Can we, for instance, see his despotism in terms of relative deprivation? Hardly. It is true that he went through some difficult times as a youth, but he knew nothing of the early poverty of, say, Hitler, Stalin or even Al Capone. Would a psychoanalytical approach be any more helpful? Again, extremely doubtful. Yes, he did have a strong attachment to his mother, and a love-hate relationship with his father, but so have countless others who have never become despots and vice versa. It doesn't seem to make that much sense to attribute despotism and all that this connotes to the outworking of Oedipal anxieties.

Even the ideological factor, so evident in so many despotic rulers, seems to be largely absent in this case. So much depends, of course, on how the term ideology is to be interpreted. Whether we take it to mean an all-pervasive belief system as in, say, Maoist China, or whether we think of it as the philosophy underpinning a preferred social order, it could hardly apply to Alexander's empire which was politically pluralistic except for the overriding demand for a cardinal allegiance to the king.

Alexander was a paradox. He can be seen as a benefactor or as an oppressor. In practice he exhibited some of the worst aspects of realpolitik;

he was a manipulator, a user of men who would brook no opposition. Even his apparent multi-culturalism can be interpreted as a means to an end. (Aristotle had actually advised Alexander to be 'a leader to the Greeks and a despot to the barbarians, to look after the former as friends and relatives, and to deal with the latter as beasts or plants'; quoted by Green, 1991: 58). Yet although he didn't forget an insult or fail to punish disloyalty, he could sometimes be magnanimous to critics and even to enemies if the mood took him. Judgments are unavoidable. Was he a military genius or an increasingly obsessed megalomaniac – or both? In some ways he displayed an insufferable superiority and treated others as his undoubted inferiors. This even extended to the Persians whom he had defeated. True, he confirmed some in their posts and incorporated many into his army, but it was quite clear that Macedonians/Greeks were regarded as possessors of a superior culture. As far as the army was concerned it is evident that he was greatly respected by most of the men with whom he shared the uncertainties and dangers of the campaigns. His personal bravery was always tinged with superstition. He was concerned to give the gods their due and, if anything, became even more punctillious about religious observances towards the end of his reign. Perhaps he felt that some precautionary celestial insurance never went amiss. In his later days he also became ever more paranoid about real and imagined plots either to assassinate him or to defraud his treasury and generally undermine his authority and administration. This resulted in a number of purges and executions which only exacerbated the situation. It was these, combined with his orientalizing tendencies and pretensions to divinity, that finally turned many of his 'old guard' against him. It is still not absolutely certain whether he died naturally of an infection or unnaturally as a result of defection. Perhaps someone helped him on his way. A little opportune regicide was always on the cards.

In a sense, despots can't win. Everything they do, even if it is seemingly altruistic, will be seen by someone in self-interested terms. If they are expansionistic – as so many have been – they are usually hated by the people they control. And even if they are not, their courts, if not actually riddled with fear and suspicion, are customarily fraught by both critical murmurings *and* by the abject sycophancy of self-serving subordinates and retainers. But what else can such people do? Their careers are so linked with that of the despot that they have little choice but to give him their complete support.

CHAPTER THREE

Primitive Despotism:
African Tribal Society

Classifications of societies vary with different theorists. Perhaps the least complicated classificatory system is that of:

1. Simple pre-industrial, that is tribal society (including both centralized and non-centralized systems).
2. Complex pre-industrial (including so-called oriental-type societies).
3. Transitional, that is Third World societies.
4. Industrial, that is modern societies.

In our overall discussion, examples of despotism will be drawn from each one of these types, though it is as well to remember that they are just *types*; actual societies cannot always be neatly categorized under these headings.

When we speak of 'primitive' or 'simple' we are thinking of societies with only rudimentary technology and with no written language and therefore no documented history. As far as we are aware there are now no undiscovered societies of this kind. All existing primitive societies have been touched by modern influences to a greater or lesser degree, though many still cannot be classified as transitional. The tribal societies we are going to look at are usually quite simply organized. They normally consist of segmentary lineage structures and reasonably uncomplicated political hierarchies consisting of king/chief, perhaps sub-chiefs of subordinated or associated clans, political advisers/councillors (including ritual specialists, executioners, and so on), the laity and slaves. It would therefore be particularly interesting to look at some of these societies as they were in their pristine, untouched states, when they had their first encounters with explorers from the West. In this way, we can get some idea of their original condition, of the way they had been perhaps for countless genera-tions before Europeans – for good or ill – had arrived to affect for ever their traditional ways of life.

Autocracy was to be found in various types of tribal society. It was not confined to any particular racial group or type of environment or area or location. George Murdock in his exhaustive study of African tribal groupings used the classification 'African Despotism' to denote those systems which exhibit all or most of the following characteristics. He adds also that at the time of his study these would be found in the vast majority of developed African states (Murdock, 1959: 37–39). Note that this is very highly generalized, almost like an Ideal-Type model, to which there are many notable exceptions in actual cases:

Monarchical Absolutism: Each king or chief enjoys what is theoretically absolute power within their respective domains. Their status is signified by the symbols and trappings of office.

Royal Possession: Everything in the land, including income derived from its resources, belongs to the ruler.

Divine Kingship: The ruler may be considered divine or someone who has a unique relationship with the gods who are the source of his power.

Ritual Isolation: Other than for some of his family and attendants, there must be no physical contact between the ruler and the ruled.

Royal Courts: Courts are established with attendants, guards and officials, and strict protocol is observed.

Royal Households and Harems: All members are given due deference, especially the Queen and Senior Wife (these need not be the same person) and the Queen Mother.

Territorial and Ministerial Bureaucracy: Districts and provinces will have their respective – usually hereditary – chiefs and sub-chiefs, and the court will include functionally titled appointees who organize the affairs of state, including war leaders, ritual specialists, executioners, and so on.

Royal Succession: Though usually hereditary, with confirmation by a council of ministers, succession can sometimes be by election. In polygamous societies where there is normally a surfeit of possible successors, rival elimination may be practised to obviate the possibility of disruptive family and/or tribal strife.

Ritual Validation: This is usually a critical feature of such systems, and sacrifices – not unusually human sacrifices – may be thought necessary in order to secure the continued favour of the gods.

In Africa, which is the concern of this chapter, divine kingship of one form or another – which is inevitably autocratic – is to be found mainly in those areas that may have been influenced indirectly in the distant past by ideas emanating from pharaonic Egypt. Certain states in West Africa, notably Nigeria, the Gold Coast (Ghana) and particularly Dahomey were well known for their autocratic rulers.

Strict autocracy was well established in Dahomey where the kings were virtually regarded as gods. Even the highest ministers of state were obliged to grovel in the king's presence and throw dust on their heads. When allowed to sit, it had to be on the ground, and there were stringent rules about both apparel and etiquette. The king had enormous wealth which was obtained by his hundreds of tax collectors by virtue of the fact that theoretically he owned all the land. He also had a vast harem – he was allowed to take any woman he wished even if, technically, she belonged to somebody else – and a huge retinue of slaves. His chiefs and subordinates either held their positions by appointment or by ratification of their inheritance by the king. This despotic power was also exercised at a lesser level by the chiefs and officials within their own jurisdictions (Lenski, 1966: 154–56).

One almost unique feature of Dahomey was that it had a large contingent of women in its army. The explorer, Sir Richard Burton, who saw them on the march in 1862 estimated their numbers at about 2,500. Although they were called the 'king's wives', these 'Amazons' had apparently been originally recruited from those condemned women whose offences had been deemed worthy of death, but who were compelled to serve in the army instead of being reserved for sacrifice. The force had been reorganized early in the nineteenth century and included some volunteers. Every recruit was sworn to celibacy, though the king was allowed to take any one as a wife to add to his numerous harem. Except on campaigns, all were kept strictly away from the male warriors, but unsurprisingly lapses did occur. Burton records that after an inspection, 150 were found to be pregnant and many were executed with their lovers by the women of the 'regiment' (Seligman, 1959: 64–65). Burton was especially interested in the bizarre and the exotic and was apparently rather disappointed with his first visit to Dahomey, writing that 'not a man (was) killed or a fellow tortured ... At Benin ... they crucified a fellow in honour of my coming – here nothing' (Hibbert, 1982: 224). In writing of the Amazons, it is obvious that he had expected to find a large contingent of attractive virgins, but he discovered that they were, in fact, 'elderly, hideous women' unsuitably equipped with elongated clitorises – a revered Dahoman custom (Hibbert: *ibid.*).

In case we are tempted to think that Dahoman women were treated well, we should note that at the annual 'King's customs' there were many days of rituals to celebrate the religious foundation of kingship. The whole process was accompanied by extensive human sacrifice (the numbers varied from king to king); the victims – many of whom were women – were supposed to take messages to the gods and the ancestors. Unbroken communication with the king's ancestors was very important and every morning he had two slaves killed, partly as an act of gratitude and partly to convey his good wishes to his ancestors.

Needless to say, the death of a royal personage, especially the king or his mother, called for extensive sacrifices; often these included important members of the king's council, and, in the case of the king, wives to serve him in the next life.

Divine kingship normally meant that sacredness was either believed to dwell in the person of the king or in his symbols of office. If, or when, he became enfeebled – often assessed in terms of his warrior potential or his ability or otherwise to satisfy his many wives – he might be killed and replaced by another, or a substitute would be killed in order that the king might be magically reinvigorated. Autocracy can be judged in terms of the *degree of control* that the autocrat had over his subjects; this was invariably buttressed by religious sanctions. In Dahomey and many other African societies, almost all human sacrifices were concerned with the life, health and death of the king; certainly no other sacrifices could be made, on pain of death, without his permission. It has been argued that it was by this means of control over human sacrifice that the kings in these complex tribal societies became godlike, and that this godlike power was 'one of the foundations of kingship' (Sagan, 1985: 132). But it would be equally cogent to argue the reverse: that the belief in their godlike powers – for whatever reasons – gave them power over life and death. After all, there have been systems of divine kingship without human sacrifice, and systems of human sacrifice without a belief in divine kingship.

Similar practices were to be found in neighbouring tribal societies. Among the Yoruba, the authority of the king is again evident from the nature of the ceremonies attending his death. Some wives were immolated with him, others were expected to commit 'honourable' suicide, and this included many prominent members of the royal household as well as slaves. A third group – often virgins – were consigned the task of caring for the graves of their departed husbands; they had to remain celibate for the rest of their lives, any infringement meant certain death for themselves and their lovers. Among the Ashanti, the main tribal group of what was known as the Gold Coast, we find an interesting variant of the same kind of system. The king's power was constitutionally circumscribed by the tribal elders, but he possessed extraordinary *ritual* power which gave him considerable de facto politico-legal authority. Great deference was paid to him as the living representative of the tribal ancestors to whom, in theory, the whole land belonged. Strictly, the Ashanti states was a theocracy, so all crimes were sins against the ancestors, thus all crimes were punishable by death. These included such offences as incest, adultery with a chief's wife, intercourse with a menstruating woman, a woman insulting a man, and, most seriously, murder and the unspeakable crime of cursing the king (Service, 1978: 360–61). Adultery with one of the king's wives, of which there were many, traditionally brought death not only to the seducer and the woman but also to the close relatives of both families. Even suicide was regarded as a form of murder, and the corpse was duly decapitated. Because suicide was also an act of 'contempt', the offender's property was also forfeit to the king. Witchcraft and sorcery were special crimes, and the accused had to be killed without the shedding of blood, that is by drowning, burning and so on. Only the king had the right to pronounce the death sentence against an Ashanti (if he failed to do this, it was said that the ancestors would be angry), and only the king had the authority to commute such a sentence, usually on the payment of a heavy fine which impecunious monarchs often found infinitely preferable.

Again we find, as in so many West Coast tribes, that the king's death was the occasion for lengthy and elaborate mourning rituals. A number of the king's wives were strangled – the aristocratic method of execution – and some members of the king's staff were killed so that both they and the women could accompany their master into the next life. In other forms these sacrifices were duplicated at district and village levels; criminals, slaves and even waylaid strangers were killed to honour the king and placate the dead ancestors.

In distant south-eastern Africa, analogous institutions existed, certainly in the late sixteenth century. In the kingdoms of Kiteve, where again we find that only the king could marry his sister or his daughter, a dead king's wives took poison so that they might attend him in the next world. And when his successor took over, it was the custom to kill some of those officials who had served the previous ruler. Although this was conducted as a necessary ritual, there is little doubt that the new man was often intent on ridding himself of those who were likely to question his policies. Again too, we have some reference to royal suicide if there was any evidence of physical deformity, including lameness, impotence, and the loss of front teeth. Gradual deterioration was closely observed, the view being that it was better to go to the next life as perfect as possible.

For our main study let us look at the Buganda (of modern Uganda), and examine the nature of despotism which – as far as we can judge – had been customary there for at least 200 years before Europeans arrived. The folklore of the Buganda would seem to indicate that they and their neighbours, the Bunyoro and the Karagwe tribes, were once part of a larger 'empire' of the Kituara peoples who moved south, possibly from Ethiopia – and settled in the area north-west of Lake Victoria (Seligman, 1959). They may have brought certain agricultural innovations with them, and these may have helped to establish them as ruling aristocracies in relation to the less advanced indigenes. It is not known for sure how long there have been organized states in this area, some may well have existed since the thirteenth century, but there is no archaeological evidence that there was any contact between these and the people of the east (Zanzibar) coast. Bugundan mythology suggests that more Bantu arrived during the eighteenth century; it is only from this time that there is any clear evidence of large-scale imports from the coast (Oliver and Fage, 1969). And it was only from this time that they were known to the outside world. Before this we have no really reliable ideas about their history. As Alan Moorehead puts it, 'Many other tribal formations existed as well, but these three little states had a certain coherency in the midst of a wilderness of utter barbarity; they formed, as it were, a tiny capsule of semi-civilization in the centre of the continent' (Moorehead, 1962: 48). Folk tradition had it that there were 29 kings in Buganda before the advent of the first white men, and that all their tombs were intact. When Roland Oliver visited the area in 1958, he was assured that the tombs of the kings could still be identified (Sagan, 1985). Until the 1860s, then, when these kingdoms were discovered by white explorers, they existed in almost total isolation. And between 1860 and 1880, they were still little known until the growing vogue for anthropology overtook academia. By the late nineteenth century they had become relatively familiar territory. They were particularly intriguing because although frightening in certain respects, they were mercifully free from many European diseases. The people were reasonably well provided for, and they were unaffected by the scourge of the slave trade.

Buganda and its people, the Baganda, were ruled by an autocratic king (kabaka). Presumably this centralized, hierarchical system had grown out of a loosely knit organization of chief-dominated clans of which one had become pre-eminent. Exactly how this had developed we can only guess. Certainly by the time of discovery, the king's wishes could not be seriously questioned by anyone. Politically, the country was divided into ten provinces with their own governors, appointed by the king, together with their subordinates. These ensured that taxes were paid and that military and labour recruitment were carried out efficiently. Each of the 30 or so clans had their own land tenure organization and respective ritual functions.

In some ways, the Baganda were very sophisticated, in others they could be cruel and unfeeling. The particularly interesting thing about them is the irregular nature of their development. The people did not live in the rather crude huts found in so many parts of Africa, for example, but had large, conical structures, sometimes as high as 50 feet, which were airy and waterproof. They travelled on the lake in huge carefully designed canoes, some 70 feet long, which were immensely useful for war purposes. And they were also expert in the making of bark cloth and musical instruments, including harps and trumpets. Yet they did not possess such simple mechanical aids as the wheel and the plough. They had no method of writing and no way of calculating time even by months or years; and they had no clearly defined cosmology or articulated religious system.

Their relative sophistication certainly impressed the first explorers, John Speke and James Grant, who were also aghast at some of the barbarities they witnessed among the same people. All the more so because they had been pleasantly welcomed to the modest court of Ruminaka, king of the more easy-going Karagwe, a vassal state, which clearly acknowledged the paramountcy of the Baganda. Ruminaka may already have encountered one or two Arab traders but certainly no Europeans. He was so fascinated with them that he not only allowed Speke into his harem of fat, force-fed wives, but also permitted him to measure one who had a 52-inch bust and 31-inch thighs. The women were so huge that many couldn't stand without assistance, and if any resisted the fat-rich milk which they had to drink in copious quantities they were lashed by an overseer with a whip to give them the necessary encouragement.

Mutesa, the king of the Baganda, was a very different proposition. He is described as young (he was in his twenties), well-built and intelligent, yet – from a Western point of view – apparently devoid of any developed moral sense. In this, he seemingly followed in the tradition of previous Kabakas. On coming to the throne he had an uncertain number of his brothers and half-brothers burned alive to obviate the possibility of rebellion or any challenge to his power (Moorehead gives the figure of 60 but Hibbert suggests 30), and now enjoyed near enough complete authority over his governors – whom admittedly he did consult – and over his subjects. His court gathered daily in what was really just a compound of huts, and consisted of his chief advisers, his servants and his wives, who numbered in excess of 200. His hair was always carefully dressed and he wore a kind of toga in which he strutted around with rather an affected gait followed by his court, including a servant carrying a chair for when he wished to sit down. His officials were similarly dressed; it was an offence for a man to enter his presence unclothed, although women usually wore a skirt or often nothing at all. When he deigned to speak to his officials, they immediately prostrated themselves before him with obsequious cries of gratitude. At first, he even treated Speke with disdain, although he was extremely curious about him and was anxious to see what presents had been brought for him. When the time came, Speke didn't actually do so badly from the transaction, he was given animals for food (including rats) and virgins from the king's own harem.

Needless to say, Speke and Grant and their bearers had been very weary by the time they reached these territories. They had only a limited display of goods and trinkets, and hardly gave the impression of being prosperous emissaries of a superior culture. But their gifts held a certain novelty for these African overlords. Grant had remained in Karagwe, while Speke had gone on to Buganda. At first, Mutesa maintained his attitude of aloofness and indifference, and actually kept Speke waiting around for some time before he condescended to pay him any attention. Speke grew impatient with this and walked out, but some courtiers, fearful lest this breach of custom would provoke Mutesa – who needed little excuse for a series of executions – prevailed upon him to return whereupon Mutesa soon surrendered to curiosity. He was predictably intrigued by the white man's weapons, and when he was inadvisedly, though unavoidably, presented with some rifles and ammunition, he characteristically ordered one of his retainers to go and shoot somebody and report how well it worked. From then on he was delighted with his visitor and carried a gun everywhere he went, with doting courtiers applauding his every shot.

Any slight infringement of court protocol was met with swift and un-contested punishment, frequently death. Barely a day passed without an execution. It only required some trifling breach of etiquette, someone sneezing in the king's presence, say, and they were hustled away to be decapitated. Not infrequently the victims were wives, but this was hardly noticed because there was always a steady supply of daughters from well-wishing subjects or from those who thought they may have offended the king or those who simply wanted to ingratiate themselves with him. Alan Moorehead, drawing on Speke's journals, likens Mutesa's court procedures to the fantastic images of the Lord High Executioner in the *Mikado*, or to the antics of the Red Queen in *Alice's Adventures in Wonderland*, except that Mutesa's actions were if anything more irrational and more bizarre – and they were *real*. The ordinary people were relatively untouched by all this, a phenomenon that we shall find in many of our studies. Those mainly affected were members of Mutesa's court or not infrequently his own family. Victims might also be tortured by burning, or mutilated by cutting off their hands or feet or – if they were more fortunate – just their ears. Sometimes the king ordered that wives must be buried alive with their dead husbands. He seems to have felt no pity for his victims, to him they were no more than irksome insects that could be squashed without pity if they annoyed him.

It is not easy to explain this callous indifference to suffering and death, although the evidence suggests that Mutesa was very susceptible to pain himself. When, towards the end of his reign, he was afflicted with gonorrhoea (presumably from European contacts) he sent out several gangs of executioners to kill unfortunate wayfarers because he had been told that this would help his condition. Some were sacrificed to the god of the lake (Victoria) by breaking their limbs and leaving them on the beach for the crocodiles.

Other tribal peoples who displayed considerable insensitivity to suffering, such as some of the North American Indian tribes (the Iroquois, for example) who thought nothing of torturing enemy prisoners to death, were also very stoical about their own pain. This was sometimes related to actual or potential human sacrifice which, with its accompanying religious overtones, was practised to a greater or lesser extent in most complex tribal societies and was sometimes conveniently used for the elimination of those suspected of lese-majesty. On the other hand, among the Baganda, it was – on a magical transference basis – sometimes employed to 'strengthen' the king. Specially chosen others – clan-leaders and even sons – died that the king might live; their blood and sinews were deemed to have the necessary recuperative qualities. In the same way, the muscles of the back of the victims were sometimes taken out and worn as anklets by the king, or possibly some of the person's skin would be made into a whip for the king to use. The death of royal notables, such as the king's mother, required wholesale sacrifice, and even a visit by the king to the grave of his father, an event which would perhaps only take place once during his reign, necessitated a holocaust of victims. It is reported that Mutesa merely dreamt of his dead father one night, and this resulted in the mass homicide of 500 people.

In the case of Mutesa, religious and political 'necessity' could not easily be divorced from wanton cruelty. He would often kill personally and gratuitously, as, for instance, when he shot a woman who was being led away for some infringement or other, or when he turned his rifle on an innocent attendant and shot her in the head just to show someone how proficient he had become with his new lethal toy. When he ordered someone's execution, they were supposed to thank him for his judgment, and when it was a 'page' – a child who had been presented to the court by its parents – those same parents had to praise him for killing their disobedient child, and were then expected to find a replacement from their own family (Sagan, 1985: 163).

Having the power of life and death was considered to be the hallmark of kingship: life inasmuch as subjects were grateful for the king's protection in allowing them to live, and death insofar as execution was the peculiar prerogative of the king. Other institutions and rituals that buttressed the king's authority were obviously important. The West African practice of kings speaking through 'interpreters', for instance, was calculated to maintain social distance between his sacred person and the laity, as was also the fact that in many cases the king was the only person allowed to procreate through his full sister. But nothing manifested his autocracy as much as the power to determine the destinies of his subjects.

CHAPTER FOUR

Despotism in Archaic Society: the Egyptian Old Kingdom

The study of ancient Egypt is as totally frustrating as it is fascinating. Unlike the Greeks, who much admired Egyptian civilization, the Egyptians produced none of their own histories. Temple priests are said to have kept records, but these are almost entirely lost to us now. There are a few king-lists, but no one to vouch for their accuracy. The best known is that of Manetho, a third-century priest, whose compilation divides Egyptian history into the dynasties that are familiar to us today, yet this is now known to be grossly misleading in a number of details. And to complicate matters even further, we are not at all sure just how many of the details are inaccurate. There are also some tablets and a very famous document (the Turin Papyrus) all dating from the New Kingdom (that is, c. 1580–c. 1080), as well as the invaluable Palermo Stone purportedly of the period that concerns us most, the Old Kingdom (c. 2800–c. 2300). Perhaps the most interesting 'history' we have is that of the Greek historian Herodotus, writing in the fifth century. Yet intriguing and colourful as Herodotus is, the problem again is to know where this account is trustworthy and where it isn't. Both Manetho and Herodotus are obviously very late for our purposes although they claim that their material is based on venerated tradition gleaned from Egyptian priests. There are also allusions in other ancient writings, especially those of the Greek geographer, Strabo, but again they are rather fragmentary and mostly later than those of either Herodotos or Manetho. So much for the paucity of extant literary sources.

In some ways what are more useful are the extensive architectural remains of this civilization, which enjoyed something approaching cultural homogeneity for the best part of 3,000 years. Yet here again there are problems. The inscriptions and hieroglyphic tomb writings are obviously there because they were ordered by the deceased, and as the deceased were invariably people of some importance it means that we have a somewhat one-sided picture of things as they were. The tomb paintings certainly give us some idea of life in ancient Egypt, or at least life as the deceased would like it to continue to be after death. If the paintings are often somewhat idyllic in style, the writings themselves are frequently quite obscure. Often they are either self-justificatory petitions to the gods, or they refer to esoteric rituals and theological ideas which are still not completely understood. The royal inscriptions, on the other hand, which are usually to be found in the temples or on stelae and pylons, are both fascinating and often – one suspects – misleading. They are generally self-laudatory accounts of the most praiseworthy events of their reign with particular emphasis on their victorious campaigns and extensive conquests. The New Kingdom pharaohs especially are commonly depicted as gigantic figures smiting their dwarf-like foes, the pharaoh being accompanied by ranks of equally diminutive soldiers. Defeat is rarely mentioned. Kings had to be seen as invincible rulers who could do no wrong. Perhaps if there were any doubts about a ruler's divinity, it could be compensated for in terms of military valour. It was vital to make a good impression and scribes had to be judiciously economical with the truth, as in the case of Rameses II (the Great) who at the thirteenth-century battle of Kadesh obviously found the armies of Hatti (modern Turkey) rather too much to handle. As far as we can tell, the outcome was something of a stalemate, but both sides unashamedly claimed it as a victory.

Egypt and Mesopotamia represent the two great 'archaic' or formative civilizations. Mesopotamia may have a slight chronological edge on Egypt, but the evidence is such that no one is quite sure about this. What we do know is that there was a long relatively undifferentiated period of Paleolithic (Old Stone Age) culture that developed into more advanced Neolithic (New Stone Age) forms with the familiar patterns of agriculture and settled villages. Then, in the fifth millennium, there was an influx of new racial types into Lower (that is, northern) Egypt, possibly from Mesopotamia, and it is in this Pre-dynastic period that two independent political entities – some authorities actually refer to them as kingdoms – grew up in Lower Egypt and in Upper (southern) Egypt. Again, we know little about this period except for a few odd artefacts that give us elusive indications as to what might have been taking place. Somewhere in the late fourth millennium, unification was effected when the ruler of the southern kingdom (possibly Narmer-Menes) conquered the northern kingdom, and what we now term Dynastic Egypt came into being. From this time onwards, Egyptian rulers were usually known as the 'kings of Upper and Lower Egypt'.

The first two dynasties, technically called the Archaic period (c. 3100–c. 2700), was the time when civilization as we understand it began and was consolidated. Typically Egyptian art forms – hieroglyphic writing, architecture, and so on – were all developed during this period. And it was also at this time that expansionism began to take place, with forays into Nubia in the south, Libya to the west, and into Sinai to the north-east in search of copper and semi-precious stones. After this, Egyptian history is conveniently divided into the Old Kingdom (c. 2700–c. 2200), the Middle Kingdom (c. 2200–c. 1800) and what some consider the full flowering of Egyptian civilization, the New Kingdom (c. 1570–c. 1090). As the chronological gaps indicate, these were punctuated by two extended Intermediate Periods when there were breakdowns in the established order. But it is significant that when order was eventually restored, the orientations were essentially retrospective; it was a question of recapturing the past that had been temporarily lost. At the end of the New Kingdom, the history of Egypt lapses into a long period of almost unrelieved decline. There were occasional revivals, most notably in the seventh and eighth centuries, but they were not really able to replicate the glories of the past. And with conquests by a succession of invaders, particularly the Persians, Greeks, and finally the Romans, what we know as ancient Egypt effectively came to an end with the Greek dynasty of the Ptolemies (dynasties 31–33) and the capitulation and death of Cleopatra in AD 30.

The Old Kingdom, with which we are primarily concerned, covers just four dynasties, three to six inclusive. It was during this period that a really powerful state was established – possibly more powerful than any of its contemporaries in the ancient world, and it was also at this time that the ideology of the god-king became most clearly articulated. (Note: the terms king, monarch or ruler will be used throughout this discussion, as the expression pharaoh is technically incorrect before New Kingdom times.) The evidence we have indicates that there was an unquestioned social hierarchy extending from an all-powerful ruler to the mass of the anonymous peasants. Strictly speaking there were no classes as such in Egypt; there were those of the royal blood and those that were not. In the latter case they were legally commoners. The priests and officials, often themselves of the nobility, and the district (nome) governors who often lived in the style of minor monarchs, constituted the upper echelons of Egyptian society. Their children were reared in special schools so that they, in turn, could take their place in what for such an early civilization was a finely graded and highly differentiated society.

Authority resided in the king and his chief ministers with the Vizier acting as his senior adviser, Chief Justice and Chief Treasurer. He was the 'eyes and ears of (his) sovereign' and the main link with the provincial governors (nomarchs) of the 40 or so nomes in the country (Kamil, 1976: 53). Egypt was administered in the name of the king by the Vizier through a highly developed bureaucracy. This consisted of tax collectors, scribes, archivists and the like through a descending order of artisans, masons and agricultural overseers to the masses of the fellahin who laboured in the fields, in workshops and on building sites, with the least skilled employed in constructing dykes and canals for the Nile irrigation system which was the life-blood of the country. Wherever they worked, they were theoretically responsible to the king from whom they received their livelihood as a kind of bounty. As subjects, they had to pay part of their crops as taxes to their superiors. They were also liable for military service and for the corvee, a form of forced labour exacted by the government for various public works. Their rights were patently minimal, and they were entirely dependent on the munificence of the monarch and his administrative subordinates for their existence. Predictably, at the lowest rung in the social hierarchy were the slaves. These were usually captives who were normally owned either by the state or by the great temple estates that were themselves part of the state machinery. They were usually allotted the most menial tasks, although in practice their lot must have been barely distinguishable from that of the serfs. Women captives, on the other hand, might find their way into one or other of the harems of their superiors if they had the requisite physical attributes, or, say, musical or dancing skills.

Some social mobility did exist, however, at the upper levels of the system, the main channels of advancement being the priesthood and the army, the two institutions which at various times in Egyptian history were to prove the principal obstacles to monarchical control. The high priest of the principal state deity, usually conceived in solar terms as Ra or Re, and his large organization of lesser priests officiated at the various cult centres on behalf of the ruler. The temples were run as economic concerns, with huge retinues of retainers, guards and servants, and during the New Kingdom it is thought that they owned at least one eighth of the land. Temples were richly endowed by ruler after ruler and it is now difficult to estimate their fabulous wealth. If size is anything to go by, the temple of Amun-Re at Thebes in Middle Egypt, with its massive columns and superb sculpture, is large enough to house five European cathedrals. Even the functions of the army were often conditioned by the state ideology. Its task was not only to maintain the security of the country and to implement instructions for military forays and campaigns, it was also to organize resource-seeking expeditions for the monarch to obtain slaves and raw materials for construction work.

Interestingly, the Egyptians had no word for state. This was because the state was not regarded as a man-made system, a consciously contrived political structure, but something that was god-given – an eternal order of unalterable rightness. The power to govern was vested in the god-king, and monarchy was seen to be as old as the world. The king alone could direct the state by virtue of the divine attributes which only he possessed. Law 'proceeded from his mouth' (Carlton, 1977: 163). Only the god-king had final authority on matters both sacred and secular, if such a distinction can indeed be made in this social context. This did not mean that his rule could be completely arbitrary. He had to govern in accordance with Ma'at, the principle of truth and right order which was said to pervade the universe. The king relied on oracular direction from his fellow gods, and was therefore theoretically infallible. But divinity requires delegation; it has to be served by its earthly helpers and these might not always be so confident about their interpretation of the divine will. So Egypt's theocratic system had its blemishes like any other, yet despite its weaknesses and disruptions it did enjoy an unparalleled longevity.

The Old Kingdom was not, as far as we can tell, a time of vigorous expansionism. Egypt enjoyed a relative isolation with the Mediterranean Sea (the 'Great Green') to the north, deserts to the east and west, and scrubland to much of the south. There was not too much to fear. In fact, the first serious invasions from 'outside' did not come until over 500 years after the end of the Old Kingdom. However, there was some state organized military activity. Expeditions were mounted to prevent incursions from Libyan and Canaanite tribesmen, and aggressive forays were made to the south, mainly, it would appear, in search of slaves. Needless to say, the supreme commander was the king, although often the actual executive functions were delegated to the Crown Prince. There was a council of high officers who deliberated matters, but the plan and its execution – especially if successful – were attributed to the divine inspiration of the ruler.

The Egyptian system was probably the nearest thing to a centralized state in the ancient world. In the Old Kingdom in particular, there seems to have been very little economic activity that was not either by royal command or carried on with royal approval. In theory at least, everything belonged to the king, which in practice meant the state. The king enjoyed appropriated rights over all state property and administered the land through his subordinates, district governors and the like as though it were a personal possession. These rights were inheritable and inalienable, although as time went on such extreme power was challenged, particularly by the priesthoods.

Throughout Egyptian history, there was always *some* free market dealing by petty producers and independent craftsmen in addition to some marketing by foreign tradesmen, though we must presume that all this was noted by diligent tax officials who ensured that the state received its accustomed dues. The key economic enterprises were the monopoly of the king, and much of Egypt's limited natural resources, especially gold, copper, turquoise and stone for special construction work such as quartzite, diorite, granite and limestone were exploited for royal purposes. Even when the power of Egypt was beginning to decline in the twelfth century, during the period of the later Ramessides, the king was still able to mobilize something approaching 10,000 men, including priests, soldiers and police as well as draughtsmen and sculptors, for an expedition to quarry stone for his monuments. The object of this expedition and of so many other ventures of a similar kind, was to applaud the deeds of 'His Majesty' which were all attributed to the favour of the gods. The whole burden of state economic activity was charged with ritual necessity.

No examination of despotism within the context of ancient Egyptian society is possible without serious consideration of the religious system. The entire culture was suffused, as it were, with religious ideas. All other institutions – education, the law, the economy and so on – were critically influenced by religious factors. But in Egypt religion was represented by a number of conflicting traditions. Perhaps, as one school insists, it was not one system but many which over time have never been satisfactorily reconciled. Other authorities, for instance J. Wilson (1956), argue that it had an essential, underlying coherence. If we include local deities and foreign gods that were introduced to the pantheon, something approaching 2,000 gods were worshipped in Egypt at one time or another. Each tradition had its supportive myths, but their derivations are historically uncertain. Some of them are undoubtedly rooted in the functions of fertility; the mysteries surrounding fecundity and reproduction in the ancient world made them centres of wonder and reverential concern. So much is a matter of conjecture. What we do know is that the principal gods were always theologically related to the ruler. Ordinary Egyptians had their own popular deities, but it would appear that those highly prized benefits which derived from the high gods of the pantheon, such as Re the sun-god, Thoth the god of learning, and the creator-god Ptah, were mediated to the people via their king. The temples were not places of public worship, but ornate sanctuaries for the gods represented by their images which had to be wakened and 'fed' symbolically. Although it is clear that the nexus of most of this cultic activity was the god-king, his actual relationship to the gods is still uncertain. It would appear that although, as the son of Re, he was divine, he still had to make supplications to his superiors. The complex rites carried out by priests, deputizing for the king at the various temple complexes, were conducted in secret. They were not the property of the laity who were only permitted to attend certain festivals when the gods were paraded publicly. The only really coherent theology, then, concerned the divinity of the ruler. Where the gods are imperceptible, the deification of a mortal may suffice as a substitute. In one sense, mythic consistency was unnecessary. There was little need to reconcile the tradition when theology could be rationalized – indeed, actualized – in the immanent authority of the god-king himself.

It follows that despotism of virtually unlimited power is made possible by this ideology of the divine ruler. If enough people can be convinced not only that their king is god, but that their eternal welfare is dependent upon his good offices, then the possibilities for total subservience are virtually unbounded. In practice, of course, this was mediated by both priests and officials who were able to influence, 'interpret', and on rare occasions even modify royal edicts to their advantage. The divine nature of the king was both recognized and qualified in what was known as the Heb-Sed festival which may even have existed in Pre-dynastic times. This was a renewal ceremony which in theory took place every 30 years and involved a test of physical prowess for the king. It is possible that in very early times the king was only able to reign for 30 years and was then sacrificed. Later, it may be that, as in certain traditional African tribes, a substitute was found whose death was then believed magically to revitalize the king.

We can get some impression of how the god-king was regarded from the architectural relics that still bear mute witness to his power and authority. The Old Kingdom is the period in which the Egyptians first began the extensive use of stone in the construction of their ceremonial centres. Still extant are the remains of part of the pyramid complex of the Third dynasty king Djoser (c. 2650 – the date is disputed) at Saqqara. It was designed by his priest/chancellor, Imhotep of Heliopolis, who was still revered in later ages as an architectural genius. This comprised the first true pyramid, usually known as the Step Pyramid, and consisted of six superimposed stages reaching to a height of over 200 feet, surrounded by a massive enclosure wall built of dressed stone, some 33 feet high and over a mile in length and punctuated by 14 gateways, only one of which was a true entrance. Within this were tombs for several princesses, and a number of courts and chapels, including Djoser's mortuary temple which contained several statues of the king. Many walls were lined with fine blue-glazed tiles, and there were thousands of precious vessels made of rock crystal, alabaster, serpentine and so on (what other riches it once contained before it was plundered in early times, we have no way of knowing). It was an incredible undertaking for its time, and may – in part – have been built in gratitude to the gods for alleviating a famine that tradition tells us took place in Djoser's reign. As far as we are aware, nothing like this had ever been constructed anywhere before; earlier, kings had just been interred in modest mud-brick mastabas. It set the standards for what was to come (Aldred, 1974).

The Fourth dynasty opened with the reign of Sneferu (c. 2600) who seems to have been something of a formidable dynast. Tradition records that he made conquests in Nubia and Libya where he is credited with taking thousands of prisoners. He probably ventured too into Canaan as his name and titles are to be found on rocks in the Sinai; and one of our principal sources of information, the Palermo Stone, also says that he was a builder on the grand scale, including two pyramids at Dahshur. It is in the Fourth dynasty that we reach what some regard as the acme of Old Kingdom achievement, the pyramid complex at Gizeh which includes the Great Pyramid of Cheops (Khufu) built about 2550 and those of his successors, Chephren (Khafre) and Mycerinus (Menkaure). About these kings we sadly know relatively little (the entries on the Palermo Stone are unfortunately mutilated). What is obvious is that they were men of enormous power; the state must have been occupied almost exclusively with the task of erecting these massive stone monuments, which required what was presumably the compulsory labour of untold numbers of serfs and possibly slaves.

These stupendous edifices almost defy comprehension. They were built, as far as we can understand, to protect each king's Ka (spirit) so that, by extension, the whole land would benefit. Nobles in particular believed that if they too could be buried near their ruler they might share something of the nature of his immortality. There is a great corpus of literature about the Great Pyramid in particular, whose mysteries have given rise to all kinds of fanciful theories, ranging from the view that it is really an ancient observatory to the more bizarre idea that it is a form of 'prophecy in stone' (Tompkins, 1973). Whatever its purported hidden significance, it is an incredible construction and it does pose some interesting questions. It is some 450 feet high and contains about 90 million cubic feet of stone – enough to build 30 Empire State Buildings. It covers an area of 13–14 acres but its level has been most accurately maintained. It contains about 2,400,000 blocks of stone, most of which weigh about $2^{1}/_{2}$ tons although some weigh very much more. (If this seems improbable, consider the fact that much later, during the New Kingdom reign of Rameses II, workers with much the same kind of equipment transported a colossal statue of the king, hewn from a solid block of stone, that weighed over 1,000 tons.) Originally, it was a 'true' pyramid faced with limestone so finely worked that it is difficult to get foil between the joins. This has been stripped away over the years to grace other buildings. Then there are the strange 'facts' about its construction. It is said to be exactly aligned to magnetic north; it is exactly at the centre of the Earth's land mass, and it has been calculated that its weight is near enough one trillionth the weight of the Earth. What these things mean and whether they can all be precisely substantiated, it is an almost unbelievable achievement for people working without pulleys, with little more than wooden sledges and rollers, copper chisels and plumb lines – and all to secure the continued survival of one man and, by extension, his family who were buried nearby.

We are now reasonably sure how the pyramids were built, though not precisely certain what they represent. It is not *that* obvious that they were just tombstones; some kings built more than one pyramid and obviously could not be buried in two places at once. In other cases, the sarcophagus containing the mummy was deposited elsewhere, but this may have been to foil would-be tomb robbers. The actual amount of labour required to erect a pyramid was staggering. Herodotus, writing 2,000 years after the event, says that the Great Pyramid took a workforce of 100,000 men (which was changed every three months) 30 years to build, ten of which were taken up with cutting the substructures and constructing the causeway. And this is without all the other buildings surrounding the pyramid which went to make up the entire complex (Fakhry, 1974: 14). These figures have been disputed by modern scholars. It is now estimated that it might have taken a corvee of about 35,000 men working in shifts to complete the construction. These may well have been serfs, rather than slaves, who were recruited during the three months or so when agricultural work lapsed. One authority has actually argued that the whole enterprise was nothing more than a work-relief programme that was also calculated to engender a sense of national consciousness (Mendelssohn, 1974). But this does not really explain why the Egyptians lavished untold resources of manpower on *this* type of economic activity. There were other ways in which these resources might have been used that would also have generated a feeling of civic pride. It is difficult to escape the conclusion that it was the ritual implications that were most important.

The predominance of the religious factor is further corroborated by the fact that kings endowed their monuments with large estates so that priests could carry out the necessary rituals and present the required offerings in perpetuity. This involved large numbers of officials, guards, scribes and so on to maintain the temple property. The fruitless poignancy of this can be seen in the continued rituals that were still taking place among the ruins of some Third dynasty temples some 2,000 years after they were built when their benefactors were no longer even memories. Perhaps the best preserved of the mortuary temples, where the kings underwent purification and embalmment, is that of Khufu's successor, Khafre. Although like other temples it is constructed of limestone, it is also cased inside and out with polished granite. The piers too are of red granite, and the floor is of polished alabaster. Inside are 23 statues of the king made from other stones, such as green diorite and grey schist, hard stones which are difficult to work but which alone were considered suitable to symbolize the eternality of the god-king. Divinity demanded the finest craftsmen. If further evidence were needed, one has only to consider the contents of the only royal tomb to have survived intact from the Old Kingdom, that of Queen Hetepheres. This was discovered in 1925 at the bottom of a concealed shaft almost 100 feet deep close to the Great Pyramid. It was shown to belong to Khufu's mother, and contained vases, knives, razors and a manicure set, all of gold, together with other copper implements. But most impressive of all was the gold-sheathed furniture, comprising bed, boxes, chairs and a carrying chair that bore the inlaid gold hieroglyphics proclaiming that she was 'the mother of the king of Upper and Lower Egypt, follower of Horus, she who is in charge of the affairs of the harem, whose every word is done for her, daughter of a god, of his loins, Hetepheres' (Aldred, 1974: 94–95).

It is probably true to say that it was during the Fourth dynasty that we see autocracy at its height. Certainly if we judge despotism in terms of its degree of control over the military and the priesthood, and especially the labouring masses, we can find no better exemplification of that control than the constructions of the Pyramid Age. After the building of the three principal pyramids at Gizeh, the style of royal tombs changed. In the Fifth dynasty some small pyramids were built, but there was a move away from the megalithic architecture of Khufu, Khafre and Menkaure to the more modest yet in some ways more aesthetically pleasing sun-temples at Abusir. These too were monumental, though hardly on the same scale as the pyramids, and consisted of a temple sanctuary with its characteristic obelisk together with a complex of subsidiary buildings. This move may be interpreted as evidence of a decline in the stature of the king and a greater emphasis on the final authority of the sun-god, which in practice probably meant an increase in the counter-balancing power of the priesthood. This too is the period of the earliest known Pyramid Texts, the origins of which may be far older than the Fifth dynasty. Their inscribed incantations and spells were calculated to ward off evil and secure the future well-being of the Ka (spirit) of the deceased. Not unusually too there were curses invoked for those who dared to violate the final burial places of the kings and the nobility. Yet we now know that the 80 or so known tombs of these god-kings throughout the Dynastic Age had all been violated in antiquity (even the tomb of Tutankhamun of the Eighteenth dynasty had been partly desecrated). The sanctions against such sacrilege should have been enough to deter most mortals, but apparently neither worldly punishments – usually either death or mutilation – nor otherworldly curses were sufficient to intimidate those who were desperate to lay hands on the untold wealth of the tombs.

These qualifications apart, it would be hard to find a system which gave more untramelled power to one man. Others, as we shall see, came close – Imperial China, for instance – but in no other state is the autocrat endowed with a greater degree of divinity. In Egypt, certainly at the zenith of the Old Kingdom, the ruler was not merely a representative of the gods, he was a god in his own person. How such ideas developed we can only guess. However, it was believed that his spirit and his mummified remains had to be protected at all costs because his immortality was the only guarantee of the well-being of the people. What greater sanction can one have for what amounted to complete despotic power?

CHAPTER FIVE

Oriental Despotism: Early Unified China

No assessment of Oriental despotism can be made without some initial consideration of Karl Wittfogel's classic text (Wittfogel, 1957) about the ways in which patterns of development facilitate certain methods of social control. Wittfogel's simple but persuasive thesis is that state control of scarce resources leads to state despotism. It has been termed an 'hydraulic theory' because Wittfogel concentrates his attention on the early riverine civilizations and argues that where large-scale irrigation schemes were needed to bring fertility to water-deficient areas, the irrigation works themselves were such that they could usually only be initiated and run by governments because they alone had the power to mobilize sufficient labour to build and operate them, and that the supply of water was a variable that could be manipulated to the state's advantage. Much, of course, depended on the respective ecologies. In Wittfogel's typology, despotism tends to develop in rainfall-based systems but is more characteristic of what he terms 'agrohydraulic' systems, those that require substantial *centralized* works of water control, which indirectly facilitate monopolization of political power. (One could compare the economic power which today derives from the control of oil supplies.) All the early riverine civilizations displayed something of the despotism that Wittfogel describes, including China, though with certain qualifications.

This control of a single, essential commodity, Wittfogel insists, led to absolutism. Rival institutions were checked and any competitive forces – insofar as they existed – were either inhibited or proscribed. Nothing was allowed to develop that would challenge autocratic rule. Power was centred in the state or despot and in the bureaucratic hierarchy that was the instrument of their wishes and even their whims. If, as was usual, this power was buttressed by religious sanctions, then it was usually that much more effective; autocratic commands were tantamount to divine imperatives.

Oriental-type society was simply stratified; the only intermediate categories between the hierarchy and the exploited masses were inconsequential groups of artisans and petty merchants. The only limitation on this form of despotism, according to Wittfogel, was self-imposed. There sometimes came a time, as so many conquerors have discovered to their cost, when it paid less and less to administer more and more – a kind of law of diminishing administrative returns.

At one level, Wittfogel is engaged in an anti-Marxist polemic. He is arguing that in Oriental-type societies no independent capitalist structure could emerge and that the consequent class struggle which Marx certainly envisaged could never take place. It is also a refutation of the theory that 'true' political freedom can be realized in centralized systems. For Wittfogel, all centralization smacks of despotism; real freedom can only stem from *independent* class relations which are quite impossible in Oriental-type societies.

Like all general theories, it has to be open to particular criticisms. As a model it is perfectly valid, but as a description of an actual type it is necessarily subject to specific historical exceptions. Resource control *is* a vitally important factor in maintaining social control, but it is by no means the only factor; an hierarchy's command of the military, for instance, may be equally important in sustaining a despotic regime. It should also be noted that not all 'hydraulic' systems breed despotism; water control was often a fragmented procedure, as in ancient Egypt, and in Mesopotamia, where it was often shared between state and temple authorities, as it was too – according to Eberhard (1950) – in parts of China. It can also be shown quite easily that many historical despotisms developed in circumstances where an agrohydraulic system was not possible, as in certain Aegean islands (for example Samos). Furthermore, not all areas where the conditions for hydraulic societies existed actually produced such systems. The riverine valleys of California, which were peopled by disparate Indian tribes, would be a case in point.

It is disputable whether any despot has been – or can be – *totally* autocratic, at least not for very long. Every despot needs some secondary supports (Eisenstadt, 1957–58); he has to have subordinates to carry out his bidding. Wittfogel seems to imply that despots have only one goal: the maximization of power. But, as we will see, especially in the case of the Greek tyrants such as Dionysios of Syracuse, motives may be mixed and may often have a plurality of competing objectives. So a 'complete' or 'pure' despotism of an entirely arbitrary and capricious kind may not have existed for very long anywhere, but insofar as it existed at all, it will be difficult to find a closer approximation than in the rule of the First Emperor of China.

The history of China cannot properly be established before *c.* 1500 BC. This was the time when the venerated Hsia dynasty, of which we know practically nothing, gave way to the oppressive Shang dynasty which lasted until *c.* 1100 when its last despotic ruler was dethroned. Chinese archaeology only really got underway in the unpropitious 1930s, and we now know that most of the accepted features of Chinese cultural life were in place during Shang times. This suggests a long preceding period of social gestation. Despite the Shang propensity for fertility rituals and the human sacrifice of slaves and retainers (and concubines?) which apparently attended a ruler's funeral, they seem to have administered a highly developed state, certainly if their art and their bronzes are anything to go by. The Shang were eventually conquered by tribes of semi-barbarian nomads, the Chou, who predictably adopted and adapted the customs and manners of those they had defeated and settled down to an uncertain existence as overlords in central China. Their rulers, who came to be known as 'sons of heaven', a title also adopted by non-Chou successors, were themselves continually harassed by barbarian tribes on the north-western borders and beset by strife within their own territories. Extensive walls, precursors of the later Great Wall, were built to try to keep them out. Their depredations were often horrific. Whole townships were destroyed, buildings were burned, rape and pillage were commonplace, and frequently everyone except potential concubines were put to the sword. Some states occasionally tried to coalesce for protection, but the jostlings for power tended to make for more fragmentation and the creation of yet more petty fiefdoms.

In the early eighth century, the Chou unwittingly sowed the seeds of their own eventual destruction, although that was not to come for another five centuries. A dispossessed prince of Chou enlisted the help of some western barbarians in overthrowing the current ruler and taking over the reins of government himself. However, once successful, the hordes didn't want to relinquish their conquests. They were finally bought off with lands in the western provinces that were thought to be potentially infertile but once properly irrigated turned out to be one of the most profitable areas in the country. Thus was born the state of Chin (hence the name China) which eventually became the Assyria of the Far East – 'without the bas-reliefs' (Rodzinski, 1984: 32).

The Chou dynasty lasted – at least, nominally – until the third century, by which time Chou had been reduced to a relatively small state in central China. During this time there were significant cultural developments, especially regarding the philosophy of rule. The conservative teaching of Kung-Tsu (Confucius) advocated a refinement of traditional hierarchical practice where strict respect for elders reflected the due reverence that was to be given to superiors. The family was a microcosm of the state. This social commitment ideology of Confucius and his later disciple Mencius, which stressed that the emperor must act as a guardian of the people, was complemented by the more 'purely' philosophical teaching of Lao-Tse, the founder of Taoism, who had a considerable influence on early Chinese Buddhists. He rejected arbitrary and artificial laws and taught submission not so much to the state as to the universal principle (Tao) of the Way of

Nature. Among the 'hundred schools' of philosophy there was also the teaching of Mo-Tzu (d. *c.* 438) – broadly speaking, another contemporary, who preached a radical pacificism and visualized a world that one day would be united by love: a radical concept that met with little sympathy from state authorities. All these philosophies were opposed to that of the Legalist school, which repudiated this high-minded appeal to moral duty and contended that subjects could only be held in check by disciplined and if necessary repressive rule. The Legalists thus provided the ideological support for despotism in general and Ch'in rule in particular.

The Chou dynasty covered what is technically known as the Feudal period, which, in turn, merged with what is commonly referred to as the period of the Warring States (*c.* 481–221). The end of feudalism heralded a time of considerable social upheaval when many became disillusioned with the airy humanitarianism of the philosophers and longed for the practicalities of those who espoused strong rule and settled, famine-free conditions. There was a weakening of central authority, and emergent states competed with each other for literati, agricultural specialists and even peasant workers. There was incessant warfare either with the ever-threatening tribes on the western and northern fringes of the Chou 'middle kingdom' or between the states themselves. In the eighth century some 200 or so feudal states had existed, but by the fifth century there were probably less than 20, a few of which were trying to establish some kind of hegemony over the rest. By the third century this number had been effectively reduced to nine: the eastern states of Yen, Ch'i and Yueh; the southern state of Ch'u and the northern states of Wei and Chao; the rump Middle Kingdom of Chou and its neighbour, the later emergent Han, with the menacing state of Ch'in in the west waiting impatiently to destroy the others one by one.

Various alliances were made between the states once they realized the danger, but all to no avail. By a process of serial conquest Ch'in dealt with each state in turn 'like a silkworm devours a mulberry leaf' (Szu-ma Ch'ien, a Han historian, quoted by Yong Yap and Cotterell, 1975: 41). Even the coalitions couldn't match the Ch'in, which by this time was a state almost totally given over to warfare. Ch'in forces had now had ample experience in dealing with the nomads, and had developed a formidable army which also recruited women to construct defences and look after provisions. Discipline was severe, but the rewards were high; the state adopted the barbarian practice of compensating every man who brought in an enemy head as proof of his military prowess. The Ch'in generals followed a policy of total war. No code of chivalry seems to have existed. It was not unknown for enemy notables to be invited for talks and then peremptorily butchered. Terror seems to have been the principal weapon of the Ch'in armies, and massacre of prisoners appears to have been a common practice, partly in order to eradicate all opposition and partly to intimidate other wavering states. Nobody made negotiated settlements with Ch'in. When the army of Chao was starved into surrender in 259 BC it is reported that virtually the whole male population of the state, 400,000 in all, were put to the sword (Fryer, 1975: 35). An interesting sequel to this was that the general who commanded the Ch'in forces was himself demoted and executed for disobedience two years later. Military discipline spared no one. Even allowing for some exaggeration, the record of Ch'in atrocities is staggering and it didn't get much better with time.

The Ch'in founder of united China, or what is formally known as Imperial China, is usually called the First Emperor. His origins are uncertain, but according to Chinese historians, he was the son of a concubine who was given to the grandson of a Ch'in ruler by an important Chao merchant, possibly to help improve relations between the two states. Soon afterwards she produced a child (c. 260) but there is still considerable doubt about who the father really was; it might or might not have been the grandson. However, when the ruler of Ch'in died, his son succeeded him, but not for long. Within a few months he too died and left the throne to the grandson (c. 250). This left the concubine's boy, Prince Cheng, as heir apparent, and in 246 he took over the reins of government aided, as was to be expected in the circumstances, by an impressive array of advisers including the formidable Li Szu who was to be Cheng's *eminence grise*. Meanwhile, his mother, after a brief dalliance with her former merchant friend, found herself a lover who she arranged to be incompletely castrated so that he could legitimately live with her in the harem as a eunuch. When Cheng eventually heard about all this, he had his mother and the conniving merchant exiled, where the merchant subsequently committed suicide. The lover – who by this time had tried to foment what proved to be an abortive rebellion – was executed by being torn apart, and any others that were implicated were also dismembered.

Li Szu, who in his early days had been attached to Confucianism but had later gravitated towards the Legalist school, became Minister of Justice. And it was he who by a mixture of diplomatic skill and duplicity orchestrated the military conquests undertaken by Ch'in before final unification. The neighbouring states had become so alarmed by the predatory Ch'in that various schemes were devised to rid themselves of the menace, including trying to assassinate the ruler. One attempt, so we are told, actually involved gaining access to the emperor's presence by making him a gift of the head of a traitorous general who had fled from Ch'in and who was then persuaded to offer his life for this very purpose. The plot almost worked, but the actual attempt ended in near farce with the would-be assassin chasing the emperor round the room bent on his destruction, and the king feverishly trying to draw a cumbersome sword from its scabbard. Needless to say, the plot misfired, the emperor survived, the assailant was killed, and all those party to the plot duly punished. After this Cheng, always a remote figure, became even more inaccessible and no one was allowed to be armed in his presence. He was constantly mobile, keeping to deliberately haphazard schedules and staying at one or another of his reputed 270 palaces. The fear of assassination, together with his horror of evil spirits, made him keep his movements secret and anyone who revealed his whereabouts could be put to death.

By 221 BC, all China was at the mercy of Ch'in, which had achieved what no other expansionist state had achieved, the complete unification or – perhaps better – the complete subjugation of all China. Cheng, who now assumed the more impressive title of Ch'in Shih Huang-Ti, a name that indicated that he was the first sovereign emperor, proceeded to initiate the measures for which he has been remembered by history, and for which he has become famous, or notorious, depending upon one's interpretation of events. He reorganized the administration of the country by rejecting the previous system of fiefs, where land was held in exchange for services to a local lord or central government or both, and substituted a system of 36 (later 42) administrative districts, or commanderies, each under appointed military and civilian officials. Subordinate to these were sub-districts controlled by yet further officials, and so on in a complex structure of devolved authority. This constituted a vast new *non-hereditary* bureaucracy with primary responsibility directly to the crown. There was a simple division between central administration and provincial administration, with several ministries whose functions ranged from care of the Royal Purse to the observation of the stars. But the main focus was always the emperor whose continued well-being was believed to be directly linked to that of the people. It was 'a fundamental pattern of despotic, centralised monarchy which was to be maintained for over two thousand years' (Rodzinski, 1984: 40).

Emperor, officials and subjects comprised the familiar broad bands into which society was stratified. There were also slaves, who might be held in private hands or owned by the government; they were employed on a considerable scale to carry out more menial tasks, but their lives cannot have been that much different from those of the peasants. Most people lived in abject poverty, and were sometimes found to sell members of their families to pay their unavoidable debts to the large land owners from whom they leased their meagre plots. Political responsibility and social distinctions were inextricably combined. Each person was treated according to his or her rank. Privilege was hierarchically ordered – and restricted, with the vast mass of the peasantry subject to corvee or military duties, as their lords required. Coercion, as in so much of the ancient world, was an ever-present reality.

Underpinning the entire system was a potent religio-philosophical tradition which regarded the emperor as the 'son of heaven'. He enjoyed a special Mandate to rule, and was believed to possess a unique capacity to do so. If, however, his authority was seen to wane, as with, say, a military or palace coup, it was simply assumed that the Mandate had been withdrawn and transferred to another, more worthy or successful dynasty. Ritual observances therefore were crucial. The government prescribed the rites that were performed to appease the spirits and financed the shrines that were built in their honour. In addition, there were more bizarre practices of an occult nature which were commonly employed to placate – even manipulate – the more capricious spirits which brought excessive rains, earthquakes or eclipses. Kin groups also had their own local shrines in recognition of the ancestor spirits, although none were venerated as highly as the ancestors of the emperor; they had the power to prosper or blight the land, a feature of Chinese life which certainly enhanced the state's capacity for social control.

The emperor spent much of his time in near seclusion, partly because of fear of assassination, and probably also to foster the image of a remote, all-wise, semi-divine being who was uncontaminated by mundane concerns. Few people had direct access to him, and those who did treated him with extreme deference. He saw his immediate subordinates, the highest officials, and was attended largely by eunuchs – who often attained considerable influence at court – and concubines who were expected to make themselves useful in the palaces and not sit about waiting for the emperor's hormones to become active. Concubines were, however, very carefully chosen and graded, the number and type being prescribed by tradition both for officials and for the emperor himself. The lot of the concubine was considered enviable, and poor parents sometimes aspired to get their girl children taken on at the palace or in the establishment of some high official. But there were also disadvantages; when Ch'in-Shih-Huang-ti died he had his childless concubines buried with him.

Much of what we know of the Ch'in period comes from the first comprehensive history of China, the Shi-Chi (Historical Records) by an Imperial Astrologer, Szu-ma-Ch'ien. He wrote during the subsequent Han dynasty and was apparently misunderstood by the then reigning emperor, put on trial, and then after a predictable verdict duly castrated – an experience which in no way endeared him to the current regime and probably influenced the bias of his writings. Nevertheless, there are certain facts which are really beyond dispute. During the Ch'in period the principle of private landownership was extended to all, *if* they were in a position to take advantage of it. There was a complete overhaul of the economic system and all weights and measures were standardized. Similarly, a rationalized form of the Chinese script was introduced. At the same time, imperial expansion continued. The armies of the conquered states, or what was left of them, were completely disarmed and the weapons melted down to make huge bronze statues and gigantic bells some weighing up to 60 tons apiece. Notorious too was the Ch'in policy of population transfer, which weakened any real possibility of revolt among the disaffected. Reputedly, large numbers from the aristocratic families in these states were deported and forced to settle near the Ch'in capital where they lived under permanent observation.

Most impressive of all were Ch'in-Shih-Huang-ti's building projects, including a vast network of roads and canals. Until recently the best known of these was the Great Wall. Little has come down to us from the historians about the actual building of the Wall except myth and tradition; we have to make what we can of the artefact itself. This monumental construction which admittedly incorporated some of the already existing walls, transverses the country for over 2,100 miles, although in Ch'in times it is thought to have been about 500 miles longer than this. One writer puts the eventual distance at 4,000 miles and suggests that only about 500 miles of this was the work of the Ch'in emperor between 221 and 210 (Fryer, 1975: 50). Its height varies, but its average height is 22 feet. Its foundations are of rock and the main structure is mainly stone and hard-baked brick bonded with lime mortar. Every few hundred yards were fortification towers measuring about 40 feet square and 40 feet high, and when the Wall was completed there were some 25,000 such towers besides the pre-Ch'in watch-towers outside the Wall that functioned as advance warning posts. The Wall passes through vast stretches of mud and quicksand near the Yellow River, desert regions near the Tibetan border where much of it is now a complete ruin, and mountainous areas to the east where the Wall is best preserved and which is now the favourite haunt of sightseers. Little of the Wall as it now exists is the original Ch'in construction; sections have been rebuilt several times by successive emperors. The ostensible purpose of the Wall was similar to that of its predecessors, to keep out the warring nomads of the north and west. It was also a wall of demarcation, the intention was to separate the developed culture of China from the barbarians outside its borders. Undoubtedly too it was designed as a monument to the emperor who had initiated it, and would be a lasting memorial to his greatness.

But the Wall was also a place of death and misery. It was a place of punishment, the Ch'in equivalent of Siberia for the dissidents of the Stalinist era. A core workforce said to number 300,000 was constantly replenished by prisoners of war, criminals and anyone else who contravened the demanding rules of the regime. Women too were recruited to prepare and transport food from the 34 enormous supply bases and to weave clothes and make tents. The emperor gave final responsibility to the military who both guarded the workers from barbarian attacks and ensured that there was no slacking or indiscipline on the Wall. How many perished in the hands of the guards and as the result of hazardous weather conditions we can only guess; one writer (Cottrell, 1964: 140) speculates that it must have been in excess of one million.

As well as the Wall, the emperor built an inordinate number of palace complexes with connecting walkways and extensive parks and gardens. Stone and timber were brought from far afield; one particularly magnificent palace, the Afang (= beside the capital) measured approximately 370 feet by 2,120 feet, and it is said that it – together with the emperor's mausoleum – involved the labour of some 700,000 men, many of them castrated prisoners. And this in addition to the 50,000 families that were deported to the south to help complete his summer palace. Archaeological excavations were begun on the emperor's mausoleum in 1974 and it was found to be even more fabulous than the historical records indicated. The site is some 150 feet high and about eight miles in circumference. As far as we know, nothing like it has ever been constructed. It was begun by the emperor and completed by his son after his death. The mausoleum houses the tomb proper which to date has not been opened, replicas of palaces, 'and a silent clay army rigidly arrayed before it in battle formation ... a monument to his majesty and a dark reminder of the suffering of his people' (Guisso et al., 1989: 179). The serried ranks of the 7,000 or so life-size terracotta soldiers, all visibly different in features, are still in excellent condition and still stand guard over the inner tomb which hopefully has never been plundered.

Ch'in-Shih-Huang-ti's intolerance did not improve with age. He became more and more convinced that he was building an ideal state based upon strict Legalist principles which, although in accord with much Chinese tradition, was in its own way seen as something different and, indeed, unique. It was felt to be rationalized and unified in such a way that it might last indefinitely – a common misconception of so many utopians. As things turned out, it had a very short lifetime, barely three generations. The emperor was encouraged in his political hubris by his ministers who argued that if he was really intent on creating something now, he should make a complete break with the past and promulgate fresh laws in response to current needs. His Chancellor, the now promoted Li-Szu, recommended a measure that has brought lasting approbrium and one that has been characteristic of other despots since: the most extreme form of censorship – the burning of the books (that is, writings on wooden strips and silk). All the official histories of states other than Ch'in were to be destroyed, as were also the works of the many schools of philosophy including those relating to Confucianism. The only works to be preserved were treatises on medicine and pharmacy (in which the Chinese were relatively sophisticated for a pre-scientific society), agriculture and forestry, and – a peculiar predilection of the emperor – works on divination. All those who refused were to be disfigured by having their faces tattooed and then sent to work on the Wall, effectively a sentence of death. Those who disobeyed the edict even by discussing the contents of the banned books in public were likewise condemned. In his frustration at the intransigence of the academic community and their inability to enlighten him on how he might obtain eternal life, the emperor, together with Li Szu, decided that they must be taught a lesson that future scholars would have cause to remember. He called them together and accused them of lese-majesty, effectively treason, whereupon – to their shame – there were protestations and mutual recriminations, but the emperor was quite unmoved. According to tradition, 460 of them were selected for execution, purportedly by being buried alive, an act which caused the expulsion of one of the emperor's sons, Fu Su, who argued that it was not only a crime, it was a political blunder. He was right, the people were growing tired of such repression; revolution was not far away.

The emperor spent much of the later part of his reign in a fruitless search for immortality. This took him along various unrewarding culs-de-sac in the vain hope that he would discover this potion or that elixir that would prevent him from dying. His alchemists prepared a variety of concoctions which they assured him would do the trick, and it may be that in taking them he was ironically hastening his own death. He is even said to have mobilized thousands of youths for an expedition across the Eastern Sea to the fabled islands of Penglai to find so-called magical herbs, but only succeeded in founding the Japanese nation. Whether this was the actual result of the venture nobody knows, but the voyagers never returned. On another occasion his quest took him to the river Si in which it was said lay the last of the nine sacred tripods of Chou. The nine tripods, reputedly made in remote antiquity, represented the nine main areas of China and Ch'in already had the other eight. The complete set was therefore necessary to legitimize his rule as the true 'son of heaven'. He sent a thousand divers in search of the tripod, and their lack of success was regarded as an ill-omen. The emperor also made sacrifices at many rivers and mountains, and at hundreds of shrines which represented a range of phenomena from the sun, moon and planets to the autumn rains. But no ritual, no herbs or drug was destined to fulfil his wishes. His growing irritation with scholars and magicians alike probably stems in part from their inability to solve the mystery. Their impotence in the face of the besetting conviction that such a panacea did exist undoubtedly fed his paranoia. He felt that perhaps they were deliberately leading him astray or perhaps they knew and just weren't telling or, on the most generous estimate, perhaps they genuinely didn't know what men of their reputation *should* have known. In despair, he had to fall back on the protective capacity of history's most bizarre burial complex in the hope that it would ensure his spiritual survival.

The decline of the Ch'in dynasty began even before the First Emperor's death. The signs were already there as a consequence of his increasingly oppressive rule. Even among his own entourage there were murmurings and uncertainties about who would be the next victims of his capriciousness and suspicion. Plagued by inauspicious omens and portents, the First Emperor finally died in 210 and was buried with his huge inanimate army, his pitiable childless concubines, and the faithful workers who had constructed his tomb. But before this an elaborate plot was devised by his Chancellor, his son Hu Hai, and the son's tutor, the eunuch Chao Kao, to convince the rightful heir, Fu Su, that his father was still alive and that he was still in disgrace and should end his life forthwith. And although warned that it might be a ruse, Fu Su obediently heeded the message that had purportedly come from his father and committed suicide. This left the way open for Hu Hai to become emperor under the unscrupulous influence of his advisers, who then set about getting rid of their most dangerous opponents. It worked for a while. Dissidents and possible rivals were put to death including 12 royal princes and ten princesses together with their families. The young emperor, however, became increasingly dissolute and the advisers fell out among themselves. At his instigation and that of Chao Kao, Li Szu the Chancellor, the principal architect of so many of the First Emperor's inhuman acts, had his due reward. After being flogged and making a false confession – the ever favourite 'treason-trial' gambit – he was sentenced to the infamous 'Five Punishments' which culminated in being publicly cut in two at the waist. His execution and that of his son (200 BC) was followed by the extermination of all his close relatives, thus invoking a law that was obviously designed to obviate any perpetuation of a feud. Chao Kao now became chancellor, and virtually ignoring the fact that the Ch'in empire was now seriously threatened by rebellion, began planning his next move, the downfall of the emperor himself. Hu Hai's reign lasted a bare two years and that of his successor only three months, but before he was overthrown, the last ruler managed to have the infamous Chao Kao assassinated. The rule of Ch'in was over, and the long-lasting Han dynasty, founded by a peasant, took its place.

There have been many explanations for the failure of the Ch'in dynasty. Its external aggressiveness and its harsh internal laws; its inhumanity to scholars and to those it alienated and dispossessed; and not least, to those who were forced to labour on its many projects. There was too the First Emperor's anti-intellectualism and his preoccupation with mystical pursuits; the ruthlessness of his ministers and successors and the apprehension they generated among all who questioned the regime. The Ch'in state was over-ambitious, its despotism demanded too much, too soon, and it was therefore largely indifferent to the amount of suffering it caused or to the means it employed as long as the ends were realized.

CHAPTER SIX

Despotism in Classical Society

Archetypal despotism: the anomalies of Greek tyranny

We have already observed that despotism and tyranny are not synonymous terms, but insofar as so many actual tyrannies were autocracies that were maintained by force we can see them as a particular form of despotism. The expression *tyrannis* was probably first used in ancient Lydia (modern Turkey) to denote a system of leadership that was not based on an hereditary principle, such as monarchy, but was established unconstitutionally, perhaps to popular acclaim, though often sustained by oppression. Tyranny took a number of fairly well-attested forms. The tyrant might well rule beneficently, or he might begin well and then degenerate into the kind of ruler who was simply concerned with personal aggrandizement. Less commonly, he might begin badly with a series of proscriptions against his immediate rivals, and then when things had settled down continue to rule with wisdom and moderation. The term dictator, on the other hand, is sometimes used for autocrats who have been constitutionally elected to office but who may then act in a despotic manner. It follows therefore that when we speak of despotism we are also speaking of tyrants, dictators and even monarchs, depending not only on their *method* of obtaining power but also on their *mode* of behaviour.

In the early days of the Greek city-states (poleis) we can see the beginnings of the perennial conflict (stasis) between the aristocracy (literally, the rule of the best people) and the lower orders (demos). The people clamoured for more popular government which would give them a greater say in affairs, while the nobility tried to cling to their privileges by making periodic yet rather grudging concessions to the people. Frequently this erupted into violence which sometimes resulted in assassination and even massacre. One side was often as bad as the other when it came to senseless cruelty. This can be seen from the events at Corfu (Kerkyra) in the fifth century BC so graphically depicted by the contemporary Thucydides (1972: III 70–85; IV 46–48). It is in these circumstances that tyrants typically arose.

The period of roughly a hundred years from the middle of the seventh century, when many of the aristocracies were overthrown, is known as the 'age of the tyrants'. But this is rather misleading as tyranny could always be found somewhere in the Greek world. Sometimes tyrants were able military leaders who took advantage of the situation to seize power, and not infrequently they were members of the privileged classes who took the side of the people. Once in power, they sometimes cancelled debts, gave poor tenant farmers more security, and enhanced the cities with public works. Some positively encouraged artistic endeavour and actually enticed well-known poets, philosophers and sculptors to their courts. Perhaps this was done out of a genuine sympathy for the plight of the poor or more probably because they saw an opportunity for personal advancement and popularity. Perhaps it was both – who ever does anything out of a pure motive? Their motives were always more than slightly suspect. They were frequently well received *at first*, but it was rare for any particular tyranny to last more than two generations. This was usually because the sons of the men who had seized power often found their father a hard act to follow. If they lacked, as they frequently did, his special appeal or abilities, yet wanted to retain the power and privileges that he had enjoyed, they had to resort to the kind of strong-arm tactics which did nothing for their popularity and they soon found themselves assassinated or, at best, deposed. A notable example is the case of Harmodius and Aristogiton who in 514 killed the would-be tyrant son of the successful military ruler Peisistratos of Athens. This act may not have been done for the worthiest motives – there were strong rumours of homosexual jealousy as the true reason for the deed. However, once done, they were hailed as liberators by the people, and when the democracy was established in Athens four years later they became symbols of patriotism and were celebrated with a sculpture by the city's most eminent artist.

Tyranny may not have had any legal or religious justification, so it was very ambivalently received in most states. Some obviously saw advantages to the system but, in general, it was regarded as the more unacceptable face of monarchy. According to tradition, Peisistratos was a wise and benevolent ruler. He reduced the incidence of border wars and settled a number of territorial disputes; he also enhanced Athenian hegemony in the Aegean and secured the grain supply from the Black Sea. On the domestic front he introduced a 5 per cent property tax, which was then redistributed in the form of subsidies to poor farmers – a problem Solon's reforms had never been able to solve (Jeffery, 1978: 96). He may even have enrolled resident aliens (metics) and foreigners on the citizen lists, something unknown in the later Classical period when metics could actually be enslaved for impersonating a citizen. Of course, he was above the law, and his mercenaries were always on hand to make sure that things stayed that way. But despite the repression, especially in the second generation, the family did much to improve the city socially, economically and architecturally.

Not all tyrannies were like this, of course, otherwise the very idea would not have been generally regarded with such deep suspicion and even opprobium. There were executions of rivals, and both enforced and voluntary exile for undesirables. Where autocratic rule was thwarted, despots could turn very nasty indeed. When the people of Kerkyra, a Corinthian dependency, rose against their overlords, for instance, and killed the son of the Corinthian tyrant, Periander, he sent 300 boys from leading Kerkyran families as eunuchs (male prostitutes?) to the king of Lydia, but fortunately they were rescued before they reached the Lydian court. In Athens, it was technically prohibited for anyone to try to establish a tyranny on pain of atimos, a term that meant loss of civil rights, but which originally meant to be 'outlawed', implying that the person could be killed with impunity. It was largely because of the fear of tyranny that the law of ostracism was first introduced to protect the state. This was the practice whereby citizens were able to vote that any potentially dangerous fellow citizen should be exiled for ten years. The person with the most votes was the loser, although he did not have to forfeit his property rights and might still live within reasonably easy travelling distance of his native city.

In reading Herodotos, one gets the impression that tyranny first became institutionalized in the seventh century in the petty city-states of Ionia (Asia Minor), though one instinctively feels that it must have existed long before this. There were certainly a number of Ionian despots, of whom we have a fragmentary knowledge, at such places as Ephesos and Miletos at a very early date. Tyranny is then thought to have spread to Greece by way of some Aegean Islands, notably Lesbos and Samos, and became established in such city-states as Corinth, Argos, Megara, Sikyon and Epidauros. Interestingly, most of the places where tyranny took root were coastal trading centres. A few states still had monarchies, though despite the distinction made by Plato and Aristotle that kingship was the good and tyranny the bad aspects of monarchy, there was not always that much to choose between some kings and some tyrants as far as *practice* was concerned. There were, however, exceptions even to this; Sparta, for instance, had a system of dual monarchy, yet real power was vested in the small council of elected men known as ephors. By contrast, Athens during the same period was largely controlled by powerful aristocratic families, but when discontentment boiled over early in the sixth century an arbitrator or archon, Solon, was elected to draw up a law code to which all were supposed to adhere. In theory, it was the answer to a number of social problems, and though it recognized a system based on economic criteria, it did sound the beginnings of something like a democratic constitution in that all citizens were to be equal before the law. Yet the intriguing thing about Athens is that before she went over to a system of radical democracy late in the sixth century, she underwent a period of tyranny under Peisistratos which, in material terms, was not altogether to her disadvantage.

It should be borne in mind that during this period considerable changes were taking place in Greece generally, especially in relation to military weaponry and tactics (Andrewes, 1966: 31–42). Many Greek states, following the example of Argos in particular, changed their style of warfare by using mass formations of heavily armed infantry (hoplites) who were drawn mainly from the middle-class farmers and artisans who could afford their own accoutrements of war. Poorer citizens comprised either light-armed troops and skirmishers or, in seafaring states such as Athens and Corinth, were recruited into the navy as rowers. It follows that those who bore the brunt of the fighting, the hoplites, came increasingly to expect a greater say in the running of affairs. This did not exactly sound the death knell of tyranny, but this emergent democratic spirit which expected some participation in the political process undoubtedly contributed to its eventual demise.

Examples of what we might term archetypal despotism of the tyrant type are also found quite late among the western Greeks of southern Italy and especially Sicily, and it is with these that we shall be most concerned. Early in the fifth century, the mainland Greeks had fought a successful series of battles against the world power of that time, the vast empire of Persia. The western Greeks, however, were menaced by lesser though important powers, the Etruscans of northern Italy (Tuscany) and particularly the Carthaginians, a Phoenician people who had established a small but powerful state on the North African coast (modern Tunisia) and whose considerable wealth was based mainly on trading, which took their merchants as far afield as Spain and France. Their wealth was a byword in the Mediterranean and enabled them to employ mercenaries to protect their economic interests in Spain, Corsica and Sardinia and to retain their control of western Sicily. But it also inevitably brought them into conflict with the Greeks, who also wanted their share of Sicily and its riches.

In these circumstances, Sicily's need for protection was paramount. Without safety and stability there was nothing. So it made some sense that the people in the island's small city-states should support the person or regime that offered freedom from internal political conflict and promised to defend them from actual and potential aggressors. We can see despotism of this type well exemplified in the regimes of some of the Sicilian city-states. Such tyrannies may well have developed in response to threats from external powers as well as to hostility from the indigenes of Sicily, the Sicels, from whom the land had been forcibly taken in the first place. During the sixth century, other Mediterranean islands had been appropriated by contending states. The Etruscans had taken Corsica, and the Carthaginians had established themselves in much of Sardinia, effectively closing it to the Greeks who coveted its corn and its metals. And it was later, in the early fifth century, while mainland Greece was engaged in a titanic struggle against the invading Persians, that Carthage did her best to wrest Sicily from the western Greeks.

At this time, northern Sicily was dominated by two Greek tyrants who were related by marriage, Terillas of Himera and his son-in-law Anaxilas of Messana. In the south there was another, more powerful, family group, Theron of Acragas and his son-in-law, the better known Gelon of Gela, the successor of the previous tyrant, Hippocrates, who had died trying to establish an hegemony in Greek Sicily. Gelon extended his domains by taking advantage of a particular set of fortuitous circumstances. The aristocracy of Syracuse, soon due to become the leading city in western Sicily, appealed to him to restore their position after having been ousted by the commoners during one of the perennial outbursts of stasis. He seized the opportunity to take the city and come to terms with both the aristocracy and the people. There is a story that having consolidated his power by conquest and by the formation of the most formidable military force in Sicily, he offered to resign his position as tyrant but was instead hailed as king. To be given this kind of formal recognition by the people was a privilege not enjoyed by many of his kind (Bury and Meiggs, 1978: 188), but this story is of doubtful authenticity. What is well substantiated is that Gelon defeated a formidable attack by Carthaginian forces in 480, ostensibly to reinstate a recently deposed tyrant. Whether there was any collusion between the Carthaginians and the Persians who (coincidentally?) launched their even more formidable invasion of mainland Greece the same year, is still uncertain, though it seems likely. Gelon had been invited to join the Greek alliance against the Persians, but had been denied command of the army by Sparta and of the navy by Athens – requests which he perhaps guessed they would refuse. He was therefore free to deal with the Carthaginians, and he also took out insurance in case of a Persian victory by sending an envoy to Delphi, the generally respected oracular shrine, with money and earth and water as a sign of submission to Persian power.

Like so many tyrants, Gelon oscillated between impulsiveness and shrewdness. He was careful about whom he backed and whom he rejected. He liked to do things his own way. He could be quite ruthless in his dealings with some states and almost uncharacteristically generous – or diplomatically indifferent – in his dealings with others. He built up a wealthy state and was often lavish with his gifts, especially to Greek cult centres such as Delphi. But he was not obviously a champion of the people which, as we have seen, was the ostensible *raison d'etre* of quite a few tyrants. Yet, despite this, he seems to have been popular with the demos, and to have been remembered with some affection for his generosity to the state. His successor in 478 his brother Hieron, was probably less well regarded despite his reputation for sporting prowess at Olympia, as well as for his military victories, which were perhaps rather obsequiously celebrated by one of Greece's most famous poets, Pindar, for whom Hieron acted as patron. Hieron, like Gelon before him, was a great benefactor, especially to Delphi; whether this was out of true piety or whether such dedications were little more than acts of autocratic ostentation is difficult to know. Pindar, for all his eulogistic versifying, hints that under the surface of court affairs problems were already brewing (Andrewes, 1966: 134). We can only make speculative inferences about this. What we do know is that Hieron's successor, another brother, lasted less than a year, and very soon afterwards the tyranny was overthrown.

There followed an uneasy period of democratic rule until the protracted and brutal Peloponnesian War between Athens and Sparta and their respective allies which eventually divided most of the Greek world (431–404). During this conflict Athens decided on an indirect approach to victory which would also enrich her coffers and secure a plentiful supply of grain, a commodity of which she was often in precariously short supply. She sent a huge task force to Sicily in 415 and, after a disastrous campaign that lasted for two years, lost most of her fleet – reputedly the finest in the Aegean – and most of her men, a catastrophic incident from which she never really recovered and which contributed significantly to her ultimate defeat. Syracuse, now the leading city in Greek Sicily, was the primary agent of this defeat which was achieved by a military junta led by one, Hermocrates, who was duly – and typically – banished after his victory because he was suspected of autocratic ambitions. Four years later (409) the Carthaginians again invaded under their leader Hannibal. He invested the city of Himera, the site of the previous Carthaginian defeat (480), and massacred 3,000 Greek captives in revenge for the death of his grandfather, Hamilcar, who had commanded that costly operation in which most of the Carthaginian invasion force had also been lost. Hermocrates tried to make a come-back to retrieve the situation, almost on a privateer basis, but was never officially recalled and was killed when he tried to press his claims. The Carthaginians returned in 406, but were now wary of tackling Syracuse directly and instead concentrated their attack on the city of Acragas (Agrigento), which finally surrendered after a lengthy siege (405). This exacerbated problems in Syracuse where there was near revolution over the conduct of the war. A subordinate of Hermocrates, who had narrowly escaped death in the abortive putsch which had left Hermocrates dead in the market-place of Syracuse but who had since distinguished himself in battle at Acragas, now presented himself as the representative of the people and challenged the government for its corruption and inefficiency. To all intents and purposes he was supporting the cause of the demos, but Dionysios was to become the most infamous of all the Sicilian tyrants.

From the outset, Dionysios made all the right moves. He attacked the rich and confiscated their property to finance his defensive measures. He got himself elected to the board of generals, hired mercenaries and ensured the loyalty of his troops by increasing their pay. By staging a mock attempt on his own life he enlisted the sympathy of the citizens, and increased the apprehension of his opponents by using the 'incident' to justify the formation of a personal bodyguard. He further secured his position by marrying Hermocrates' daughter and executing those generals – actually his main rivals – who were deemed to have failed the state in its time of national emergency. He brought back exiles from the former democratic regime and put his family and friends into key military and political posts. But he had his share of problems too. He soon had to deal with a revolt in his own ranks, and then had to come to terms with the Carthaginians who gave him a free hand in Syracuse providing he left most of the island under their control, an arrangement which just couldn't last. He broke the treaty by progressively taking over some of the neighbouring cities, often transporting the inhabitants to Syracuse where he needed labour or else selling them off as slaves. Some, however, were endowed with Syracusan citizenship and given lands, as were also some of his mercenaries, an honour that placed them under a deep sense of obligation to the tyrant and ensured that in future their fortunes were inextricably bound up with his.

To ensure his own personal safety and that of his family and bodyguard, Dionysios fortified the island of Ortygia in the harbour and lived there much of the time in near seclusion. In the city itself, life went on as usual. Dionysios retained most of the constitutional trappings of government. The magistrates and other officials were duly elected – though it is doubtful if any could have remained in office long without Dionysios' approval. The assembly of citizens still met and passed resolutions, but nothing was allowed to disturb the existing status quo. Trade was good, though much of the income was devoted to military expenditure. Dionysios campaigned both summer *and* winter – something of an innovation in the ancient world – so needed increased wealth to finance his expansionist policies and especially to maintain his on-off wars with the Carthaginians. Like so many despots, he found that it paid to have a permanent enemy on the doorstep; it helped to divert public attention from disturbing domestic issues. In 392 he embarked on the conquest of southern Italy, where many Greeks had settled, and by 387 was master of most of these western Greek states. He also controlled territory, especially harbours, on the west coast of Greece where he suppressed much of the piracy, as well as parts of eastern Italy. In fact his conquests were such that Syracuse became, albeit briefly, one of the most powerful states in the ancient world. Dionysios was so well known that even the fierce and barbarous Gauls from northern Europe, who had made incursions into

Italy in 400 and had actually sacked a still unpretentious Rome in 387, offered to make an alliance with him.

In many ways, Dionysios was an unpredictable and complex character. He was a man of obscure birth, a one-time official in a public office who had risen to prominence through a combination of energy and ruthlessness. He was unscrupulous when it paid, and quite insensitive to others' needs when it served his interests. He was capable of selling whole populations into slavery, yet he could sometimes be uncharacteristically merciful to his enemies, even when they had actively rebelled against him (Finley, 1968). During his long and turbulent reign he did much for his own city, and was generally well-thought of by his own people, though he was so distrusted by other Greeks that at the Olympic Games of 388, the orator, Lysias, made such a condemnatory speech that many of the spectators attacked the tyrant's ambassadors and prevented them from offering their sacrifices (Haywood, 1971: 271). Dionysios revolutionized warfare, especially in the development of the catapult which reputedly could hurl two hundred-weight stones over 200 yards and – complementarily – in the art of constructing fortifications capable of withstanding the most challenging sieges.

Yet there was another side to Dionysios. He was a great patron of the arts, and even harboured the fanciful notion that he had been touched by the Muses himself. He tried unsuccessfully to get his tragedies published at Athens, and it was only shortly before his death in 367 that he was allowed to have a modest but immemorable chorus at the festival of Dionysos. Although his whole reign was unconstitutional, and maintained by the ongoing fiction of re-election, there is no record of personal violations either to his supporters or to his adversaries. This sort of thing has been the undoing of many a despot. It is said of Dionysios that there were never complaints from fathers or husbands or lovers; he never violated their families or friends out of personal lust or whim, or was guilty of arbitrary affronts that they could never forget, as was the case with, say, Caligula. Perhaps the secret of his tyranny was that of true political cunning. He apparently never committed outrages to gratify purely personal desires; his rule was that of the shrewd despot whose oppressiveness was part of his political craft.

Monarchical Despotism: early Imperial Rome

One could hardly find a worse concentration of despotic rulers than those of early Imperial Rome, that is from Augustus (d. 14 AD) to Nero (d. 69 AD), although there were a number of pretty unsavoury characters throughout the Imperial period. In theory, they each acted as princeps, that is to say a kind of first among equals, but almost from the outset this became something of a constitutional fiction. They were supposed to be ultimately answerable to the Senate, the highest deliberative body in Rome, but in practice it was they who were usually firmly in control. This succession of emperors, for that is what they really were, are known as the Julio-Claudian dynasty, and seem as though they had some kind of congenital defect or proclivity for despotic behaviour.

Octavian, later – and better known – as Augustus, was the nephew of Julius Caesar who was assassinated because he was seen by many of the traditionalist Republican faction in Rome as a dictator. Octavian was anxious to become Caesar's successor, but he was still only in his teens and, what is more, he had some well-placed rivals, especially the opportunistic Mark Anthony, one of Caesar's lieutenants. So he had to wait. As an initial step a triumvirate was formed, consisting of Octavian, Mark Anthony and another candidate, Lepidus, as a junior partner. This threesome effectively divided up the Roman world between them, each one taking responsibility for a portion of the empire. To make such an arrangement work they had first to suppress all opposition. This meant the proscription not only of political enemies but also those who were no more than strident critics of their policies. Even those they intensely disliked were sometimes included, thus Mark Anthony insisted that one victim should be Cicero, perhaps the most brilliant of the Roman intelligentsia, because he had denounced in his speeches what he regarded as Anthony's inordinate pretensions. Cicero was but one of many. The proscription lists also included certain wealthy citizens simply because the triumvirs wanted their money to pay their troops and to confiscate their lands in order to settle their veterans. In all this Octavian was particularly unscrupulous, and pitilessly demanded the death of a number of leading members of the Senate, mainly because they might prove an obstacle to his overweening ambition.

Predictably, the triumvirate began to dissolve by disagreement. The lesser member, Lepidus, virtually retired from public life except for certain ritual duties, so the main conflict of interest was between the remaining two partners who actually became related by marriage. A redivision of the empire was agreed, with Anthony taking the East, and Octavian taking the West, shrewdly guessing that the real power would always reside in Rome. Octavian thus bided his time in the capital, gradually building up support in influential quarters, while Anthony pursued his amorous adventures with the Egyptian queen, Cleopatra, preparing further campaigns in the east and awaiting the showdown that he knew would have to come. When it did, at the battle of Actium (31 BC) Octavian was victorious. Anthony and Cleopatra fled back to Egypt and both committed suicide, though not until Cleopatra had tried her reputed wiles on Octavian to secure an amicable settlement for her and Caesarion, her child by Julius Caesar. But it didn't work. She was now nearly 40, the last reigning member of the Ptolemaic (Greek) royal family that had ruled Egypt since the late fourth century. The implacable Octavian – no respecter of age or of faded beauty – was quite unmoved. After her death, he had her child killed, and made his own dispositions about the province; in future it would become, in effect, the personal property of the emperor. Such was the inauspicious beginning of the political career of the 'pale assassin'.

Octavian was now master of Rome. The ruthless young man who had traded on his relationship with the dead Caesar and who had triumphed over all his adversaries by his own brand of lethal guile, now metamorphosed as Augustus, the father of his people. His rule was not called despotic, because most of the conventional constitutional forms were still observed, but nothing of any importance was decided in Rome unless it had the imprimatur of Augustus. He was voted special honours, and his continual re-election to office became just a matter of form for the rest of his life.

Augustus always had very clear ideas about where he was going. He was not a great general, but he was an astute administrator and had the gift of choosing capable subordinates to do his work for him. After over a century of civil strife he brought relative peace and stability to Rome (the Pax Romana), and although he had a number of personal tragedies in his family, his work for the state was long remembered. Indeed, his influence was such that he was allowed to nominate his own successor, his stepson Tiberius, who had proved to be one of his most able commanders. It was the beginning of dynastic rule – and of quasi-legal despotism.

Tiberius actually became emperor by default. He had not been Augustus' first choice by any means, but others had either died prematurely or had been considered unsuitable for the task. Apparently a rather disgruntled and enigmatic character, he was already in his middle years before he came to power. He proved to be an able statesman, certainly until his later years when he tended to procrastinate and leave many important decisions to others. In general, he not only continued Augustus' policies but also managed to maintain relative peace throughout the empire.

The historical sources, particularly Suetonius, have not been altogether kind to Tiberius – perhaps with good reason. It is acknowledged that he disdained the trappings of power and hated outward show, high-sounding titles and the like. Neither was he keen on festivals and the gladiatorial Games which so excited the Roman public. But he did like power *itself*. He usually managed to impose his will on the Senate, and some of its members suffered from his intolerance. He appears to have been a stickler for the rules and was keen to observe the prescribed ritual niceties and to show that he honoured the gods. When abuses were detected, for example, in various foreign cults, notably that of Isis, he had some priests crucified as punishment. His austerity and aloofness are perhaps well illustrated by his apparently genuine retort to his critics that he didn't care if the people didn't love him as long as they respected him.

The despotic nature of Tiberius' rule can best be seen in the various treason trials that took place during his reign. These were largely carried through by his chief lieutenant and by common consent, his sinister but influential daimon, Sejanus, though whether they were instigated by Sejanus or whether he simply acted as a front-man for the largely absent Tiberius is difficult to say. As Prefect of the Praetorian Guard, Sejanus had considerable power already, but he was a man of unlimited ambition. One way or another he gradually did away with the opposition. He seduced the emperor's daughter-in-law and poisoned his son, and generally fomented trouble between different branches of the family to his own advantage. Yet still the ultimate prize was denied him. In his impatience he overplayed his hand. He concocted a plot which was then betrayed to the incredulous emperor who, if Suetonius is to be believed, was wiling away his time in deviant sexual pastimes on the island of Capri. Once the plot was rumbled, the now indolent emperor acted with ruthless dispatch: the plotters were arrested, and Sejanus was executed together with his family. Tacitus also indicates that this was followed by a brief reign of terror in which a number of judicial murders took place.

Tiberius has often been depicted as a lonely, morose and yet in some ways rather pathetic paraphiliac. The very fact that he left Rome and retired to Capri some 11 years before his death in 37 AD, indicates that he had become somewhat disillusioned with conventional court life, and not only wanted to divest himself of everyday administrative activity, but also of the scheming and general in-fighting that went with work within the hierarchy. Yet he continued to be a wary soul, prey to the whispers and suggestions of his favourites. Not easily able to verify or otherwise the stories they brought him about life in the capital, he gradually changed into an old and disgruntled misanthropist – a rather inglorious end for the master of the world.

Tiberius may or may not have died a natural death, there have always been suspicions that he was helped on his way by his enigmatic successor, Gaius Caesar (Caligula). Aside from the murder – if, indeed, there was a murder – Caligula started well, almost too well. In contrast to the frugality of Tiberius, he spent lavishly, and, being liberal with tax concessions and imperial pardons, was instantly popular with both people and Senate. All in all, it was a promising beginning. However, in September of 37 he had a serious illness, and when he recovered he began to exhibit the worst signs of arbitrary despotism both in his private pursuits and in his public activities. He almost certainly had an incestuous relationship with his sister, and thought nothing of forcing members of his court to lend him their wives for sexual diversions. He became even more profligate with treasury monies, spending frivolously, especially on his favourites who were more often than not either athletes or actors. Much more sinister was the way in which he abused his position by ordering the deaths of a number of innocent but wealthy citizens – even to the point of commanding some to fight as gladiators – mainly, it seems, so that he could confiscate their estates. He also ordered the murder of his own cousin, the youthful Gemellus, possibly because of some vague suspicion about threats to his authority. In fact, such evidence as we have suggests that he actually derived some perverted pleasure from exercising power in this brutal and irresponsible way.

In the autumn of 39, he set out on what was meant to be a great campaign against the Germans and the British. But the German expedition turned out to be little more than a ludicrous pretence, and the 'token' invasion of Britain consisted mainly of the emperor's intrepid visit to the French seashore. He did confiscate a few Gallic fortunes, and when he got back to Rome in 40 he counted it all as something of a triumph. On his return, his rapacity and cruelty increased. He now declared himself divine, something dangerously novel to the Roman experience, as normally emperors had to wait until they died before they received such honours. He prescribed sacrifices that were to be offered to himself, and actually had a high bridge built on the Palatine Hill in Rome which he could climb in order to speak to his brother-god, Jupiter, the chief deity in the Roman pantheon. Finally, his behaviour became too much even for the rather obsequious Senate, which had gradually abdicated responsibility, and he was murdered together with his family in January 41 by his own Praetorians who seem to have had personal reasons as well as the good of the state in mind when they killed him.

One wonders why the Senate put up with Caligula for so long. Some contemporary opinion attributed his behaviour to madness resulting from his illness. How else, they asked, could one explain the change that had taken place at the end of 37? Others have maintained that his upbringing with an embittered mother and the company of eastern princelings fostered his despotic leanings. Maybe: perhaps these were contributory causes. On the other hand, it may have been largely a matter of too much too soon: the situation of a young man, not without ability – especially, reputedly, a ready facility for public speaking – who, reared in an atmosphere of suspicion and proscription, found himself suddenly able to indulge his most despotic fantasies. It seems never to have seriously occurred to him that unlimited power brings with it unlimited responsibilities.

Caligula's successor, like Tiberius, came to the Principate in his middle years. During the upheavals attending Caligula's assassination, his uncle,

Claudius, who thought that he too was to be killed, was found hiding behind a curtain by the Praetorians and to his amazement was proclaimed emperor. The guard was suitably rewarded by a donation, thus establishing a precedent which was to become customary in the empire. Claudius, possibly due to some congenital illness, was generally regarded as the least suitable of Augustus' family for high honours, and had spent much of his earlier life in scholarly pursuits. Not that he was an unrecognized genius or the benign and bumbling old scholar depicted in Robert Graves' *I, Claudius*. It is probable that in the circumstances there was little else for him to do.

It is quite conceivable that the Senate, who were at first critical, agreed to the army's choice, and were then ready to endorse his succession because he seemed to be the safest of the possible choices, and someone who could be manipulated at will. They were to discover how wrong they could be. Claudius was open to persuasion, but much depended on who was doing the persuading. He was particularly susceptible to the influences of his freedmen (that is, men who had been freed from slavery), and even more to that of ambitious women. And he also had that wilful streak that sometimes displayed itself as a kind of irrational stubbornness.

Given his natural disadvantages, Claudius turned out to be a remarkably energetic emperor. He introduced all sorts of beneficial fiscal measures, and had a positive mania for law reform. He also gave Rome a much-needed harbour and reclaimed large tracts of land by lake drainage. Besides adding new provinces to the empire, he also put into operation the one great military campaign that had long been anticipated – the conquest of Britain. We do not know how much all this was directly due to Claudius' own initiative and foresight, or to what extent it was really the work of gifted subordinates, but at least he saw the wisdom of such schemes.

Claudius had singularly bad judgment when it came to women. Before he became emperor, he married a woman of the aristocracy, who soon became a byword for her flagrant sexual indiscretions – even to the point, so it is said, of posing as a prostitute. For a while Claudius does not seem to have been aware of Messalina's behaviour, but it could hardly be kept secret when she went so far as to go through a form of 'marriage' with one of her lovers, Gaius Silius. Claudius had Silius executed, not just because of his adultery with Messalina, but because what he had done constituted a presumption to the throne. Yet, in spite of all this, he still could not bring himself to punish his wife. This was left to his freedmen who, acting on their own initiative, had her put to death – something which Claudius seems to have resignedly accepted as politically necessary. As an act of diplomacy, he later married his niece, Agrippina, who allegedly had married and then murdered her former husband for his wealth. This expedient of Claudius' caused something of a scandal in Roman society but was eventually condoned by a compliant Senate.

Agrippina's dominating ambition was to ensure that her son by her previous marriage would inherit the throne instead of Claudius' son by Messalina. She was quite unscrupulous in her methods, and she used her considerable influence with the Praetorians and the Senate, with whom Claudius was increasingly less popular, to achieve her ends. Eventually, when all was set, and her son had been adopted by Claudius and had married his own step-sister, Claudius' daughter, Octavia, when she was only 15, she arranged to have the aged emperor poisoned. As the mother of the new emperor, she regarded herself as the real power behind the throne, but she miscalculated – the new emperor was Nero.

Claudius' affliction, which apparently gave him nervous spasms and often rendered his speech unclear, made him an unattractive personality, and he was kept out of the limelight during his earlier years even though these disabilities probably disguised a lively intelligence. When he came to power, he tried to restore the dignity of the court by replacing, where possible, monies and works of art that had been stolen and by having some of Caligula's worst minions put to death. But having said all this, it would be unwise to overlook the more unpleasant aspects of Claudius' reign. He purported to follow those practices favoured by Augustus, and like Augustus he did not easily tolerate opposition. Any hint of criticism was often interpreted as treason and was ruthlessly crushed. His court was alive with conspiracy, and although he claimed to disdain professional informers, he was ever ready to listen to malicious gossip and rumour which, not unusually, reached him via his wives and his freedmen. There was a dark, cruel side to Claudius' nature. It says a lot when the sources tell us that he was an avid fan of the gladiatorial contests and that he liked the defeated contestant's vizor to be lifted so that he could see the expression on his face when his throat was cut. It is not surprising to read that his unpopularity was such that plots became rife, and that over 300 senators and nobles were executed during his reign.

Nero's accession in 54 was achieved without protest, not least because the Praetorians had been promised an appreciable donative to secure their cooperation. The first year of his reign passed relatively uneventfully. He was only 16, personable and, in theory, full of royal promise. What is more he had the guidance and support of the Praetorian Prefect, Afranius Burrus, and his tutor since 49, the eminent Spanish philosopher, Lucius Seneca. And keeping a synoptic eye on everything was his ambitious mother who, in these formative years, acted as a kind of regent to her inexperienced son with whom it is suggested, she had an on-off incestuous relationship. But Nero learnt quickly. He soon began to resist his mother's influence and go his own way. To what extent this was aided and abetted by his advisers, no one is quite sure. Certainly in the case of Seneca, what we know of his writings makes modern authorities rather reluctant to cast him in the role of Svengali. However, someone appears to have catered to his baser instincts because we soon see evidence of the kind of depravity for which he later became infamous. In 55, he had his adoptive brother poisoned and, to his mother's distress, later took as his mistress Poppea Sabina, the wife of the future emperor, who was to reign for a mere three months (January–April 69), Marcus Otho. By 59, he had become thoroughly impatient with Agrippina's interference and tried first of all to have her drowned in such a way as to look like an accident, and then when this failed, in tragi-farcical circumstances, he contrived to have her butchered inelegantly by one of his aides. Such was his gratitude to the woman who had schemed and murdered to ensure his eventual succession to the throne.

Fratricide and matricide apart, things didn't go so badly at government level during these early years. But once Nero had assumed fully the reins of government the situation changed. Increasingly he began to live only for the gratification of his own interests. After the death of Burrus (in 62), who was replaced by the notorious new Praetorian Prefect, Tigellinus, Seneca was able to exert less and less influence over the ruler. Nero's wanton extravagance depleted a treasury that was already at a very low ebb and he had to resort to more oppressive measures to bolster his revenues, especially to finance the building of his famed Golden House. During this period too, there were serious problems in the empire. There was a rebellion in Armenia (60–61), which was only subdued with considerable difficulty by one of Nero's most able generals, Corbulo (62–63), who was later condemned to death, perhaps partly out of jealousy, despite his reputation as a first-rate military commander. At about the same time, a revolt broke out among the Iceni and Trinovantes tribes in Great Britain in which Colchester, St Albans and London were destroyed and some 70,000 Romans (including families) were reputedly killed (60). It is now generally accepted that this was largely due to repressive Roman administration although the vengeance of the tribespeople got completely out of hand. The rebellion was finally checked and the Britons were decisively defeated and their moving force, Boadicea, the queen of the Iceni, subsequently committed suicide.

At this time, Nero was distracted by domestic matters. He was running down his liaison with Acte, a Greek freedwoman, having simultaneously conducted various affairs with a motley assortment of men and women – bisexuality being something which seems to have been almost *de rigueur* in court circles, if Suetonius and Petronius (Satyricon) are to be believed. He had grown tired of his young wife, and in 62 divorced her on the trumped-up charge of adultery with a slave and had her exiled to the island of

Pandateria (Pantellaria) where she was conveniently put to death after only a few days. Having become enamoured of the Roman beauty, Poppea, who Tacitus said had every possible asset except goodness, he married her within days of the divorce.

In 64, fire broke out in Rome and continued unabated for nearly a week, and when it looked as though it had finally petered out, it broke out again. The city was devastated. There is no evidence that it was started at Nero's instigation, but he undoubtedly took advantage of the tragedy to rebuild Rome on a grander scale. He also looked around for a suitable scapegoat, someone to blame for the fire; in such circumstances it always pays to divert public attention towards a possible culprit. It was decided, possibly at the suggestion of Tigellinus, to blame an obscure but (to Roman eyes) deviant religious sect, the Christians, because they appeared to have no great love for the state or its emperor, and – what is more to the point – were particularly vulnerable because of their pacifistic attitudes. People were rounded up and treated with inconceivable cruelty. Some were cast to the beasts in the arena, others were butchered by gladiators, and some were even tarred and used as lighted torches in Nero's pleasure gardens. They received little sympathy from the public, though some were impressed by their courage and the sect continued to grow, one day to take over the empire itself.

Nero, perhaps uncharacteristically, was not particularly keen on the arena, rather his interests were artistic and aesthetic. Gladiatorial combat did not appeal to him that much, but he did pride himself on his athletic prowess; he took part in the Greek Olympic Games of 66 and despite making something of a fool of himself was still dutifully awarded all the prizes. He was so overjoyed at his reception by the Greeks that he magnanimously granted them their 'freedom'. He also fancied his chances as a poet, singer and musician – not unlike Dionysios – and appeared in public, much to the disapproval and embarrassment of the Roman aristocracy, among whom his talents were largely unrecognized. It may be that he actually did sing during the fire – it was the sort of spectacle that would inspire him. However, his artistic temperament did not rule out those bursts of anger and irrationality which vitiated his behaviour, especially when he was criticized or thought that he was in any kind of danger – a sure mark of the despot. Previously, in 65, he had even been instrumental in causing the death of his beloved Poppea Sabina – albeit unintentionally – by kicking her when she was pregnant with their second child. She was laid to rest with considerable ceremony; Nero took charge of the obsequies, delivered the funeral oration, and had her proclaimed a goddess. But none of this prevented him from taking a fancy to a young eunuch whom he called Sabina, or very soon taking another wife, Statilia, who may already have been his mistress. That she had been married four times already probably added a certain piquance to the occasion (as was once said in quite a different context, 'he knew exactly what to do, the problem was how to make it interesting'). The fact too that she was currently married also presented few difficulties – the imperial executioners simply visited her husband's house one evening and cut short his dinner party.

Since at least 62, when there had been a number of treason trials, there had been ominous rumblings of dissension in the city. Nero's behaviour, as we have seen, was becoming increasingly erratic, and inevitably conspiracies began to take shape. By 65, the sense of unease and insecurity was such, especially among the senatorial classes, that plans to overthrow the despot were formulated by one particular senator, Gaius Piso, and some of the Praetorians. This was discovered, and there were widespread repercussions. It is not known how many were caught and condemned; the common use of torture was very effective in uncovering a wide network of plotters as well as those who just maintained a silent disapproval. Among those who died for complicity were the aged Seneca and his nephew, the poet Lucan, and Corbulo who was forced to commit suicide in 67.

By 68, the situation had become so intolerable that open rebellion took place among some of the legates in the Roman provinces. Perhaps surprisingly, other legates declared for the emperor or maintained that it was the Senate's task, not theirs, to decide on such high political issues. Nero could probably have weathered the crisis if it had not been for his own cowardice in the face of some of his own suborned Praetorian guards. He fled from Rome and eventually killed himself with the aid of one of his freedmen, just as soldiers were arriving to capture him. Thus concluded the reign of a despot who, unlike, say, the unpredictable Caligula, could always be relied upon to react to frustration or opposition in much the same way. He was cruel, superstitious and self-deceived to the end; almost his last words are alleged to have been, 'what an artist dies with me'.

CHAPTER SEVEN

Dynastic Despotism: the Ptolemies

The period from the death of Alexander in 323 BC to the death of the last of the Ptolemies, Cleopatra VII, in 30 BC, is commonly known as the Hellenistic Age. The Roman takeover of the kingdom of Egypt marked the end of some 300 years of Ptolemaic rule and set the seal on Roman domination of the Mediterranean world.

The Hellenistic Age was characterized by the struggles of Alexander's generals to carve out territories for themselves. The empire that Alexander had created was too unwieldy and too unstable to survive his death. Even before he died, fragmentation was beginning to take place, and when his autocratic rule ended the struggle for succession began. At first, his generals tried to keep the empire in being, but this period lasted almost no time at all. Within ten years Alexander's 'natural' successors, his wife and son, were murdered and it was obvious that unity could not be maintained. The struggles intensified and the situation became complicated by all manner of shifting alliances. One of the contenders, an elderly general, Antigonus, tried to exert his authority over the others, but this was finally scotched at the battle of Ipsus in 301, whereupon three men emerged as successors and proclaimed themselves kings: Lysimachus in Thrace and Asia Minor, Seleucus in the East and Ptolemy in Egypt.

The Egyptian people, especially the poor fellahin, were accustomed to the day-to-day drudgery of agricultural life. The lot of the peasant had never been exactly enviable. Ptolemy saw no reason to disabuse them. He was more than happy that things should go on as before, and he merely injected a little more rationality into the system, which he ran as a personal fief. Careful land registers were kept, and although some personal ownership of land was allowed, considerable proportions were administered for the king through his agents. This was not really that dissimilar from the way things had been under the earlier pharaohs. Demobilized troops were often given allotments of land as a reward for their services and, no doubt, to neutralize any possible agitation; retired soldiers, and especially mercenaries, could be more trouble than they were worth once they had no more campaigning to do. Each peasant's allotment was rationally calculated, and he was given seed and told just how much he was supposed to produce. Needless to say, the bulk of the yield went to the crown; not too much was left for the peasant and his family. Furthermore, peasants were mobilized for work on the canals, the irrigation system and other public works, their labour counting as a form of tax to the government. Little wonder that slavery, as we normally understand it, was not well developed in ancient Egypt as it was largely unnecessary with such a huge reservoir of conscripted serf labour. However, slave estates did exist, a practice later to be copied by the Romans, and little could rival the horrors of the Nubian gold mines which were almost exclusively worked by slaves.

A good example of how agricultural production was organized and regulated can be seen in the olive oil industry (Haywood, 1971: 399). This was a typical government monopoly, as is evidenced by a papyrus known as the Revenue Laws of Ptolemy Philadelphus. Before the Greek takeover in Egypt (it was broadly a conquest – Alexander, en route to Persia, 'liberated' the country from the Persians in 332), oil was derived mainly from seeds such as sesame, safflower and so on, and olives were usually only eaten as fruit. But the Ptolemies encouraged the pressing of olives and thus established an indigenous olive oil industry which obviated the need for expensive imports. Every step in the process was regulated by the government from the distribution of the seed to the allocation of the lands. No private initiatives were allowed. The gathering was strictly supervised as were the government sponsored 'mills' where the processing took place. Even the marketing networks were government organized, as were also the tariffs and price controls.

Or again, take the matter of wheat, of which Egypt was one of the main producers in the ancient world. The 'gift of the Nile', as Herodotos called it, and the vast irrigation works that were developed, enabled Egypt to become not only a producer but also a principal exporter of wheat throughout the Mediterranean. Her harvests were often so rich that she could afford generous gifts of wheat to those countries, such as Greece, with whom she had particularly strong ties. Egypt redeveloped the old caravan routes to Mesopotamia, and even restored the canal linking the Nile to the Red Sea in order to foster trade with the East. She also formed important commercial alliances with other trading nations, especially the island republic of Rhodes, which was one of the great maritime powers at this time. Besides this, she ran a useful trade in slaves from Nubia, and was able to import spices, ointments and dyes from remote, exotic lands such as Arabia and India. Yet despite all this, the government nearly always seemed to be in need of more income. This was due, in part, to the fact that although Egypt was rich in some natural resources, she was sadly deficient in others, such as timber for building and ships – which came largely from Macedonia and Phoenicia (Lebanon) – and iron for tools and weaponry. But it was also due in no small part to the munificence and extravagance of the king and his court.

It has been argued that the Ptolemaic government was one of the most capable and rigidly hierarchical bureaucracies ever devised (Bowman, 1986: 36ff). Although not geared exclusively to satisfy the requirements of the royal family and the nobility – the system was too functionally differentiated and its economy too multifarious for that – it undoubtedly did oppress the poor for the benefit of the rich. It appears to have recorded and regulated all political and economic activities, sometimes down to the minutest details. An extant text of 258 of the king, Ptolemy Philadelphus, illustrates this point well. It concerns orders given for a census of the entire kingdom, a task allocated to the finance minister, and shows that detailed returns were required from scribes and officials for information about types of holding, sources of water, irrigation methods, kinds of crop, and so on. The state also had a carefully controlled monetary system which was later copied by the Ptolemies' successors. Interestingly, this high degree of royal organization, which traditionally was the focus of religious veneration, was complemented – perhaps we should say, offset – by an increase in secular control. The Ptolemies maintained the customary religious observances and built temples in quasi-pharaonic fashion, yet there was still a decline in the wealth and influence of the native Egyptian priesthood.

In the governmental machinery, the king was unquestionably the key figure: he was the chief executive who issued detailed instructions that were to be followed precisely by his subordinates. The tone of the royal decrees gives the impression of autocratic fiat, but as we know from the state of affairs in earlier times, this was a formal requirement which might not always be adhered to in practice. Orders had obviously to be mediated via subordinates at appropriate levels in the hierarchy. In this carefully graduated system, everyone had *some* responsibility. Absolutism had to be tempered by necessity.

Sophisticated as the system was, there was no clear demarcation between civil and military or religious and secular matters; an official might well function in more than one capacity. There was evidently a considerable amount of nepotism within the system; the bestowal of favours and the granting of offices was very much the prerogative of the king. Strange as it may seem to us, there was no proper salary structure for officials, and this, combined with the fact that vital operations such as the collection of taxes were farmed out to private contractors, left the system open to peculation and graft, crimes for which punishments could be extremely severe.

What seems very clear is that Ptolemaic society was reasonably clearly stratified along cultural lines. It was a question of Greeks and Egyptians, although distinctions could be blurred where Egyptians were prepared to become Hellenized, learning Greek (the language of the administration) and taking on the cultural appearance of their overlords. Greeks had been settled in the Nile Delta since pharaonic times when they had been allowed to set up trading stations (emporia) at Naukratis and elsewhere. As time had gone on, and especially since the founding of Alexandria in the fourth century, these trading stations had become established communities. With the takeover by a Greek nobility, the status of ordinary Greeks had been enhanced from settler-colonists to ruling elite. And cultural differences were not all. The Greeks were politically and economically dominant, and even had a different judiciary from that of the native Egyptians. Some towns were almost exclusively Greek, in which case citizenship, which effectively meant having certain social and political rights, was strictly regulated. These towns maintained the traditional Greek institutions – assemblies, magistrates, and the like – and civic amenities such as gymnasia, all of which contributed to their distinctiveness.

Gradually, however, these distinctions began to be eroded, partly by intermarriage and partly by the inevitable and necessary process of integration. This was particularly evident in certain areas of activity – the military, for example – but by-and-large it did not take place because of some form of egalitarian conviction but rather out of sheer expediency. So we have the emergence of the Graeco-Egyptian as a kind of intermediate category (usually a Hellenized Egyptian), much the same as in Britain under Roman occupation there developed a stratum of Romano-Britons. Even the very different religious cultures did not entirely separate the Greeks from the Egyptians. Some degree of syncretism was bound to take place. The Greeks, in particular, interpreted certain aspects of Egyptian religion in their own terms. The royal family took on some of the trappings of traditional pharaonic ritual, largely, one presumes, as a matter of policy, although there is just the suspicion that they were not a little seduced by the exotica of the display itself.

The relative orderliness and rationality of Ptolemaic rule can be contrasted with the often turbulent lives of the rulers themselves. The founder of the dynasty, Ptolemy Soter, was obviously an able general and – like his late king, Alexander – something of an opportunistic adventurist. Just a year before his death, Alexander had put one of his subordinates, Cleomenes, in charge of the financial administration of Egypt, but Cleomenes had taken advantage of the situation to amass a large fortune and establish himself as virtual master of the country. When Ptolemy became satrap of Egypt in 323, he quickly brought charges of exploitation against Cleomenes, who was effectively his rival, and had him put to death. He then had a rather protracted struggle against other contenders and would-be dynasts, and did not become king officially until 304. Ptolemy controlled more territory than any earlier pharaoh. As well as Egypt, this included part of Libya, a number of Aegean islands, Cyprus, some areas of Asia Minor, and – perhaps most importantly – Palestine and Phoenicia, which remained a permanent bone of contention with his one-time fellow general, Seleucus, who eventually ruled the greater part of Asia Minor.

Ptolemy laid the foundations of the administrative system, restructured the army, and refined the monopolistic organization of the state economy. He also moved the capital from Memphis to Alexandria where he founded the famous library and museum; henceforth Alexandria became possibly the most celebrated cosmopolitan centre of learning and commerce of its time. Ptolemy encouraged immigrants, especially Greeks, and it is estimated that there came to be more Jews in Alexandria than there were in Jerusalem (Grant, 1982: 75). Although, like his successors (except Cleopatra) Ptolemy never learned Egyptian, and did not wear Egyptian dress except on ceremonial occasions, he did not denigrate the national culture. The key factor here was religion. And in this Ptolemy was essentially a pragmatist. In particular, he did not want to antagonize the priesthood. He encouraged the worship of Isis, and redeveloped and modified the ancient cult of Serapis as a kind of tailor-made focus of veneration that combined elements of both Egyptian and Greek culture. Little wonder that after his death in 283, and that of his wife Berenike four years later, they were both proclaimed 'saviour gods' because of their generous benefactions to the state cults.

Their son, born in 306, became co-ruler with his father in 285 and came to the throne as Ptolemy II Philadelphus in 282. He ruled Egypt in the same tradition as his father, extending the process of rationalizing the administration and the state economy, and even extended its territories in the Mediterranean and beyond. The prosperity of the state was greatly enhanced by a system of taxation unprecedented in the ancient world. And along with this went a considerable development in banking which both facilitated the expansion of trade and helped to make Alexandria's reputation for financial activity. It was, incidentally, during the reign of Ptolemy Philadelphus that the famous 400-foot Pharos lighthouse at Alexandria was completed which because of its monumental size and ingenious construction became numbered among the Seven Wonders of the World.

Brother-sister marriage, or perhaps more precisely half-brother-half-sister marriage, had been practised by earlier pharaohs, but it became the custom among the Ptolemies, who seem to have had a preference for full siblings. Thus Ptolemy II married his sister Arsinoe II (c. 277), a very determined woman who exercised a considerable influence over her husband. She was the daughter of Ptolemy I and Berenike I, and when only 17 was married to another of Alexander's subordinates, Lysimachus, an oppressive pretender to the Macedonian throne, who actually had his own son killed when a dispute arose between his wife and his daughter-in-law. After his death in battle in 281, Arsinoe contracted a marriage with her step-brother, Ptolemy Ceraunus (Thunderbolt) who killed two of her children but failed in his attempts to have her mother murdered as well. She fled to Egypt where she then married her younger brother, Philadelphus. Exceptionally, she was accorded divine honours during her lifetime and was frequently identified as a personification of Isis (for the Egyptians) and Aphrodite (for the Greeks), another convenient fiction which did no harm at all to the popular image of the royal family. Needless to say, the royal couple came to be seen as Brother and Sister gods (Theoi Delphoi) with their own separate cults and priesthoods. Religion served its customary purposes in Ptolemaic Egypt as it had since time immemorial, but with the introduction of Greek Dionysianism, with its stress on personal liberation and carefree living, it also functioned increasingly as a soporific for those whose often joyless lives needed display and colour, in short, a festive escape route.

Philadelphus' son, Ptolemy III Energetes (Benefactor), succeeded his father in 246 and continued the policy of expansion, and his agents may have penetrated as far as the Hindu Kush (Grant, 1974: 63). In the same year (246) he married Berenike, the daughter of the king of Cyrene, who had successfully disposed of her first husband and who was now looking for greater things. She too shared a cult with her husband during their lifetime, a practice that was now becoming the norm for royalty and which further enhanced the social distance between them and their subjects. It may be assumed that Berenike II was also a masterful woman, a trait that did not always pay dividends. Her son, with whom she shared the throne after Energetes' death in 221, obviously grew a little tired of her interference and had her murdered in a typical act of Ptolemaic filial piety. Energetes continued the cosmopolitan policies of his father, and immigrants – especially Jews – were welcomed to Egypt, mainly as part of the trading community. He also encouraged cultural development by commissioning agents to purchase copies of the works of classical Greek dramatists and historians. But although he supported scholarship, his not always successful military ventures imposed such a heavy financial burden on the state that it gave rise to considerable public disquiet in his later years.

Energetes' son, Ptolemy IV Philopator (devoted to his father), came to the throne while still a youth. As Polybius puts it (1979: v.34, 2ff), '[from the outset] he showed himself inattentive to business and difficult [to] approach, and treated with complete negligence and indifference those charged with affairs outside Egypt'. It was perhaps inevitable that he came under the influence of dubious court personalities, often eunuchs, whose influence was questionable, to say the very least. The dominating figure was Sosibius who really ran the show and whose reputation for cunning and ruthlessness was a byword even by current court standards. Philopator also married a sister, Arsinoe III, and, although the evidence is rather flimsy, it would appear that in the same lethal tradition she was murdered about the time of her husband's death in 205, possibly at the instigation of Sosibius. Soon after his accession, Philopator's armies had won a notable victory over the Seleucids at Raphia (217) but, in order to do so had to pay a heavy price. He had to recruit large numbers of native Egyptians into his army, who then wished to cast off their image as a rather despised underclass and looked for greater equality with their Greek overlords. This eventually led to civil disturbances and revolts during which the king – who saw himself as a kind of latter-day Dionysios – became ever more disengaged from society. As far as can be ascertained, he gave himself up to a life of profligate indifference, retiring to his 300-foot floating 'pleasure palace' on the Nile which was fitted out with shrines, arcaded courts and a winter garden.

Ptolemy V Epiphanes (god Manifest) was a mere child at the time of his accession (205). And it almost goes without saying that he too was 'guided' by largely self-seeking and unscrupulous mentors, including Sosibius. The famous Rosetta Stone dates from this period (196). This trilingual inscription was of invaluable help to scholars in their efforts to understand and unravel the intricacies of Egyptian hieroglyphics. It proclaims the coronation of the king at the traditional capital, Memphis, and is obviously an attempt to conciliate the native priesthood despite the fact that real control still lay with a foreign power. And despite Epiphanes' concern with internal affairs rather than overseas conquests, it also makes clear that the weakness of the government had led to serious revolts in the south (Thebes) which were severely dealt with:

> King Ptolemy, the ever-living, beloved of Ptah, the god Manifest and Beneficent ... has conferred many benefits on the temples and those that dwell in them and on all the subjects of his kingdom, being a god born of a god and goddess ... when he came to Memphis to avenge his father and his own royalty, he punished in a fitting way all those who rebelled ... (quoted by Bowman, 1986: 30).

During Epiphanes' reign much of the Ptolemaic empire was lost, particularly the territories in Asia and the Aegean. This was largely the result of unsuccessful wars with the Seleucids in Asia Minor. It was possibly to cement relations between the two powers that Ptolemy married into the Seleucid family. His bride was the first of a line of queens named Cleopatra, who may have been of Persian blood (interestingly, as far as we know, no Ptolemy ever married an Egyptian). The loss of many of its overseas possessions led to a marked impoverishment of the Egyptian economy, and this, in turn, encouraged more native unrest, workers' strikes, and then incursions from Nubians in the south. Epiphanes just lived to see the beginning of the decline in Ptolemaic power; he died in 180, to be outlived by his wife by only four years during which time she acted as regent to yet another child-king.

Ptolemy VI Philometor (Mother-loving) married his sister, Cleopatra II, in 175, a lady who was to have a very chequered career. His reign, like his father's was marked by internal dissension – not helped by rapid inflation – and very serious external threats to the existence of the state itself. In fact, at one point (168) Egypt would have been conquered by the Seleucids, had Rome, the now ascendant power, not intervened. From 170, he ruled jointly with his wife and his brother (the future Ptolemy VIII). There were the predictable disputes. But after a period in exile, he returned to take on the sole sovereignty from 163 until his death in 145. The obsequies were hardly over when his brother returned from Cyrene, where Rome had installed him as king, and established himself as Ptolemy VIII Energetes II (Benefactor). His title in part derived from the fact that he made a number of 'amnesties' which were not so much expressions of goodwill as concessions to the growing power of the native population (Walbank, 1981: 122). Out of filial devotion, or more probably in order to secure his position, he married the widow, his sister, in 144, and in the same year – in by now predictable Ptolemaic fashion – murdered their brother who had reigned very briefly as Ptolemy VII. Then taking royal incest a stage further than his forebears, he married Cleopatra III, his sister-wife's daughter, in 142, an arrangement that continued until 132 when Cleopatra II revolted, and Energetes II temporarily lost control of Egypt. But in 127 he regained control of Alexandria, and later a rapprochement was reached and he again ruled jointly with his two wives until his death.

Ptolemy VIII was regarded as a heartless tyrant by some of his fellow Greeks, but then they may have been unduly biased. There was even a strange story that he murdered one of the children he had by his sister, and served the corpse up to her as a meal. He is also known to have banned certain intellectuals from his court. But on the plus side, he was also responsible for dispatching one, Eudoxus, to explore the sea-route to India in the interests of trade and discovery. Physically, he was a person of ample proportions (not for nothing was he nicknamed Physcon – 'fat belly') and sometimes could barely walk for his bulk. Yet despite this congenital tendency towards personal overindulgence, and regardless of the many disruptions during his reign, he did manage to maintain a precarious grip on the political situation, and was probably the last Ptolemy to do so.

From now on it was a matter of continuous decline. Court life became increasingly a matter of fratricidal intrigue. Ptolemy IX Soter II, nicknamed Lathnos (Chick-pea), the son of Cleopatra III with whom he shared the throne after his father's death, was in almost permanent contention with his brother Ptolemy X Alexander. He divorced his sister-wife, Cleopatra IV, in order to marry another sister, Cleopatra Berenike III. For a while he sought exile in Cyprus (108) while his mother ruled jointly with Ptolemy X. In 88 Ptolemy X died and Ptolemy IX returned to rule, but in all these fluctuations there had been heavy borrowing from Roman financiers in order to hire forces to help the rival contenders to secure their positions. For some time it had paid the Ptolemies to maintain good relations with Rome as, in turn, it paid Rome to have a friendly client state that was so strategically placed as Egypt, and Rome badly needed friends for this was a period of considerable upheaval for Roman imperialism. The king of Pontus, Mithridates VI, had embarked on an expansionist policy in Asia Minor which brought him into direct conflict with Rome. This resulted in the massacre of thousands of Rome's eastern settlers before Mithridates – a cunning and elusive foe – was initially subdued by the Roman dictator Sulla (87–86) and finally defeated by Pompey in 66.

By 80, Ptolemy IX too had died, and after the brief and rather anonymous reign of Ptolemy XI, the son of a concubine came to the throne as Ptolemy XII (Neos Dionysos), often referred to as Auletes (Flute-player). For some time, Rome did not recognize his right to the succession as it was assumed that Ptolemy X's wish to bequeath the country to her Roman protectors held good. However, Auletes eventually secured recognition in 59 by offering a huge bribe of reputedly 6,000 talents of gold to Julius Caesar, who had incurred vast debts in securing his own position and who was now intent on becoming supreme in Rome. But the Egyptian people revolted under the burden of the taxes imposed for the repayment of the debt. Auletes fled from Egypt to Rome in 58 and, although disparaged as a foreign voluptuary, he was treated as a generous and potentially useful exile. He succeeded by presenting his case to the Roman Senate after having suborned as many as he could with the promise of rich rewards.

The Senate was tempted to put Egypt under full Roman jurisdiction, but hardly trusted any one man to become sole governor of such a rich territory without the presence of a 'counter-balancing' royal family. Meanwhile, one of Auletes' daughters seized the throne and ruled as Berenike IV. She had difficulties in finding an eligible male to share the monarchy with her, and, in fact, had one suitor strangled after only a few days. In order to thwart her father's return, an embassy was sent to Rome from Alexandria to protest against his possible reinstatement. Whereupon Auletes again resorted to bribery, and those of the embassy who were not bought off were promptly assassinated. This did not endear him to his protectors, and again he was forced into exile, this time to Ephesus, where he eventually persuaded Gabinius, the Roman governor of Syria, to ensure the consent of the Senate to his reinstatement as king of Egypt. The inducement was a colossal offer of 10,000 talents, which also had to be borrowed. This time it worked because Gabinius was also short of funds. Roman Legions successfully invaded Egypt and Berenike was killed at her father's command. Auletes was reinstalled as king (55), in which position he remained until his death in 51. Because of the extreme uncertainty and unpopularity of the monarchy, the Romans decided to keep a closer hold on Egypt. Gabinius – that 'thieving, effeminate ballet-boy in curlers' as his counsel Cicero called him (Grant, 1982: 41) – and his financier friend, Rabinius, exploited the situation for all it was worth, but they were later arraigned on charges of corruption before the Senate.

In order to consolidate their control, the Romans left a garrison in Alexandria; one of its officers was the young Mark Anthony who was later to send an execution squad to silence Cicero for his outspokenness in impugning his authority (43). Anthony's future amoureuse, the person with whom he was to be inextricably linked, Auletes' daughter, Cleopatra VII, was as yet only an appealing girl of 14. Precocious or not, Cleopatra – effectively the last of her line – proved no less treacherous than her ancestors. Though apparently no great beauty, she obviously had a way with her. She was clever – she spoke several languages including Egyptian – and was manipulative, as evidenced by the influence she had on her two most famous lovers, Julius Caesar (assassinated in 44) and Mark Anthony. All of Auletes' other five offspring eventually met violent deaths; two were Cleopatra's youthful half-brothers, nominally Ptolemy XIII and Ptolemy XIV, with whom – as custom decreed – she had gone through a form of marriage. True, Ptolemy XIII with the connivance of the Egyptian hierarchy had deposed her in 48, but after she was restored in 47 by her lover, Julius Caesar, the boy was drowned mysteriously in the Nile. The younger brother was also removed, probably on Caesar's initiative, though possibly at Cleopatra's suggestion. Things were so much neater that way. Certainly, at least two of the five offspring were murdered at Cleopatra's instigation, including her half-sister and ostensible rival, Arsinoe, who was actually dragged from a shrine where she had been seeking sanctuary and killed on Anthony's orders (41). And so it was with anyone who proved a threat – sometimes only an imagined threat – to her ambitions, which were originally to remain unquestioned queen of Egypt, and later, to rule 'the East' with her equally ill-fated partner, Anthony. Their joint aspirations came to nothing when their forces were decisively defeated at Actium, as we have seen, by Anthony's one-time triumvir and co-conspirator, Octavian (later Augustus), after which both committed suicide.

The fortunes of the Ptolemies are not particularly well documented and the dynastic complexities and various comings and goings are not always easily disentangled. The generational repetition of names hardly helps. But the general outline is reasonably clear. The original Ptolemy came as a liberator (or saviour as the name Soter implies) but stayed to exploit the country more thoroughly and more 'rationally' than it had ever experienced before – not that it made *that* much difference to the ordinary Egyptian fellahin. The Ptolemies were never servants of the people, and as time went on and the quality of the leadership deteriorated, it just became a matter of survival. There were plots and counter-plots, often with lethal results. And with increasing degeneracy, the rulers and their courts became more and more divorced from the realities of state. Actual administration was left to the top-heavy bureaucracy whose members – not unnaturally – manipulated affairs to their own advantage. As far as the practice of despotism is concerned, there was precious little difference between the women and the men. Ptolemaic rule certainly calls into question the old idea that women have harmed the world less than men. This may well be factually true, but then it could be countered that they were never given the opportunity. The contention that women are naturally less aggressive (with its implications of moral superiority) similarly cannot be sustained. The truth of the matter is that women *in power* – or perhaps just seeking power – can be just as ruthless as their male counterparts. Gender has little to do with it. It's really a *structural* phenomenon, and lends itself to a similar kind of interpretation as the ruler-ruled dichotomy. As so many revolutions have shown, the ruled can be just as bad – if not worse – than the rulers when they are given, or have seized, the power to do so. Despotism is as much to do with position and opportunity as it is to do with human disposition.

CHAPTER EIGHT

Depredatory Despotism:
Timur the Tartar

It is probably true to say that there was nothing in pre-industrial society to compare with the devastation wrought by the Mongol invasions. The Mongols, who were related to both Tartars and Turks, were a collection of nomadic tribes that swept out of the steppes of eastern central Asia to attack the settled societies in Asia and Eastern Europe. In terms of the sheer destruction of human life and property they remain unsurpassed until modern times. Indeed, most modern armies with their technological capacity for mass slaughter find it hard to match the record of Chingis (Genghis) Khan who is estimated to have caused some 18 million deaths in China alone (Carlton, 1990). His entire life as leader of the Mongol tribes (1206–1227) was spent in conquest, and when he died he left an empire larger than anything the world had ever seen. His sons continued the pattern, and took their armies to Korea, Russia, India, Iraq and Hungary. They even ventured as far as Silesia in Germany, and then just when it looked as though nothing could save Europe, one of the sons, Ogdai, died. This caused some disruption in the Mongol ranks, and the invasion of Western Europe never did materialize (Chambers, 1979).

In its early stages, Mongol conquest simply meant subjugation. But as these tribespeople began to appreciate the virtues of the societies they conquered, pillage and murder gradually gave way to administration and exploitation. Many of the eastern Mongols espoused Buddhism, while those of the west were influenced by Islam. (In fact, one tribal leader, the khan of Moghulistan, not only adopted the Muslim faith but compelled 160,000 of his men to be circumcised in order to do likewise. This 'unkindest cut of all' was not to everyone's liking, and many did not take readily to the new faith.) These uncivilized nomads began to see advantages in the settled life, that is until the advent of Timur-i-Lenk or Leng (that is, Timur the Lame) – a throwback to Chingis himself – who happened to be related to Chingis' family by marriage. Timur despised the assimilation that was taking place and became leader of the Tartar groups in AD 1369, determined to emulate his hero. He was 33 and had already served his apprenticeship in numerous tribal wars, in one of which he may have received the wound that made him lame. Although illiterate, he is said to have excelled at 'intellectual games' such as chess, perhaps a particularly suitable pastime for a military strategist.

At this time, both Europe and the Middle East were recovering from the catastrophic effects of the Black Death. In the Middle East this recovery took more time, and there is evidence to suggest that the plague decimated the ranks of the military in many states and this made them more vulnerable to attacks from the less ravaged societies of the East. The prizes, as usual, went to the strongest, and at Timur's accession this meant the rule of the Mongolian Golden Horde in Russia, the rising power of the Ottoman Turks to the South, and the rise of the Tartars in the East. There were also other important states whose destinies were bound up with the Tartars, such as Jalayrid-ruled Iraq, Mameluk-controlled Egypt and the not inconsiderable monarchies of north-west India. Further west, the Genoese were strong both militarily and economically because of their mastery at sea, and there were still some vestiges of Crusader power left in the Aegean.

Some of the main obstacles to Tartar expansion were other Muslim societies. From its earliest years in the seventh century, militant Islam had been a force to be reckoned with. By the late eighth century, its influence extended from the Atlantic to Central Asia. In the conquered territories of the East, Buddhist temples were converted into Mosques, and Arabic became the lingua franca of state authorities and merchants alike. In particular, Islamic art and literature had great influence on the cultures of subjugated peoples. In most instances, the Muslim conquerors left local administrations intact and retained local princes as vassals, although in a number of larger cities they appointed their own governors and installed protective garrisons. Such states were then required to pay special taxes to their Arab overlords, and in the circumstances it was not surprising that some people looked for help from tribal nomads such as the Tartars.

Timur spent his first years as 'emir' (he was hesitant about employing the term 'khan') prudently consolidating his power in his own territory of Transoxania. A year later, he began to move against his neighbours. Between 1375 and 1390, he carried out a series of campaigns against Moghulistan, a country that he obviously found difficult to subdue, besides major expeditions in other directions. There were numerous insurrections to deal with in these early years from rival khans who disputed the hegemony of the Tartars. Even the *potential* competition of a neighbouring state was enough to start Timur thinking; the newly independent state of Khwarazim (later a republic incorporated into the Soviet Union), ruled by a Muslim Sufi dynasty, is a case in point and clearly demonstrates how sometimes Timur had to conquer the same enemy again and again. Timur sent an envoy demanding some of its southern provinces, probably guessing – rightly – that he would be refused. Invasion was thus 'justified'. Timur intimidated its ruler by assaulting one of his cities, slaughtering the men, and selling the women and children into slavery. Resistance continued, but then abated when the old khan of Khwarazim died and a marriage alliance was arranged between his daughter (the new khan's sister) and one of Timur's sons. When the conditions of the contract were not fulfilled, Timur mounted a second expedition (1373) and this was enough to impel the bride to set out for Timur's capital, Samaqand, with a huge dowry of gold and jewels. All was relatively peaceful until 1379, when there was another revolt, and yet again it was only subdued when a second city was attacked and destroyed after its treasures had been looted. Actually, it was not until 1388 after a further revolt, this time instigated by Timur's rival, the khan of the Golden Horde, that Khwarazim was finally brought to heel. Its dynasty was liquidated and the chief city, Urganch, levelled to the ground except for its mosque because Timur was, at least nominally, a conscientious Muslim.

By the time he was 40 (1376), Timur's armies were engaged in predatory expeditions as far abroad as Mongolia. But it was not until 1381–82 that he ventured to eastern Iraq and Afghanistan and – among other conquests – took Herat, one of the most heavily fortified towns in central Asia. The city was spared on the payment of a huge ransom. But here too there was a revolt, and Timur's son, Miranshah, a mere youth, returned with his forces and imposed an even larger indemnity after erecting a tower of the heads of all those he had killed.

As success followed success, Timur drew on able men from conquered territories to augment his forces, but the backbone of his army remained the tough nomads who were recruited on a tribal basis and commanded by their own officers. Like so many despots, Timur could be quite arbitrary in taking decisions about the fate of a conquered enemy. In his 'Instructions', a book dictated for the benefit of his successors, he says that the 'enemy soldier who is firmly loyal to his master, has my friendship. When he passes beneath my banner I reward his merits and his fidelity and have confidence in him' (Nicholle, 1990: 11). And it is reported that when an enemy Syrian was found among the dead and dying after one campaign, he was brought to Timur who, on seeing his numerous wounds, 'marvelled ... at his bravery and endurance ... and ordered that he be given medical treatment' (Nicholle: *ibid.*). On the other hand, he was just as likely to order a prisoner's execution on the grounds that he was a 'revolutionary', or because he had had the effrontery to resist the conqueror, or – failing that – just because he felt like it.

As with so many conquerors, Timur bit off more than he could successfully chew. In driving his armies further and further from their heartland, he found insurrection a common problem in places he had overrun but where he had left no adequate Tartar garrisons. When he did turn on the rebel territories, his treatment of the people was absolutely merciless. At Isfizar, for instance, he had two thousand captives taken, put one on top of another and cemented them together with layers of clay and brick to form a living tower as a warning against further resistance. And thus the Tartars continued their campaigns, 'making mountains of the bodies and towers with the heads' (Hookham, 1962: 107). At another city in the territory of Sistan where there was heavy fighting and where Timur had his horse killed from under him, the walls were razed, the inhabitants killed, and the whole place given over to the desert sands.

From 1386 to 1388, Timur campaigned in Persia (Iran), where one of the principal ruling dynasties was that of Hulagids, descendants of Hulagu, a grandson of Chingis Khan. Here the story was much the same. Travelling with frightening rapidity, the Tartar hordes everywhere spread death and destruction. Mountain tribesmen who were deemed guilty of unwarranted attacks on caravans were either killed in battle or captured and cast over the precipices. Timur moved on relentlessly to Azarbayjan and its capital city Tabriz, which had already been devastated by the armies of the Golden Horde led by Tokhtamish, a protégé of Timur's who, if anything, was even more bloodthirsty than his mentor. Regardless of the extenuating circumstances – the surviving inhabitants of Tabriz had been forced to pay a huge ransom to Tokhtamish for their lives – and Timur, now his rival, held them responsible for submitting to the wrong conqueror so they were killed anyway. Timur then travelled north to Georgia, part of the one-time Soviet Union, where the capital, Tiflis, was taken by storm and the army again came away laden with spoils. It is said that when Timur returned to his family and their entourage, he showered them with so many gold coins and precious stones that they grew tired of picking them up.

In the spring of 1387 Timur set out to conquer Armenia. His forces assaulted the citadel fortress at Lake Van, and all those that resisted were put to the sword or bound and thrown from the summit on which the fortress was built. His next target was Isfahan in Persia. Its indemnity was fixed and the citizens feigned compliance, but one night they attacked the soldiers Timur had left to garrison the city. Some 3,000 Tartars were killed, and in a terrifying act of revenge, Timur ordered each unit of his army to collect their quota of heads. Those Muslims who were reluctant to kill other Muslims are reported to have bought their heads from others with fewer scruples in order to fulfil their quotas. Some citizens escaped but their tracks were followed in the snow, and in the end 70,000 heads were piled outside the city walls.

Despots can be strange, contradictory creatures. They are not always full of ungovernable rage or conscienceless cunning; only some have been idle, indulgent voluptuaries wiling away their time in the harem with houris and dancing girls. Some, like Alexander (the Great), could be given to drink and a little depravity when the occasion allowed, but they could also be almost ascetic when on campaign, sharing the rigours of war with their troops. What is more they could often be eccentrically generous and persevering in certain circumstances: Hitler was inordinately fond of his dog; Al Capone was kind to newsboys – the list goes on. And, in many ways, they were often intensely superstitious, one might almost say religious, despite their cruelties. Timur comes into this category. He was undoubtedly hardy – note his continued campaigning even in old age; he was also pious in his own way, preserving certain religious buildings and observing the appropriate Islamic festivals; and – so typical of the despot – he was often remarkably indulgent to those he liked, as was the case with his protégé, Tokhtamish, who eventually became his bitterest enemy.

As a youth, Tokhtamish had fled to Timur after his princeling father had been killed by opponents in another tribal group. He was received at Timur's court where he was welcomed as a son and no doubt also as a useful political pawn. He was given presents of armour, jewels and slaves and even assigned territories on the border between the Tartar 'kingdom' and his homeland. He was also allocated troops with whom to attack his rivals, who were also enemies of Timur. In this he was singularly unsuccessful, but this was continually overlooked by his protector who supplied him with fresh forces with which to make yet another foray. On one occasion, he barely escaped with his life, and returned to Timur, having been found wounded and naked hiding in some undergrowth. Yet again he was re-equipped, and yet again he failed, but on being given a much stronger army, he ultimately succeeded in establishing himself as khan of his own people, the White Horde in 1378.

It was here that the break occurred. Tokhtamish, a powerful figure in his own right, was also bent on military expansion. In 1382 he invaded the Russian principalities, sacked and burned Moscow, and compelled the Russian princes to pay him tribute. He then also attacked cities which Timur considered his own particular preserves, most notably Tabriz, where the slaughter lasted for ten days (1385). The young man whom Timur had cultivated as a possible vassal, now became his most persistent rival, and there followed over the years a series of clashes between them, beginning in 1387, in which the honours usually went to Timur. But even when Tokhtamish was finally defeated (1395), and his troops either slaughtered or brought back in chains, the main prize – Tokhtamish himself – always eluded capture. However, despite all the animosity that had built up between them, and contrary to all expectations, the two apparently became reconciled shortly before Timur's death in 1405.

In 1392, after a serious illness, Timur, now 56, set out from Samarqand on a five-year campaign in Persia and Iraq. Again there was the storming of cities, although this time one of his purported justifications (if, indeed, he ever really worried much about justifications) was that this was a holy war. He intended to bring the true Islamic (Sunni) doctrine to the 'heretical' Shias. En route, he attacked the recalcitrant Kurds and detoured somewhat to make a second invasion of Georgia (1393). In Persia itself, the Tartars were confronted by one of their most formidable opponents, Shah Mansur, who, like Timur, was not given to delicate susceptibilities (he had seized the throne from his brother and blinded his own cousin). His resistance caused a major hiccup to Tartar plans even though his forces were greatly outnumbered. Eventually he was defeated after nearly killing Timur himself, and his head was brought back and symbolically thrown at the conqueror's feet. Such were the niceties of Tartar protocol. It was, of course, a lesson to other local nobles, who hurried with their gifts to pay due homage to the victor.

Timur moved on to Iraq and the city of Baghdad to which he came as a self-proclaimed liberator. The city had been ruled by yet another despot who had now fled to Cairo leaving his family and much of his treasure behind. The city offered no resistance, but Timur still deported those citizens who could be useful to him back to Samarqand, and forced the others to pay a huge ransom for their lives. This, of course, was the way he rewarded his troops. After disporting themselves the Tartars made for a rebel fort at Takrit which really had no chance; here the citizens were left unmolested, but the surviving soldiers were first tortured and then put to death. Almost as a ritual act, their heads were used in the construction of minarets. Later, Timur used some of his wealth to build less gruesome shrines to the memory of local saints.

The Sultan Barquq of Egypt, who had given sanctuary to the deposed ruler of Baghdad, decided that if he was going to have to face Timur it might as well be somewhere other than on Egyptian soil. So he took his troops north to Damascus in Syria where the Mameluk dynasty also held sway, and there awaited the Tartar hordes. Meanwhile, Timur was making his familiar predatory way through Armenia, where his army was becoming depleted by both battle and the extremely adverse weather conditions. Sultan Barquq's intelligence services kept him duly informed of Timur's movements and he moved his army even further north in an attempt to meet the Tartar threat, but Timur decided to avoid the challenge. Instead of continuing in a westerly direction, he turned his forces north to Russia against the reformed armies of his erstwhile friend, Tokhtamish – with considerable success, as we have seen. It was the customary brutal story. At Tana, non-Muslims were butchered and their churches, banks and depots destroyed, although if they were people of obvious means – especially Europeans – they were often ransomed instead. At Astrakan and Savay, people were driven out into the snow in mid-winter and their cities put to the torch once their treasures had been confiscated. There is indirect evidence that the rich may have been subjected to unspeakable tortures in order to get them to give up their valuables. At

Savay, for instance, excavations have unearthed skeletons without heads or
hands or feet (Hookham, 1962: 160). The losses to the Tartar army in such
a long campaign were considerable, but the booty in gold and furs, and not
least slave girls, more than compensated the survivors for the rigours of
battle.

Never content with what he had, Timur began to cast covetous eyes
on India and her fabled riches. There had been exploratory raids over the
Great Snow Mountains (Hindu Kush) by Muslims since the eighth century,
but there were no really serious invasions until the tenth century, after
which a Muslim dynasty was established at Delhi and conquest was
extended as far as Bengal (Bangladesh). It was when Timur learned of
dynastic disputations within the Sultanate of Delhi that he felt that an
opportunistic attack at this time was likely to produce rich rewards. As
ever, he was not looking for long-term occupation, only for the treasures
that were known to exist in the palaces. Yet again, there was the
pretence(?) of a holy war against idolatrous infidels. Delhi was seen as a
seat of spiritual declension and therefore badly in need of Timur's personal
brand of religiosity. After all, hadn't the Prophet himself enjoined his
followers to make war on enemies of the faith so as to achieve their highest
rewards. So the Tartar army, supported by troops from their dependencies,
set out in 1398 to bring well-deserved punishment to the spiritually
degenerate of northern India and – hopefully – to acquire a little booty on
the side.

The army traversed the mountains with some difficulty, the now aged
Timur having to make some of the journey carried on a litter through the
deep snow. Having dealt ruthlessly with the rather wild hill tribesmen and
leaving the usual mounds of decapitated heads to commemorate their
victory, they marched on to Kabul where Timur received envoys who
brought him gifts and protestations of fealty. The celebrations over, Timur
divided his forces for a two-pronged assault on Delhi. Any signs of resistance were summarily dealt with and, with supplies running low, the troops
were allowed to confiscate what they could regardless of the needs of the
population. Indeed, it was reported that the plight of the inhabitants was
such that many had been reduced to cannibalism.

Towards autumn, disease struck the invading army and local princes
took advantage to attack the Tartars, but to little effect, and by the end of
the year Timur had reached his goal. In the surrounding area of Delhi
people were either killed or flogged and enslaved, and the despair of the
Hindus was such that a number set their houses alight and whole families
jumped into the fires rather than face the Tartars. Having devastated the
environs, the Tartars were now free to deal with Delhi itself and its not
inconsiderable army. Before the actual attack on the city, its ruler, Mallu
Khan, ordered an attack on Timur's forces, not only with the intention of

defeating them, but also in an effort to free the thousands of captives that were already in Timur's hands. This attempt proved abortive, and absolutely disastrous for the prisoners. Timur feared that a revolt might break out behind his lines to coincide with Mallu Khan's attack, so he ordered a general massacre of the captives of whom about 50,000 were put to the sword. He argued that it was all a question of means and ends, saying that at a feast the guests should be more concerned with the meal than with the blood on the hands of the cook who had prepared it.

However, the Tartars did not have everything their own way. So anxious were they about the outcome, especially when the court astrologers insisted that the planetary portents were by no means favourable, that Timur commanded extra prayers to be said and re-emphasized that they were all engaged in an essentially religious crusade. Perhaps they shouldn't have been so worried. Indian forces made the fatal misjudgment that they could defeat the Tartars in open battle instead of waging an operation from a strong defensive position. They were routed by Timur's battle-hardened troops and the Sultan and Mallu Khan fled, leaving their families behind. The next day the conquerors entered the city and the notables did obeisance to their new master and were granted mercy. Nevertheless, they had to pay the customary huge indemnity for having had the city and its people spared. The collection of this ransom led to serious disputes which developed into large scale resistance by the citizens, who felt that the Tartar demands were so extortionate that they had little more to lose. But they really had no chance. The Tartars turned on the people with renewed fury and the city was sacked and burned. Beyond this the accounts are confusing. It is clear that there was a massacre, though how general this was we are not sure. We do know that a great deal of wealth was amassed, and that huge numbers of people were taken as slaves back to Samarqand where they were paraded to the delight of its citizens.

In 1399 the apparently indefatigable Timur began preparing for yet another campaign. This time, he planned a seven-year expedition to the west, particularly to Egypt and Syria, both of which were said to be in a state of governmental chaos. Meanwhile, he had to deal with various rebellions and inefficient rulers, including members of his own family, who received a variety of sentences ranging from flogging to execution for their reported misdeeds. En route (1399–1400), two attacks were launched against the ever-recalcitrant Georgians who were treated with unmatched severity; all those who survived the onslaught but who did not accept Islam were promptly beheaded. This movement westwards meant that the Tartars were on an unavoidable collision course with the empire of the newly emergent Ottoman Turks who established a European province in Serbia after defeating the flower of the Franco-Hungarian forces at Nicopolis (1396). The Turks had advanced on and threatened

Constantinople (Byzantium, modern Istanbul) and appeals had been made to European states, many of which were in turmoil at this time. Their governments were either having disputes with one another or trying to cope with fractious elements within their own borders and therefore hardly had the time or the resources to devote to yet another uncertain Crusade against the infidel Turks. Nevertheless, they responded surprisingly well to the emotional call of their compatriots and a very large army was assembled to contest Ottoman power. But it was no match for the Turks. Their ruler, Bayazid (who, as was not unusual among the Ottomans, had murdered his brother to secure his position) had all the prisoners killed when he saw the scale of his own losses, except, of course, those who could fetch a large ransom. Timur was obviously about to meet a fellow spirit, and this time there could be no claim to ideological rivalry – Bayazid was an Islamic competitor.

Timur had good reason for challenging Bayazid, who was now con-testing Tartar suzerainty over several territories, and it flattered his sense of irony that the Europeans saw him, Timur, a potential enemy, as a possible ally against their more *immediate* enemy, the Turks. They should have known that if they were going to sup with this particular devil they needed an especially long spoon. Timur's treatment of the Turks followed what was, by now, the usual pattern. With the defeat of their armies, Timur required the mandatory ransom for sparing his fellow Muslims including – so it is said – 9,000 virgins. For the rest, however, the future was decidedly bleak. In this respect, the conqueror introduced a nice refinement: because he had promised that no blood would be shed, he had those that had offered resistance buried alive in pits, lepers strangled, and others drowned.

The main Tartar target, however, was to be the Mameluk Sultanate of Egypt, at that time probably the strongest of all the Muslim states and one that included Syrian Damascus. The Egyptians had so little respect for the Tartars that an envoy sent to the Sultan from Timur, with what amounted to an ultimatum, was promptly cut in half. The Tartars attacked Syria first, and despite robust opposition the cities fell one after another. The treatment of Aleppo was particularly brutal; women and girls were raped in public and in front of their relatives who were unable to do anything about it. Jewish people were slaughtered in their synagogues, and it was reported that the heads of 20,000 Muslims, including some theologians with whom Timur disagreed, were built into mounds five metres high. Damascus, the chief city of Syria, well known for its wealth and crafts-manship, was then approached and its citizens were inclined to accept Timur's promises of leniency if he spared the city. But when they saw the arrival of an impressive combined Egyptian and Syrian force, they decided to muster a makeshift army and attack the Tartars themselves. Timur concentrated on one group at a time. First, he cut the Damascus units to pieces, then he turned on the city itself where optimism had turned to fear because as suddenly as the Egyptians had appeared they also went, apparently – but who knows? – because of trouble that was fomenting at home. The Damascenes now found themselves alone and facing a truly formidable enemy. Their city was well fortified, however, and they had ample supplies so they decided to brave it out.

Timur, whose guile had not decreased with age, again offered terms. Delegations were exchanged, limited numbers of Tartars were allowed in the city by its one open gate, and as an ostensible act of good faith, Timur even had some of his own men – who were already guilty of looting – crucified in the city's bazaar. Although the city had surrendered, the fortress within the city continued to resist, but this proved to be a brave but fruitless gesture. The ransom required of the city was increased tenfold, a demand which virtually brought the city to a standstill. Once the money had been collected, Timur accused the city elders of short-changing him and had virtually everything of worth confiscated. He then threw the city open to his troops to rape, murder and pillage as they pleased. Some prisoners were taken, especially artists and craftsmen, but many thousands perished, some in the Great Mosque – one of the architectural marvels of the Islamic world – which was burned to the ground (1401). The people of Egypt, anticipating the worst, made plans to meet the Tartar threat, but the Tartars had had enough. Glutted with booty they made their way slowly northwards and prepared for their meeting with Timur's main adversary, Bayazid. He was still harbouring the Sultan of Baghdad and another of Timur's enemies, Qara-Yusaf, who subsequently had the Sultan strangled and, when the opportunity came, seized Baghdad for himself.

Timur sent word to Bayazid that he was prepared to come to terms providing Qara-Yusuf was surrendered, but the Sultan prevaricated and the conqueror lost patience and gathered his reluctant troops for battle. Bayazid withdrew his army from the siege of Constantinople and prepared to counter the Tartar attack. Neither ruler underestimated the other and knew that they must deploy maximum strength in the field. Consequently, they both went to great pains to mobilize even their non-Muslim vassals; in these circumstances just one more unit could make all the difference. Because of the vast numbers involved, the battle was considered to be perhaps the greatest of its time (Angora 1402). The tide was turned when an appreciable number of Turkish units defected to the Tartar side, and by evening Bayazid and his bodyguard had fled. They were pursued and captured and taken back to Timur and, as far as we know, not harmed, although Bayazid died the following year, possibly by suicide. Tartar troops then raced to various cities of the Turkish empire to take what booty they could before it was spirited away by the Turks themselves.

Timur then switched direction westwards to the seemingly impregnable city of Smyrna on the Turkish coast held by the Knights Hospitallers. After a desperate siege the city was taken and everyone in it killed, a massacre which Timur regarded as an appropriate culmination of his holy war against the infidels. The ideological divide was such that Timur even ordered the heads of the defenders to be thrown from the battlements on to the decks of ships that were belatedly arriving with reinforcements for the city. Suitably intimidated, his opponents withdrew, and various island states in the Aegean sent tokens of submission together with offers to pay an annual tribute. The West feared that the Tartars would continue to expand what was, in a sense, a European foothold, but Timur had his voracious eyes set in a quite different direction: to the 'celestial' empire of China.

The Mongols under Chingis Khan had devastated China in the thirteenth-century, but their successors had since been effectively expelled by the time of the Ming dynasty which was contemporaneous with the rule of Timur. It was the conqueror's wish to emulate Chingis; moreover, it was believed that the conquest of China would release wealth in excess of anything the Tartars had known from their previous campaigns. But this time it was not to be. The army set out in the late autumn of 1404, not a very auspicious time for such an expedition, with an old and ailing Timur carried on a litter. By the time they had travelled some 250 miles from Samarqand on what was intended to be a 4,000-mile journey, they had encountered fearful weather. At one point the snow was so deep that nothing could move and the air so cold that men and animals froze in their tracks. Fortunately, Timur's 'minarets' were never to grace the Eastern skyline, for it was in this desolation that Timur died in February 1405.

It is not easy to know exactly what kind of a man Timur was. Various observers have left us accounts of the conqueror's life both on campaign and at court, but actually to understand him is still difficult. As far as personal details are concerned, we know that he had numerous wives and concubines; and well into old age we find that he was not at all averse to the embraces of quite young nubile girls, perhaps on the assumption – or experience – that they stimulated the jaded sexual palate. All seem to have been treated quite liberally, a fact that appears to have offended contemporary Muslim opinion. It is well-attested that even strong patriarchal societies are not unambiguously repressive, and much the same seems to be true of Tartar society, where it is reported that there were some female warriors – to be one of the military was a singular honour for anyone. In common Tartar tradition, Timur enjoyed feasting and drinking; in fact, his drunkenness – in between military engagements – was proverbial.

Like most autocrats, Timur was inordinately suspicious and he had agents at home and abroad, often in high places, sending him reports on all and sundry. The fate of those who fell into disfavour was unenviable, to say the least, as was that of troops or commanders who failed in their duties. One observer, whose own treatment gave him no cause to praise the conqueror, obviously admired some of his qualities. He writes that Timur, 'did not love jest or falsehood; wit and sport pleased him not. He was not sad in adversity nor joyful in prosperity. He did not allow in his company any obscene talk or talk of bloodshed or captivity, rape, plunder or violation in the harem. He was spirited and brave and inspired awe and obedience' (the writer Amad Arabshah, quoted by Nicholle, 1990: 9). Also on the positive side, we note that Timur beautified his own cities, most especially Samarqand with its Great Mosque, though admittedly this was done largely with the treasures looted from elsewhere and by the skills of artists and craftsmen 'imported' from subjugated territories.

We have already chronicled something of Timur's use of terror. This is the characteristic for which he is most remembered. He devastated whole provinces, killed and enslaved entire populations. In some cases, as in parts of Russia, there were cities that never recuperated. His practice of erecting towers of human heads set in clay ('as high as one might throw a stone' is how one witness described them), and the additional nicety of cementing live prisoners into so-called minarets has not exactly endeared him to posterity. Muslims suffered (usually those whom Timur regarded as heretics) but not as much as non-Muslims, who in Georgia were thrown from city battlements, in Armenia were buried in moats, and in Delhi perhaps as many as 100,000 Indians were burned and flayed alive, as compared with captive Muslims who were 'privileged' to have their throats cut. Some writers (Beatrice Forbes Manz, for example) are inclined towards the Great-Conqueror-who-was-a-child-of-his-day approach, and tend to de-emphasize Timur's cruelty and remain uncritical of his unbridled aggression. Though, to be fair to Manz, her main intention is to show how Timur gained and maintained his power by reducing the authority of the old tribal leaders and promoting a new elite with a personal allegiance to himself. His control rested on strict discipline – his troops could only rape and pillage when he let them off the leash. Similarly, feasting and celebrations – usually as a kind of social catharsis – were only possible with his permission. He was generous to those who were prepared to give him unwavering obedience, but woe betide those who failed or faltered; or who did not think as he thought they should. They were infidels and traitors of the deepest hue who did not deserve to exist. This, of course, is the mark of the true despot: they alone know what is right and wrong, they alone decide what is acceptable and what is not, who should live and who should die.

CHAPTER NINE

Constitutional Despotism: Henry VIII

The accession of the Tudors can best be understood in the light of the turbulent events which immediately preceded their rise to power, critically what we term the Wars of the Roses, which historians are generally agreed heralded the demise of the Middle Ages. This period of fratricidal strife which convulsed England came within a century of the Black Death which may have killed as many as a third of the population. And as if plague weren't enough, the rivalry between political factions broke out into armed conflict, the whole sorry period being punctuated by sporadic trouble with England's traditional enemy: France.

With the death of Henry V, the victor of Agincourt, in 1422, the throne was inherited by Henry VI, a nine-month old child, a situation which was virtually made for baronial factionalism. With the collapse of English power in France (1449–53), the barons prepared to contest the question of authority at home. It was fundamentally a matter of who would support the king against those who now challenged his rule. The nobility was divided on the issue. On one side was ranged a formidable opposition which consisted principally of the Duke of York, aided by the Earl of Salisbury and his son, the Earl of Warwick. The king, on the other hand, was supported mainly by the Duke of Somerset and by his queen, Margaret of Anjou. First blood went to the Yorkists at St Albans in 1455. They tempered their victory with moderation and simply replaced a number of the king's ministers. They were again triumphant in 1460 at Northampton, but fortunes were quickly reversed when the queen, a resourceful if ruthless woman, defeated and killed the Duke of York at Wakefield (1460) and had his second-in-command, Salisbury, beheaded. She then went on to defeat Warwick at the second battle of St Albans (1461), but unaccountably failed to prevent Warwick and the Earl of March, the dead Duke of York's son, with the remainder of their forces from entering London where the Earl was proclaimed as King Edward IV. The situation was again reversed when in the same year, Edward's forces decisively defeated the queen's army – the Lancastrians – at Towton, a battle that turned into a bloody rout and subsequently consolidated Yorkist rule.

Warwick remained in the new king's favour until his retirement in 1467. But only two years later he returned, having switched his allegiances, and with considerable popular support in the south raised a rebellion against the king. At first Warwick was victorious, though after he had come to terms with Edward, hostilities broke out again and Edward was deposed and replaced by the earlier king, Henry VI (1470). But still Edward was not finished. He mobilized yet another army and defeated and killed Warwick, his one-time comrade-at-arms, at Barnet (1471), and went on to beat the queen's forces at Tewkesbury the same year. The queen's son was slain and soon afterwards the former king, Henry VI died (most probably murdered) in the Tower of London.

Edward's reign lasted until 1483 and he was succeeded by his brother, the enigmatic Richard III (formerly Duke of Gloucester) who, although probably not much worse than many other medieval kings, has a reputation as a despot of the worst kind because it is believed that he was the instigator of the infamous murder of the Princes in the Tower, although this may be a calumny of later historians to justify the Tudor takeover of power. Richard's reign was brief, a mere two years. He was killed and his army defeated at Bosworth by a young Henry Tudor, Earl of Richmond (later Henry VII), whose claim to the throne was, at best, extremely tenuous.

Edward IV had a substantial inheritance, but Henry VII's was even better. He learned his lessons well – especially the lesson of the Wars of the Roses. He, and even more so his son, the future Henry VIII, determined that never again were the barons going to get out of hand. He was no respecter of privilege and legal immunity. His intention was to suppress the pretensions of the nobility, so he abolished their custom of having units of armed retainers, and he set up a special court, the Star Chamber, which became his principal instrument of political control. Henry was a shrewd operator. He drew his councillors from those of undistinguished birth who thus owed their positions and their futures to the sovereign. Of course, there was opposition, but this was dealt with peremptorily, and even armed rebellions by pretenders – always a hazard where the claim to royal legitimacy is uncertain – were ruthlessly crushed. His aim was a true united kingdom so he expediently married his daughter to the Scottish king, James IV, in order to secure a useful alliance, though Ireland (always a thorn in the English side) was dealt with very differently. Henry's solution there was repression; Ireland was to be under English control and its parliament made subject to English law, a move that was to prove ruinous for the English exchequer. The king displayed his intolerance in his treatment of any who dared to raise their hands against their temporal lord. He followed the examples set in the Wars of the Roses and condemned to death – under the procedure known as attainder – those who failed in their rebellion; and their property, their legacy to their families, was duly confiscated.

The Tudor monarchy probably represented the greatest concentration of royal power in England since the time of William the Conqueror. But it was not an 'absolute monarchy' in the sense in which that term came to be understood (Woodward, 1970: 70), though arguably it had all the makings of a despotism. Regardless of their profits from certain opportune confiscations, the Tudors did not dispose of huge revenues – the depredations of the baronial wars had seen to that. However, Henry VII did begin to amass wealth by being prepared, for payment, not to dispute foreign (usually French) claims to territory which he could not easily have contested anyway. Neither did the Tudors command immense armies, nor could they afford bands of mercenaries. They did not employ unwieldy bureaucracies which were very expensive, and Henry VII, like his granddaughter, the future Elizabeth I, was rather mean with his wealth. Henry VIII, on the other hand, was perhaps typical of the minor monarch who wishes to compensate for his modest position by spending freely on display in order to give the impression of unbounded magnanimity. Or perhaps it was just a reaction against having a somewhat parsimonious father.

In many ways these were exciting times. Education at the universities was undergoing interesting changes; the invention of the printing press made literature available to a wider public. With the translation of the Scriptures into English, more people began to question the nature of institutional religion and particularly of some of its professional functionaries whose life-styles seemed strongly inconsistent with the simplicity found in the Scriptures. Though, to be fair, some of the higher clergy were debating social and political issues – especially as they related to widespread crime – and what they considered to be abuse of power. John Colet, dean of Saint Paul's preached about the evils of the bishops and the worldliness of the clergy (1512), and Sir Thomas More wrote his *Utopia* (1516) as a reaction against the oppression of the poor.

Tudor society, especially the upper echelons, was run very much on a patron-client basis. There were no objective selection procedures or public competition; it was all a matter of personal recommendation, a favour-for-favour system. This had its advantages. It enhanced the status of the patron, demonstrated his influence and thus gilded his reputation. Furthermore, it held out the promise of future rewards; one day he might approach the client to return the favour either in economic terms or perhaps in some tangible but less conspicuous way. Obviously, the more important the patron, the more important the favour, and no one was more prestigious than the king. Thus people anxiously vied with one another for the king's attention; his approval often ensured their loyalty and allegiance (Ives, 1979). Yet though it increased his personal power, it made for factionalism among his nobles and within his immediate entourage.

Henry VIII succeeded his father in 1509 at the age of only eighteen. He was an active, ambitious and popular king with quite a healthy bank balance who had every prospect of reigning long and successfully. His athletic body, which he regarded as handsome, had no signs, as yet, of running to fat, and there were only the barest hints of the irascibility and cruelty of his later years. He was gifted as a musician and was also something of a linguist; and the Venetians reported that he was the best dressed sovereign in the world. In his early years, his interests centred on foreign affairs as much as domestic matters, and in these he was opportunistic and hardly inhibited by moral considerations. Sir Thomas More, who probably had more integrity than most of Henry's subordinates, put it succinctly: 'if my head could win him a castle in France, it should not fail to go' (quoted by Feiling, 1966: 337).

Henry did little about social reform for the first half of his reign. He seems to have been more interested in keeping up with the other royal Joneses, his more prosperous European counterparts, by putting on pageants, entertaining lavishly, and generally making free with his father's carefully accumulated wealth. He effectively silenced any serious political opposition, sometimes on trumped-up charges, as in the case of the Duke of Buckingham who was arraigned in 1521 accused of high treason. This really meant that he had spoken out indiscreetly about the king of whom he initially had high hopes. For this he was summarily found guilty and beheaded. The threat of the block was a potent reminder that heterodoxy didn't pay.

There was, however, a semblance of participatory government. Partly to celebrate his accession, the king called a Great Council, an assembly of peers, to consider any breaches of 'laws and customs of our kingdom of England' (quoted by Starkey, 1985: 41). A series of high-powered investigatory committees were organized (the commissions of oyer and terminer) to look at complaints and infringements and general mismanagement. The result was that two previous councillors were executed, possibly as a token gesture that the Council was prepared to admit mistakes. Then, within less than six months, the whole initiative just fizzled out – social justice was deemed to have been done. But all was not well with the kingdom. The Irish question remained unsettled, and there was disorder in Wales. As usual, there were also border problems in Northumberland and Scotland, a matter that was temporarily settled in 1513 at the battle of Flodden when the Scottish king and the flower of his army were killed. On the domestic front, when uprisings or outbursts of public indignation occurred, as in 1517 when there was an outcry over foreign imports which indirectly affected the employment situation, the government could be prudentially ruthless. Troubles of this kind were put down by the soldiery and the ringleaders executed or imprisoned.

Abroad, the king was also having some success. He joined in a Holy League with Spain against the ubiquitous enemy, France. This was backed by the mandatory religious sanctions of the Pope, although one suspects that here the motivations were more political than spiritual. The Great Council was against such a move, but Henry – possibly envious of French power – overrode all opposition and defeated the French at the 'battle of the Spurs'; also in 1513. He then made a separate peace with them which was cemented by the marriage of Henry's sister, Mary, to the French King, Louis XII. But the following year Louis died, and the ungrieving widow contracted another marriage, this time with an English nobleman. Meanwhile, Louis' successor, Francis I, a much more aggressive character, effectively abrogated the alliance by embarking upon a successful policy of expansion against Italy and Switzerland, and deliberately antagonized the English by supporting the claims of their Scottish opponents. Thus, Henry's costly wars and extensive manoeuvrings had netted him practically nothing except the ill-will of his Council.

All this political jockeying for position was vitiated by the beginnings of the Protestant Reformation that was occurring in Germany and quickly taking hold elsewhere, particularly Holland and Switzerland. While the Hapsburg Emperor of Austria and Germany felt some constraint to help the Pope, he also had obligations to his nobles many of whom sided with the lapsed priest-cum-heretic, Martin Luther, who had taken his stand against what he regarded as the abuses of the Papacy. They thought of him as someone who gave theological justification for their break with the traditional Church which they saw as overbearing and meddlesome – a wordly institution that insisted on interfering in their political arrangements. Henry, perhaps already anticipating that it would pay to maintain good relations with the Papacy, came to its aid and wrote an anti-Lutheran text which earned him the title of 'Defender of the Faith'. Ironic really, when history has come to see him as the initiator of the Reformation in England.

The traditional English Church itself looked for changes. There were just too many infringements among the clergy to be ignored. Some priests were charging for their spiritual duties, and were even found appropriating the garments of the dead. They were also active in inquisitorial enquiries and persecutions, and thus generated a certain amount of cynicism and opprobrium from the public at large. Reform, then, was something that was generally felt to be necessary, but not the kind of reform implied by the Lutherans, which entailed not only doctrinal changes and modifications in ceremonial practices but also a reorganization of administrative procedures and the curtailment of peculation. The English Church was not out to undermine its own authority, let alone free itself from Papal tutelage – something that had previously been unthinkable. It was more a matter of tidying up procedures, and bringing them more into line with what Rome felt was required, and into harmony with the development of independent national sovereignties. But who was to carry this out?

Among Henry's subordinates in the earlier years of his reign, none was more important, or interesting, than Cardinal Wolsey. A man of modest beginnings and, if his many opponents are anything to go by, even more modest abilities, he shared the king's distrust of Lutheran doctrines. He particularly disliked their subversive implications; radical reform was just not on his agenda. He had embarked on a political career on the personal recommendation of the Marquis of Dorset to whose sons he had acted as tutor. Wolsey was a man of consuming ambition and came to prominence as Papal Legate, charged with correcting the abuses of the English Church in keeping with the ideal Roman model. But it was a matter of using Beelzebub to cast out Beelzebub. Wolsey, in his own way, was as corrupt as many of his clerical colleagues, and with a great deal less excuse. (For example, he was uncanonically married and had natural children; but worse, he gave his son a number of valuable ecclesiastical preferments, something that was hardly in line with his commission.) As a minion of the king, he rose to become not only cardinal but also Archbishop of York and eventually chancellor, effectively the most important office in the kingdom, and it was strongly suspected that he had an eye on the Papacy itself.

But Wolsey ultimately proved to be a disappointment. Henry was not notably faithful to his subordinates, or to his friends for that matter. And he lost patience very quickly with those who let him down or who failed in their allotted tasks. It was Wolsey's misfortune to founder over an issue dear to Henry's heart, the not inconsiderable matter of the annulment of his marriage. (Henry claimed, rather belatedly, that his marriage was technically illegal because his wife, Catherine of Aragon, had previously been married to his now deceased older brother.) An annulment could only be given by the Pope and presumably the king felt that if anyone had influence in that direction it was the Papal Legate. But there were both ecclesiastical and political reasons why the appropriate dispensation should be refused, not least because the queen's nephew was probably the most powerful monarch in Europe. To Henry, Wolsey's failure was unpardonable. He was of no further use to the king, and moves were soon afoot to effect his political demise. He was accused of usurping the rights of other clergy and of taking bribes for favours either given or promised, and was deprived of his palaces. He was detested by many for his ostentation and for what was regarded as his ill-gotten wealth, and was finally dismissed from office in 1529; he died in disgrace just a year later.

Henry now sought other means to get his way over the divorce. He tried both to intimidate and conciliate the Pope at the same time, and it is still difficult to know whether he was really seeking a good excuse to break with Rome and rid himself and others of the need to pay the dues that Rome imposed. These were a drain on his Exchequer, and he and the nobility had other uses for the money. However, his threats to take the English Church out of the system did not move the Pope, nor did the burning of a few Protestants here and there do anything to humour the Pontiff. Henry grew more and more exasperated with the delay and with the comings and goings of various officials who were trying to achieve an amicable settlement. Acting on clerical advice he explored a new and somewhat exculpatory gambit. He referred the matter to the universities both in England and on the Continent, and on receiving favourable responses, decided finally to break with Rome and go ahead with the divorce. He was duly excommunicated by the Pope who also declared the divorce invalid.

The severance with Rome had reasonably popular support. There were, of course, some objections, but these were waived aside. In 1533 the king secretly married his mistress, Anne Boleyn, who was already pregnant, and who had apparently held out for royal status – a fatal move which eventually brought this poor, ambitious woman to the scaffold. The culminating move was the Act of Supremacy (1534) which effectively made Henry head of the English Church. Wolsey's successor, Sir Thomas More, a high-minded traditional churchman, refused to swear the necessary oath of allegiance to the king in his new capacity as ecclesiastical supremo, and so he, like so many others, ended up on the scaffold. It wasn't necessary to rebel against the king, merely to slander him or question his authority rendered that person technically liable to a charge of high treason.

As we have seen, some rulers start well but become more autocratic with time, and as circumstances permit. Henry was a case in point. The tendencies had always been there, but with the assumption of these additional powers, his despotism and his general discontentment certainly became more evident. Anyone who incurred his displeasure was liable to be arraigned on whatever charges were deemed appropriate; the more plausible the better. The Act of Supremacy, for example, claimed any number of victims. Those who had the audacity to impugn the royal title were now guilty of a form of sacrilege. As head of the Church, Henry was in a position to punish its ministers, and those who did not acknowledge his overlordship were liable to suffer the death penalty. These included friars who were executed and Carthusian monks who starved themselves to death rather than recognize Henry as their spiritual leader.

The king's next move concerned the monasteries, whose wealth was too much of a temptation for someone as permanently in need of money as himself. It was well known that many of the monasteries had become notoriously lax in discipline and worldly in practice. Their dissolution could therefore be seen as a long overdue act of 'purification'. Henry's agent (like Hitler's Bormann) was Thomas Cromwell, who had inherited the position but hardly the mantle of Sir Thomas More. He, like his modern counterpart, was ever the dutiful functionary, doing the bidding of his master and *out*doing in assiduousness and zeal all others who sought Henry's favour. Cromwell wanted all the monasteries to be destroyed, but modified his terms because of the importunate pleas of the archbishops. By the Compromise Act of 1536, 370 houses with incomes of less than £200 were closed, many of the clergy were pensioned off and others were found work as parish priests. Again there were objections, but Parliament had its way and the measure was carried through without too much fuss. The closure of many important monastic schools meant that education as a preparation for university became very restricted and the numbers offering themselves for ordination fell sharply, a phenomenon that may well have contributed to the rise of Puritanism in later Elizabethan times (Feiling, 1966: 357). It is reasonable to suppose that doctrinal disputes meant less to the 'average' person than variations in ritual. The main protagonists in the Reformation issue probably would not like to admit it, but no other explanation is really adequate to account for the relatively rapid success of these changes among so much of the public. Perhaps it was because 'neither movement required a fundamental and revolutionary change of outlook towards [the basic questions] of human life and destiny' (Woodward, 1970: 74).

Considerable financial benefits accrued to the Crown as a result of these measures. By the end of his reign, Henry had disposed of about two-thirds of all monastic lands, some by gift but most by sale, while the rest remained on Crown leases. By and large, the laity went along with the confiscations and even made their own contribution by stripping lead from abbey roofs and dismantling the buildings for their stones. Henry's depredations affected only selected members of the public, mainly the clergy and some of the nobility and lesser aristocracy. The bulk of the citizenry remained largely unaffected, and the poor just stayed poor. Hence Henry's popularity was not greatly diminished.

We can probably date some general change in the king's practices and policies from as early as 1527. Until this time, his reign had been unexceptional, indeed, there was even room for praise. He had made a considerable contribution to the updating of the navy and to the improvement of facilities for the English merchant fleet. And he had also initiated changes in the general administration of the capital, particularly in the running of its, admittedly, rudimentary medical services. But gradually we see a vigorous and personable young man change into a gross and often morose autocrat. His protracted divorce negotiations took six years, which probably did little to lighten his disposition. And by 1531, some kind of character change, perhaps in part due to illness, seems to be evident in his behaviour (Cartwright and Biddiss, 1991: 74ff.). Punishments were usually pretty fearful, but in that year he agreed to the enactment of a law decreeing that those guilty of certain offences should be boiled to death. By 1533, anyone who slandered his marriage to Anne Boleyn or who, by extension, cast aspersions on any children from the marriage was deemed to be guilty of treason. And by 1534, as we have seen, he was executing Protestants and non-Protestants alike if their views came into serious conflict with his own or if he detected in them any ominous signs of subversion.

In 1536, Catherine of Aragon died, and the king had no longer to fear the political complications that had arisen as the result of the divorce and his remarriage. Ironically, at about the same time, he was obviously growing rather tired of his new wife and would be glad to see her out of the way. She was arraigned on a charge of adultery for which, it should be noted, there was no firm evidence. Henry claimed that 'more than a hundred had had to do with her' (quoted by Starkey, 1985: 126), but it was only a few intimates of Anne plus a young musician who actually suffered with her. It seems quite likely that there were underlying political motives present, although Henry seems to have been only too willing to be rid of a wife that he considered demanding and abrasive; she presented fewer difficulties dead. He didn't want yet another divorce and he had already had the experience of one resentful wife. It is curious though that such a proud man as Henry should declare himself a cuckolded husband – especially if it wasn't true anyway. Anne Boleyn went to her death in May, and within ten days the king had married Jane Seymour, a much more compliant, almost docile, woman who was to die giving birth to Henry's only legitimate son, Edward.

There took place too in 1536–37 the rather inaptly named 'Pilgrimage of Grace'. In effect, it was a rebellion of conservatives who were violently opposed to the suppression of the abbeys. It began in Lincolnshire and soon took over much of the north and recruited both high and low with sundry grievances ranging from the burden of increased taxation and the higher price of goods to peasant complaints about land enclosure. The rebels largely represented the traditional Catholic element and, at first, their efforts were ill-organized and uncoordinated; some wanted a full-scale revolution, but others wanted simply to intimidate Cromwell and the government and challenge their laws. The Lincolnshire 'wing' of the rebellion was particularly hesitant, but the Yorkshire forces gathered more and more supporters until they had about 40,000 men under arms and had taken over Hull and Pontefract and even the stronghold of Lancaster. They were joined by a number of discontented peers, but were actually led by a lawyer, Robert Aske, who kept remarkable control over those who were agitating for outright civil war. Their programme included the burning of

Protestant literature, the restoration of at least some of the monasteries and the recognition of the Pope as the spiritual head of the Church. They also wanted Princess Mary (the future queen), who had been declared a bastard, to be given her legitimate status.

The king temporized. He ordered his officials to make the necessary promises, and he would deal with the leaders himself. Suitably conciliated, or mollified, the rebel forces largely disbanded, trusting that the king would attend to their grievances even if the Chancellor and his ministers were out of sympathy with their cause. Perhaps they should have known better. Henry was a past master in the art of dissimulation. The doubts of the few were justified when the king repudiated his promises, declared martial law, and instructed the Duke of Norfolk to put down the rebellion by force. The leaders were hanged, drawn and quartered – a barbarous punishment that was thought fitting for those who questioned the king's edicts. Others too were put to death, possibly as many as 200 in all, including a number of recalcitrant Yorkists, among whom was the aged Lady Salisbury, whose reward – in Henry's view – was long overdue. So ended a well-intentioned but half-hearted attempt to effect a mini counter-Reformation without sufficient popular support. By comparison, three years earlier there had been a rebellion in Ireland which had a great deal of popular support. Predictably, this too was forcibly suppressed and a number of its leaders executed, but Cromwell's policy of terror was never thoroughly successful and the king was never really accepted as head of the Irish Church. As was to be expected, government policies were much more enforceable on the mainland. Henry was determined that his reforms should be carried through, and the Chancellor made sure that this was done without question. Cromwell's creatures were everywhere, and the least sign of dissension was pounced upon immediately, 'the slightest word spoken in an ale-house or a shop ... reached his ear ... fourteen died at one blow in Somerset for a corn riot [and] another dozen in Norfolk for criticism of the King's tyranny' (Feiling, 1966: 362).

By such means Henry was able to keep a tight hold on the country; such repressive measures were technically constitutional as the king, being head of state, still had the firm backing of his Parliament. This was confirmed in 1539 by the Six Articles, a statute directed towards those who challenged the king's self-appointed position as head of the Church. This legislation rendered Protestants liable to be burned as heretics and Romanists hanged as traitors.

The king's domestic life was still unsettled. Some felt that it was high time he married again. Was it possible to contract the kind of marriage that would both please the king and effect a useful political alliance at the same time? Cromwell obviously thought it was. In an act of cardinal misjudgment he persuaded Henry to consider Anne of Cleves, who was not the most prepossesing of nature's children. The marriage took place in January 1540, and the nuptials were hardly over when Henry decided that he had to be rid of this 'Flemish mare'. It was all a disastrous mistake, and the marriage – presumably unconsummated – was dissolved in July of the same year. The king was angry and humiliated. The marriage did little for his relations with other anti-Protestant states, and its failure made him look foolish to his own court. Ultimately, of course, he had no one but himself to blame, but, being Henry, that was one fact he was unable to face. So he cast around for a victim, and who better than the person who had instigated it all, the redoubtable Cromwell. The Chancellor was unpopular with the Commons and he also had enemies among the nobility, one of the most pre-eminent being the Duke of Norfolk who just happened to have a young and attractive niece, Catherine Howard, who might well appeal to Henry's diminishing sexual libido. So, at last, Cromwell's time had come. He went to the scaffold together with clergy of polarized persuasions; those who favoured a Protestant rapprochement, and Romanists who fervently opposed it and denied the supremacy of the king. Afterwards the king lamented that it was other councillors who had 'upon light pretexts and false accusations ... made him put to death the most faithful servant he ever had' (quoted by Elton, 1962: 10).

By the standards of the time, Henry was now middle-aged, indeed, he looked older than his 50 years. His huge frame had become obese and he was plagued by ailments that partly incapacitated him. In 1538, an ulcer had been noted on his leg, and later he began to suffer from headaches, insomnia and sore throats, all indicative of the possibility of syphilis, a common disease at this time. (The fact too that his daughter, Mary, who sent her own share of people to the stake, may have been abnormal because of congenital syphilis also indirectly points to the same conclusion.) But Henry was entranced by the young and vivacious Catherine Howard and was unwilling to listen to those sage voices who countenanced caution. She soon became his mistress, and it was rumoured that she was already pregnant by him at the time of his divorce from Anne of Cleves. Within three weeks of the divorce they were married, and Henry seemed deliriously happy. But it was yet another union that just couldn't last. It transpired that the king was by no means the first of her lovers, as one writer has put it, 'she seems to have been free to do as the fancy took her. And the fancy took her pretty often' (Starkey, 1985: 127). What was more to the point, her fancy took her after she was married, with fatal results. It was understandable that she should be attracted to handsome, younger men, but she was hardly discreet with her favours. When the king was told, he was extremely reluctant to believe what he heard and actually wept when the charges were proved beyond doubt. Although many were implicated, the number of those indicted was kept to a minimum; only four were executed including Catherine herself who died in February 1542. Needless to say, Henry took full advantage of the forfeiture of all the property involved.

A year later, to just about everyone's surprise, the king married the woman who was to be his last wife, Catherine Parr. According to tradition, she was about as different from her predecessor as a woman can be, small, unprepossessing (although at least one of her portraits depicts her as a proud and not unattractive young woman) and extremely devout; perhaps the kind of person he really needed in his declining years. Yet Henry didn't exactly mellow with age. His advancing years and increasing ill-health had their effects. 'Unquestionably his physical grossness, suspicious arrogance and ... political dexterity all grew more marked [with] self-indulgence and adulation' (Elton, 1962: 8). In 1544 he went to war with France, but bankruptcy forced him to come to terms, and soon afterwards he was provoked into a war with Scotland. If anything, his failing health made him even more bad-tempered and more impatient with members of his court. Many prominent men were sent to the Tower on little more than suspicion. In the Council all sorts of factional manoeuvrings were taking place at the prospect of the king's demise and of the possibility of a royal successor who was a sickly and impressionable youth, ripe for manipulation.

Henry died as he had lived – a despot to the last. He had inaugurated his long reign with the execution of two nobles, Richard Empson and Edmund Dudley, on charges of high treason. He died safe in the knowledge that he had sent two more of his erstwhile subordinates, the Earl of Surrey and his father, the Duke of Norfolk, to the scaffold only days before his own death in January 1547. Thus expired 'one of the most egotistical temperaments known to history' (Elton, ibid.).

CHAPTER TEN

Absolute Despotism:
Ivan the Terrible and Louis XIV

The term 'absolute' in this context does not quite mean what it says. It is used in a semi-technical sense to distinguish between what is often called absolute monarchy and the somewhat later conditioned monarchy associated with the inaptly named 'enlightened despots'. Just a glance at the political situation in post-medieval Europe will give some idea of the various forms of despotism exercised by different rulers. Their authority was no more absolute than others we have considered, indeed, in many cases less so. But they were not constitutional monarchs in the sense that we understand monarchy today even though there were some constitutional curbs on their autocracy. The two instances we are going to discuss here have much in common but, as we might expect, are quite singular in their own particular ways.

Since the early Middle Ages at least, there had been a continuing debate in Europe about the power of kings in relation to the well-being of their subjects. There was too the allied dispute between rulers and popes as to who was the final arbiter of men's fortunes, which had been uneasily resolved by distinguishing between temporal and spiritual spheres of interest. With the gradual breakdown of the feudal order, when rights and duties were well understood, this distinction was no longer so clear. Kings and queens often claimed to rule by divine right, which now meant that rulers took on a kind of priest-king role which neutralized the power of the popes and actually made for a special type of royal absolutism. This was keenly contested by those who wished to circumscribe the power of the monarch and who wanted to define the reciprocal duties of both the ruler and the ruled. England was probably in the vanguard in this respect. The Magna Carta issue of the thirteenth century between King John and his barons, which was, admittedly, an argument about rights between two levels within the hierarchy, addressed this very problem. By the end of the fourteenth century in the reign of Richard II, this same issue, in another form, found popular expression in the abortive Peasants' Revolt, the suppression of which provided an interesting lesson in royal duplicity.

The discussion about mutual rights and obligations continued through the sixteenth century, and was in full spate in the seventeenth century when the English mathematician and political theorists, Thomas Hobbes, wrote the treatise called *Leviathan* (1651). This was the period of the

English Civil War which was essentially about this very matter. Hobbes agreed that qualified despotism was not only permissible, it was positively desirable if governments were to realize their aims. Justice was the servant of the state – a principle that suited the quasi-Republican Cromwellians as much as the Royalists. Governments should, by definition, be strong and efficient. The sovereign should make and implement, the laws and appoint officials to see that they were properly administered, although Hobbes conceded that the citizen had the right to resist a weak and incapable ruler. But alongside this there was also the growing conviction that governments existed for the people and not the reverse. It was felt that the state should not interfere with the lives of its citizens unless it was necessary for the social good. The philosopher John Locke, in his *Treatise of Civil Government* (Plamenatz, 1963), argued that citizens too had inalienable rights and that the state or sovereign could only govern by consent.

The two doctrines, then, stood in opposition. The principle (or method) of absolute government was adopted, for example, in Russia by the tsars, in Spain by Philip II, in Austria by the Habsburgs, by the French monarchy, especially Louis XIV, and unsuccessfully by Charles I in England. This constituted a kind of divinely validated despotism which came to be seriously questioned, especially when it proved to be neither particularly wise nor efficient. It was only much later that some sort of inconsistent synthesis was arrived at which we, in modern times, call constitutional monarchy. Practically speaking, this is – nor ever was – either fish, fowl or good red herring, and really satisfies no one, least of all the monarchs who cease to rule and who have become mere political cyphers. Perhaps this is all to the good. Royals are no longer seen as exemplars, only as members of an outdated institution that persists because of a strange amalgam of lingering sentiment and public apathy.

Ivan the Terrible: repression in sixteenth-century Russia

The Mongol conquests beginning with the depredations of Chingis (Genghis) Khan in the thirteenth century and continued by his successors took in much of eastern Europe including the territory we now broadly think of as Russia. These conquests were consolidated and the conquered states exploited, but gradually Mongol control lessened with the fragmentation of the power structure into four groups, one of which, the Golden Horde, had Muslim affiliations and its members were commonly known as Tartars. Its leader held Russian lands, and these territories were required to pay him their requisite taxes – or perhaps, more correctly, tribute. Tax collection was normally entrusted to compliant members of the indigenous nobility, in this case the Grand Duke of Moscow

(Muscovy), except that by 1480 the Grand Duke had decided to take the risk of not remitting the appropriate dues. Muscovy was already a powerful independent state, yet the Tartars were still able to carry out punitive raids on Moscow and take captives as slaves as well as destroy property on the outskirts. But they were unable to take the citadel itself (Kremlin) which was virtually impregnable. Horse-borne archers, the Tartar strength, were no longer sufficient to challenge the Muscovites, who had come to the conclusion that it was time Tartar supremacy came to an end. The Muscovite leader, Ivan III (the Great), formally renounced his allegiance and took the title of tsar, an act that had more than a mere symbolic significance. It heralded a new age for the Muscovites and announced to the Tartar overlords that henceforth their suzerainty was at an end. Ivan determined too on the conquest of new territories, and was supported by the Orthodox Church which endorsed neither Catholicism nor the Reformation.

His successor, Vasili III (1505–33), furthered the policy of military expansion, and a later more renowned successor, Ivan IV (born 1530), earned his sobriquet, the Terrible, from his ruthless purge of his own nobles (boyars) who are said to have treated him badly as a youth when he reigned while the boyars ruled. He was formally proclaimed tsar in 1547 after a considerable tussle with the nobility whose strict and inflexible ranking system led to bitter disputes. What was meant to enhance stability actually did the opposite. No boyar could be expected to occupy a position inferior to one enjoyed by a member of his family, and the system was further exacerbated by the rivalries over court precedence. The boyars were the beneficiaries of a state largely based upon serf labour. Although serfdom was not officially recognized in law until the seventeenth century, it was commonly practised long before this. Serf labour developed for basic economic reasons. The taxation system inherited from the Mongols put such a burden of debt on the peasant population that they could only discharge their debts, buy the seed and implements they needed, and so on, by binding themselves to local landowners. This, together with the increased demands made for military service, generated a substantial reservoir of discontentment which could only be dealt with by a process of accommodation or of repression. The tsars – especially Ivan IV – chose the latter.

There are stories which relate how Ivan was cruel even as a child, when he was fond of torturing animals (Bowle, 1980: 360) and ordered his first murder at the age of only 13. He made it clear from the start that he was the person who was really in charge by putting down a rebellion with considerable ferocity. Having asserted his authority, he then set about reforming the law code and the taxation system (1550). He also reorganized the army, mainly by creating a body of regular infantry equipped with muskets, something of an innovation at the time. Two years later, with his troops, he embarked on a career of military conquest. His first expedition was against Kazan, a Tartar fortress on the Volga, and by cutting its water supply he forced the surrender of the garrison, which was subsequently destroyed. After this victory, he went on to annex the entire territory of Astrakhan.

This dynasty of tsars adopted the Asiatic absolutism that they had experienced as subjects of the Mongol state, which was founded upon the principle of universal service and the total submission of all classes and persons, from nobility to serfs to the supreme ruling power of the khan. Mongol absolutism, then, became the model for these one-time Dukes of Muscovy (Charques, 1959: 34). But the tsars wanted more. They, and especially Ivan the Terrible, felt the need to validate their rule, so either out of genuine conviction or by self-conscious persuasion they came to see themselves as the heirs of the Eastern Roman Empire (Caesar = Tsar), and conducted themselves accordingly. Ivan III had married the orphan niece of the last emperor, thus formally establishing the connection, and he and his successors adopted some of the pomp and manners of the earlier Byzantine court which had ceased to exist after the capture of Byzantium by the Turks in 1453.

Once in complete control, Ivan IV encouraged visitors from the West. This brought increased trade and western expertise, particularly in medicine and the arts. The English established trading relations in 1553, and the first English ambassador was received in 1559. Ivan was still inordinately jealous of those he thought wished to usurp his power. His anger with those who questioned his authority was fuelled by his growing conviction that he ruled by divine right, perhaps a validatory device to justify autocratic power and territorial ambition. His rule was still contested by the boyars, and exasperated and frustrated he packed up such goods as could be easily carried and left Moscow together with his family, household and bodyguard. He left a letter for the people justifying his departure by insisting that the fault was not theirs but that of the nobles and officials. As he anticipated – or possibly planned – they sent a message to him via the chief clergy pleading with him to return. This he duly did, but under a very specific and somewhat unusual set of conditions. Although once again nominally tsar of his country, he set up a kind of state within a state; an oprichnina, which comprised a separate realm with its own citizens and troops (who wore black) and which was supported by the revenues of numerous towns and extensive – often confiscated – estates.

From now on we see Russian absolutism at its worst. Enforced deportations and confiscations were the very least of offences. Torture, depravity and mass murder were commonplace in Ivan's Russia, in a reign that lasted some 50 years. He had inherited a court that was riddled with suspicion and intrigue. His own mother was murdered, and he, in turn, appears not to have balked at the murder of some of his many wives and ultimately – to his lasting remorse – his own son. Working through his security police and the all-too-familiar denunciations of informers, he decimated the old independent nobility by a process of deportations, confiscations and executions. Traitors, the accused, and even the suspected all suffered the same fate. An example of Ivan's methods can be seen in his capture of Novgorod in 1570. Those men deemed guilty of defying the king's authority were burned and thrown into the river; their wives and children were then tied up and also flung into the river with them while soldiers with pitchforks prodded them under until they drowned. Add to this sort of thing the mass executions carried out in other cities, especially Moscow, and one begins to understand Ivan's appellations 'Terrible' and 'Dread'.

In order to strengthen his position Ivan developed relations with various European powers, and it says much for his own status and that of Muscovy generally that these were recognized at the international level. But his political policies were secondary. His main claim to fame came from his wars of conquest. After taking Kazan and Astrakhan, and treating the inhabitants with utmost cruelty, he moved on to gain access to the Caspian Sea. Also, though indirectly, through his use of semi-independent Cossack bands – who were little more than brigands – he made important incursions into Siberia, in particular to exploit the fur trade (1581). His main efforts were directed against Tartar states and enclaves, as the nomads were still capable of invading non-Tartar territory and taking off thousands of slaves to be sold in the Crimean markets. In trying to ensure access to the Baltic Sea, he involved himself in a protracted and ultimately unsuccessful struggle against Sweden, Poland and Lithuania, and was eventually saved from a devastating defeat by the intercession of Rome which hoped for a reconciliation with the Russian Orthodox Church.

Ivan's cruelty was evident in both his personal and his public life. He was obviously far from being just an ignorant, brutal tyrant, and he was certainly not unintelligent. He recognized how backward Muscovy was in so many respects, and tried, as we have seen, to change matters by encouraging the importation of goods, especially from England, and by welcoming specialists and artisans from abroad in order to develop the skills of his own people. But the cruelty was there and, in later life, there in abundance. These tendencies were recognized in his youth when he was known to be guilty of such gratuitous acts of violence as throwing his hunting dogs off roofs. He was undoubtedly quick-tempered and could not – or would not – tolerate contradiction. Only two years before his death, in a fit of anger, he even killed the son who was due to succeed him.

Ivan's typical daily routine seems to have consisted of religious devotions followed by a session in the torture chamber – he liked nothing better than to devise new and exquisite entertainments – and then an evening engrossed in some form of elaborate sexual orgy. But in all this, he had just taken the precedents established by his forebears to greater and more ingenious lengths.

Ivan married early, at the age of only 17, and chose his bride from several hundred virgins who were brought to him from all over his kingdom in the same year as his coronation (1547). The death of his wife, in 1560 seems to have temporarily unhinged him; subordinates were accused of witchcraft and some were exiled and others imprisoned for life. He had four more wives after this, besides concubines, but he seems never to have quite recovered from his first wife's death. His creation of the oprichnina is said to have brought dismay to the general populace who thought that they were about to lose their tsar. This strange arrangement, whereby he stood aloof from the public yet remained their ruler, merely served to enhance his power – and to increase his cruelty. In effect, Muscovy was now divided into two states, his own 'model' state (oprichnina) consisting of his own army and officials with its own separate court, and the remainder of the country (zemschchina) which appears to have comprised the less prosperous areas. Both, according to Ivan, were undermined by deceit and treachery. Thus all those suspected of disloyalty and dissension had to be extirpated, a situation that allowed full rein for Ivan's sadistic instincts. Perhaps the worst incident among many was the 'punishment' of Novgorod, said to have been seeking union with Poland. As we have seen, the town was devastated and some 60,000 people killed. The slaughter here and elsewhere was relieved only by Ivan's 'macabre donations' so that religious services might be held in honour of the spirits of those he had murdered. Extreme measures they may have been, but he regarded them as just by virtue of divine right. He seems to have assumed that this made his absolute rule indisputable: the king could do no wrong. His ongoing onslaught, however, was on the boyars, whom he replaced with landowners of his own choosing, and who therefore owed their position to him personally. The boyars later attempted their own 'counter-revolution' in subsequent centuries, and 'produced an amalgamation of the state and the landowners to which the only threat would [one day] come from the peasants and the intelligentsia' (Kochan, 1967: 55).

The first years of Ivan's reign had been eventful, but the scale of horrors became much worse in his later years. One hypothesis suggests that this may have had something to do with his failing mental condition. As his health began to deteriorate, he turned for help to soothsayers and witches. When this did not work, his desperation drew him back to other forms of superstition. He would be taken to his treasure chamber to fondle precious jewels which he hoped had curative powers. But all to no avail. As one contemporary wrote: 'The Emperor began grievously to swell in the cods [genitals] with which he had most horribly offended over fifty years together, boasting of a thousand virgins he had deflowered and thousands of children of his begetting destroyed' (quoted by Kochan, 1967: 59). It is not known exactly what disease he had, but it is a reasonable bet that it was syphilis, probably contracted before his first marriage. Ivan had three legitimate sons: one died (or was murdered) in infancy; another, the tsarevitch, was killed by Ivan in a fit of temper; and the third (from a current description) sounds as though he may well have been a congenital syphilitic (Cartwright and Biddiss, 1991: 167). Some support is given to this conjecture about Ivan when one considers his bizarre behaviour in retreating from Moscow and setting up his strange quasi-monastic oprichnina. It is plausible that the sickening litany of tortures, floggings and executions were related to the onset of cerebral syphilis, though, if so, why it should take *this* form is anybody's guess. It is obvious that he took a peculiar delight in cruelty either as a voyeur or as an actual participant. For instance, when the executions in Moscow took place in July 1570, Ivan, and the son (also Ivan) whom he later killed, participated in the ghastly operations. While one of their noble victims was being hanged and simultaneously sliced with knives, the tsar was raping his wife, and his son was raping the eldest daughter. And these are just incidents in a reign of terror that lasted for over 20 years.

Ivan died in 1584 preparing to play a game of chess. At this time, he was in the midst of negotiations with the English court to marry a kinswoman of the queen. Elizabeth I had already refused, politely but pointedly, an offer of marriage with herself, but was pleased to suggest the possibility of a consolation prize from her court. Fortunately for some unsuspecting girl, these plans never materialized. After suffering what he felt were the torments of the damned, Ivan expired, leaving the country close to con-stitutional chaos. There followed what has become known as the 'time of troubles', and some semblance of unity was only achieved with the accession of the Romanov dynasty in 1613.

Louis XIV: authoritarianism and the French monarchy

We should properly distinguish between the policies, the practices and the style of Louis' reign, and then decide whether or not he can be justly classified as a despot. His main aims which were expressed as policies can really be seen as a continuation of those established earlier by Cardinal Richelieu and then by his one-time assistant and successor, Cardinal Mazarin. The general aim was that of raising the prestige of France among the warring nations of Europe. There were two subsidiary aims: that of lessening the intransigence and independence of the French nobility and, in effect, bringing them to heel; and that of depriving the Huguenots of any political power. The Huguenots, French Protestants, had already suffered terribly in the earlier Wars of Religion; many thousands had been massacred in France in the previous century. In 1598 their rights had been recognized in the Edict of Nantes, but infringements and abuses still took place. Hence the intention of Richelieu to keep them in their place. Once these 'domestic' issues were taken care of, the government would then be free to pursue its larger aims elsewhere.

In all these matters, Richelieu had qualified success. The administration of the state was gradually reorganized along more centralized lines. This reduced the influence of the nobility and the effectiveness of the traditional administrative districts by augmenting the power of the intendants who reported directly to the central administration. It is probably no coincidence that it was at this time that Richelieu set up his Cabinet Noir whose task was to 'advise' on all matters of intelligence. This included the interception and analysis of correspondence, the work of the police, and the sifting of intelligence reports from a large network of spies and informers. This intelligence-service-within-an-intelligence-service kept the government in touch with the thinking and scheming of all sectors of society, especially the aristocratic milieu, and was therefore able to monitor the potential centres of subversion and neutralize dangerous plots before they could develop (Deacon, 1990: 18–19). Richelieu generated antagonism by his extravagance and his often questionable ways of raising revenues, not least by the debasement of the coinage and the creation and sale of titles and sinecures. Although his plans for overseas colonization came to little, he was relatively successful in his foreign policy. France acquired a number of not inconsequential territories at very little expense; he made sure that France profited from other people's wars.

On Richelieu's death in 1642, his place was taken by Mazarin whose methods were different but whose aims were virtually the same. His domestic policy too was found wanting, especially his oppressive tax laws, and he had to face a minor revolution (the Fronde) when the nobility made an uneasy and temporary alliance with the Paris underclass and called for reasonably modest reforms. Promises were made, and – except for a few minor concessions – predictably not kept once the commotion had died down. The whole affair had been simmering on and off for five years, and it finally petered out in 1653. The king, Louis XIII, had been rather overshadowed by his more energetic ministers but things were to change dramatically when his son, who succeeded to the throne in 1643 when only four, became of age in 1661.

Louis XIV (the Sun King) came to the throne at a time when France, though not militarily dominant, exercised a kind of cultural hegemony in Western Europe. It was foremost in architecture and the visual arts; its designers set the standards and styles for others to emulate. There were developments in the then embryonic sciences which became diffused with the persecution and flight of the Huguenots. This, in turn, was helped by the fact that the French language was the normal medium of international intercourse. In polite society it was the customary mode of expression (Beloff, 1963: 47), and was the accepted vehicle of communication between social and intellectual elites. French had even begun to replace Latin in the preparation of treaties between states, and even political ideas that originated elsewhere often remained parochial philosophies until they were taken up by the French and disseminated via French writings.

As we have seen, absolute monarchy did not mean the unlimited or arbitrary exercise of power. The king, in theory at least, had to heed the advice of his Council, although it seems to have been accepted without serious qualification that the final decision was his. The hereditary principle was not, at this time, open to challenge; indeed, it is doubtful whether it was ever really questioned except by a few radical extremists. It is usually conceded that the great advantage of a monarchy is that it often obviates unnecessary and sometimes fratricidal wrangling over the succession, but it has also been suggested (for example, Beloff, 1963: 50–52) that at this time it was so popular that unwelcome social measures were often thought not to be the work of the king himself but of his more untrustworthy subordinates. Be that as it may, it was only the king who had the power to tax at discretion, restrict religious freedom, and order arrest and imprisonment *without trial* for an indefinite duration. The ordinary citizen, although he had the rights of petition and association providing it was for *non*-political purposes, was unacquainted with the idea of general liberty as we understand it today. Seventeenth-century France presents us with a bewildering series of class and territorial divisions, the most characteristic of which was the Estate. This was a legacy of the feudal system by which land was given as fiefs in exchange for military service. Every member of society, unless he was a serf or a resident alien, was a member of an estate. Traditionally this mode of stratification involved royalty, nobility, ecclesiastics, the lesser gentry, free tenants, serfs and even slaves, but we can say for simplicity that, for France at this time, if a person wasn't a noble or ecclesiastic he was then a member of the Third Estate, effectively the free poor. Of course there were all sorts of corporate bodies that cut across these distinctions, including the professionals and officials who held administrative offices that were both hereditary and, in many cases, subject to purchase. Territorially, the 'pays' or provinces and many towns and cities, especially those which had come under French jurisdiction as the result of some post-war settlement, were virtually self-governing.

In Europe at this time, there was almost permanent rivalry between many states, especially those seeking political and economic hegemony. But the entire scene was complicated by shifting alliances that were sometimes inconsistent or frankly inexplicable, and often stemmed from rival dynastic claims; witness, for example, the War of the Spanish Succession (1702–13) towards the end of Louis' reign. There were also the conflicting religious allegiances occasioned by the Reformation which helped to initiate the fearful Thirty Years War that was still in progress during Louis' youth. Much of the time, then, from his coming of age in 1651 and the beginning of his personal rule in 1661, was taken up trying to recuperate from the ravages of revolution and war while preparing for yet further trials of strength.

Louis actually took over his formal duties as king the day after the death of Mazarin whose place was taken by Colbert, another shrewd administrator who had been one of Mazarin's assistants. It was Colbert's economic reforms that enabled Louis to pursue his grandiose schemes in art and architecture, and in building up his military forces, especially the navy. He went on to become Controller-General of Finances in 1665 and Secretary of the Navy and the Royal Household in 1669. His duties were wide-ranging: he was responsible for shipbuilding, extending the canal system, establishing many of the Academies for which France became famous, and for overseas ventures such as the attempted revival of the French East India Company.

It has been argued that Colbert's reforms were largely dissipated in an effort to maintain and finance Louis' aggressive policies (Revill, 1962: 410). On the other hand, Louis' reputation has been defended by those who see him in quite a different light, especially French historians (for example, Mousnier, 1974). It is here that we encounter a fundamental debate: Louis is seen variously as a tyrannical militarist bent on French expansionism and, alternatively, as a calculating, clever and generally benevolent despot who, despite the extravagances of his court and the colossal expense of his wars, really only had the interests of his country at heart.

Let us examine the record. There was almost perpetual war during Louis' reign, something which he is said to have regretted as a dying man. Even the periods of truce can be seen simply as opportunities to get ready for yet more war. In 1667, France went to war with Spain – not for the first time; this ended with a treaty in 1668. In 1672, Louis invaded Holland, something he had planned for at least five years. (Admittedly, the Dutch were getting rather cheeky in threatening others' commercial interests, including England's. Holland was only a small trading nation but had a relatively large fleet. She wanted to be up with the big boys, and in 1667 her fleet even had the temerity to sail up the Medway and play havoc with English shipping.) Louis succeeded in a lightning campaign conducted by his best general, Turenne, and most of Holland was overrun in just a few weeks. The Dutch saved themselves by opening the dykes and flooding much of the country, but they still had to come to terms and cede territory to France. Eventually, many other European states became involved because they were anxious about Louis' intentions. The coalition against him was formidable, his only allies were England and Sweden, and after the English opted out in 1674, France and Sweden continued to battle it out against virtually the rest of Europe. After more fruitless years of fighting both sides were exhausted and terms were agreed. France and Sweden didn't come out too badly in the circumstances. Both gained territories from the Peace of Nijmegen in 1678, although neither had yet dealt as intended with the irrepressible Dutch.

Spain was obviously unhappy with these arrangements and declared war in 1683, but had to sue for peace the following year. In 1683 too, Louis sent troops to help the emperor of Austria when Vienna was threatened by the Turks. He also attacked Algiers and Tripoli which were nominally under the suzerainty of Turkey, notwithstanding the fact that he had treaties of friendship with Turkey which, in this case, were obviously overriden by ideological considerations. In 1686 the League of Augsburg was formed, consisting mainly of German states plus Sweden and Spain, in order to enforce the treaties that had been made and finally secure some measure of peace in Europe. Louis, whose problems had been mainly with the maritime powers, rightly saw this as a united front against him and decided to strike first, so again he went on the offensive. Many other states were drawn into the conflict which continued until 1697. This time, it was Louis who had to make concessions.

Maybe this can be judged as a preventive war by the French who naturally feared encirclement by their enemies, while for the allies it was an understandable attempt to curb French aggression. It is quite impossible to isolate any one reason for these continuing conflicts. As we have seen, there were dynastic disputes which often derived from intermarriage between different European royal families. These were intended to foster good relations between states, but actually they sometimes caused serious problems when rival claimants tried to secure their inheritance or some form of compensation in lieu. This was certainly the case in what is termed the War of the Spanish Succession, which was fundamentally about territorial appropriations. In 1702, England, Austria and Holland all declared war on France in order to wrest Italy and the West Indies from French control. The great victories of Marlborough at Blenheim (1704), Turin (1706) and Romillies in the same year against the French-Bavarian alliance effectively spelled an end to Louis' ambitions. France lost out all round.

Treaties were signed in 1713, 1714 and 1715 when many of her possessions were distributed among the victors. Much of Canada went to England, but Louis did manage to secure recognition of his grandson's claim to the Spanish throne, and was allowed to keep his American colonies.

Nevertheless, the reasons for these interminable wars are complex. In addition to the dynastic dimension, there were also insoluable economic rivalries – especially over the profitable Mediterranean routes, and over who had the lion's share of the slave trade from Africa to America, which at this time was the monopoly of the Spaniards. Louis' hatred of the Dutch arose partly because of their republicanism, but much more because of their successful commercial ventures.

Towards the end of the seventeenth century, warfare had changed considerably from the relatively minor hit-and-miss affairs of the Middle Ages. Armies were larger and better organized, and weaponry much more sophisticated than it had been only 100 years before. So it was no longer a matter of simply finding a plausible rationale or justification for war, there was also the matter of the *mode* in which warfare was conducted. It had ceased to be an expression of knightly valour or a question of honest chivalry, for instance: the barbarities of the Thirty Years' War had seen to that. So Louis' often precipitate and seemingly unprovoked attacks on other states look suspiciously like naked aggression. And the brutal French treatment of such cities as Mannheim and Heidelberg in the League of Augsburg cannot easily be excused. Indeed, it is arguable whether massacre and atrocity can ever be justified, regardless of the situation (Carlton, 1994).

There is little doubt that Louis can be classified as a type of despot, although there is no sense in which he governed unconstitutionally. He had his Council who advised him on the various constitutional issues, but it was he *alone* who made the decisions, especially the decision to go to war. Strictly speaking, he didn't have ministers, only officials. Even the chancellor did not have a place on the Council *by right*. The post of superintendent of finance was abolished, religious dignitaries and nobles were actually barred from the Council, and not even Louis' family and heirs were allowed to have any executive function. Louis concentrated all power in his own person. He reduced the importance of magistrates, suppressed many offices, and abrogated to himself the authority to make all important appointments. He radically curtailed the right of office-holders to make 'remonstrancies', that is, complaints concerning the outcome – or possible outcome – of his edicts, and in the end they gave up and didn't offer any. On the other hand, it was possible to ask the king and his Council to reconsider their decision on any particular issue, but if Louis chose to reject it, it was rejected (Mousnier, 1974: 11–12).

Probably Louis' most serious political blunder was in revoking the right of religious toleration; an issue on which he vacillated and changed course more than once. Protestants, who constituted a substantial skilled minority and who themselves could be quite intolerant and even bigoted in their own way, fared rather badly in seventeenth-century France. Not only was their theology anathema to Catholics, their general religious views were regarded as dangerous because of their implied republican orientations. Their colleges were suppressed, synods forbidden and rituals curtailed. In 1669, the government relented and tried to woo them back to the Catholic Church. It didn't work that well, and in 1679 persecution was resumed. Protestants were barred from public office, and various forms of intimidation were used to obtain Catholic 'conversions'. Louis set himself up as the defender of the 'true' faith, discrimination became outright persecution and torture. Needless to say, Catholics who had been tempted to stray were re-converted in huge numbers. In October 1685, there was the official revocation of the Edict of Nantes granting limited toleration, an act that may have been partly inspired by the anti-Protestant views of Louis' second wife, the former Madame de Maintenon. Life became even more unbearable for the Protestants. Emigration, which was officially forbidden on pain of death or consignment to the galleys (which was much the same thing), increased. Thousands of people who had once been a real asset to France escaped to Germany and Holland, to England – after the flight of the Catholic James II, who had promised to help Louis, and the accession of William of Orange in 1688 – and to America where the first 'state' to give *full* religious freedom was probably Rhode Island. They were generally well received by these countries, who regarded their skills as a valuable acquisition.

Louis' fiscal policies were also typical of the ambitious, autocratic ruler. The tax levied on most sections of the population was truly excessive. His building schemes at Versailles, with its huge park and the later, smaller palaces, the Trianon and Marly, and his very expensive wars imposed a heavy financial burden on the nation. (Interesting for a man who in his early years had clapped one of the richest men in France, Nicholas Fouquet, in gaol for his ostentation on the young king's behalf. Louis may have been getting rid of a threat to his independence, but was not above confiscating some of Fouquet's possessions.) Poverty was widespread. Admittedly, France endured some severe winters during Louis' reign which diminished population numbers, and this combined with huge losses in military personnel and massive emigration meant that there was something in the order of 20 per cent fewer people in France at the end of his reign in 1715 than there had been at the beginning. In the wider arena, it is arguable that the Sun King left Europe more impoverished than it might have been. His unnecessary wars and vaunting ambition were ultimately to no one's benefit – least of all that of France.

CHAPTER ELEVEN

Ecclesiastical Despotism: the Borgias

The papacy has had a very chequered career, most notoriously so in what we broadly term the late Middle Ages. Serious disagreements over who should be elected to office resulted in the Great Schism in which two Popes 'reigned' at the same time (1377–78), one in Rome and the other in Avignon, each supported by his own particular group of European states. This farcical situation which had resulted largely from political rather than spiritual considerations continued until 1409 when a determined attempt was made to resolve the problem. A Council was called but only succeeded in making matters worse by declaring both reigning Popes deposed, and electing a third Pope to office. Neither of the reigning Popes accepted the ruling, and the whole affair lingered on until the Council of Constance (1414–18) was called by the emperor of Germany. There was a magnificent array of ecclesiastics and other notables including the ardent Bohemian reformer, John Huss. As always, the proceedings were very protracted, but the matter was effectively settled to most representatives' satisfaction. Yet the price of this precarious unity was considerable. It involved closing ranks against any who questioned the fundamentals of Papal practice and authority. Any criticism that was raised against the Church was also seen as a denial of the sanctity of the state. Consequently, Huss, who was there on a solemn pledge of safe conduct by the Emperor, was seized, condemned for heresy, and burnt without appeal, all on the same day (6 July 1415). This was seen as a direct attack on radical reform and did nothing to assuage the grievances of the critics. It consequently resulted in a religious war in Bohemia which lasted, on and off, until 1436.

In the longer term, the Council of Constance was shown to have done little lasting good, so another Council was called at Basle in 1432 and likewise dragged on for ages, indeed until 1449, a period that was punctuated by the calling of several lesser Councils which, yet again, had little effect. And all this while the most serious squabbles, often culminating in armed conflict, were taking place between the shifting alliances of European states. As if this were not enough, all this was taking place while the West was facing the menace of Turkish expansion in the East.

Absolutely fundamental to the problems of the papacy was the still ongoing issue of where spiritual matters end and political ones begin. Indeed, it may be that it is a false dichotomy and that there can never be a clear all-purpose answer, merely tentative solutions to specific problems. We can still only give highly qualified answers to particular questions that arise from time to time (such as, in our own day, the matters of abortion, contraception, and so on). In the period which concerns us here, the issue was very much one of authority. Did the Pope have the last word on all matters? Did the church make political decisions, or was the final prerogative with the state? And how could the secular powers think of the Church in spiritual terms when the Pope courted them for political purposes? And how in Italy specifically could anyone take the Papacy really seriously when ecclesiastical dignitaries comported themselves like kings and princes with all the trappings of wealth? How could the Pope enlist the services of the Papal States (theoretically under his jurisdiction but 'leased out' to his quasi-ecclesiastical representatives) to deploy their armies in his temporal interests? It was issues of this kind, and not least disgust at the corruption and simony within the Church, which generated the reforming movements both within and outside its boundaries that came into their own in the following century.

Rome at this time has been described as a sink of iniquity. Out of a population of about 50,000 there were some 7,000 prostitutes mostly working in brothels licensed by the Papacy in which disease, especially venereal disease, was common. Crime was rife, and there was an average of 14 murders a day (Hibbert, 1979: 205). The city itself was nominally autonomous and was effectively ruled by ecclesiastical officials within the bureaucratic structure known as the Curia. This comprised a number of departments which were mainly concerned with financial administration. The income of Papal Rome was literally incalculable. By the end of the fifteenth century, it was one of the richest of the Italian states, for besides its normal revenue there were the unrecorded but considerable gifts of money and jewels many of which went into the Pope's private treasury. Monies from the sale of offices, special dispensations and annulments, and, not least, the remission of penances, all contributed to the Pope's personal coffers. Technically, his authority was subject to the will of the College of Cardinals, but it was often possible to circumvent opposition by the bestowal or withdrawal of Papal patronage, somewhat like that of a modern British Prime Minister vis-à-vis the Cabinet. In practice, therefore, Popes enjoyed virtually unlimited power. They were rich, often fabulously so; they were temporal princes, and lived accordingly in vast palaces with a large retinue of servants. And they were also religious leaders, which gave them considerable coercive authority because they alone had at their disposal the spiritual sanctions which at that time were generally recognized. Even kings feared the threat of excommunication. It was as well to keep in with the papacy; a little celestial insurance might be all to the good, and certainly it did no harm.

The abuses of the higher clergy produced an adverse reaction among both priests and the laity. Even prior to Martin Luther and what is often misleadingly referred to as *the* Reformation early in the sixteenth century, the religious ferment of the fifteenth century produced pre-Protestant reformers who, like Luther, also came from within the Church. One of the most influential was Ginolamo Savonarola (b. 1451), a near contemporary of Rodrigo Borgia who later became Pope Alexander VI. Savonarola became extremely famous as a preacher and in some ways was more extreme than John Wycliffe, the English scholar who became known as the 'morning star of the Reformation', or even than Luther himself. Savonarola denounced both the princes and the Papacy. In Florence, where he was a Dominican friar, he entered the political fray and helped to foment a revolution which ushered in a period of more ameliorative oligarchic rule in place of the control exercised by some of the more autocratic members of the Medici family. This made him a good many enemies, especially among the nobility in Florence and those in other neighbouring states who feared the possible impact of such ideas on their own governments. His radicalism soon attracted the notice of the Papacy, and the Pope (Alexander VI) forbade him to preach what was regarded as tantamount to heresy. Needless to say, he defied the ban, and in doing so denied the authority of the Church, and was thus excommunicated (1497). Being *persona non grata* he found that his support began to diminish. Once isolated, he could be arrested without too much commotion, and once in prison, he was tortured, hanged and finally burnt for heresy (1498), a 'victim of his own fanaticism and moral fervour' (Revill, 1962: 331) and – one might add – the intolerance and despotic certitude of the Papacy.

The position of cardinals was somewhat like that of the Pope, although they obviously lived on a less lavish scale. Keeping up appearances was important; status was related to expenditure and not all cardinals enjoyed the privileges of a rich benefice. Some, indeed, were often very much in debt, perhaps because they had already paid out a great deal to obtain the living in the first place. Others lost out in the scramble for preferment which often followed the election of a new pontiff. If at all possible, many cardinals welcomed an appointment as 'ambassador' to one or another of the Papal States where they might secure the favours of the local nobility, although this not infrequently put them in an invidious position when one state was in conflict with another which was also nominally within the province of the Church. Who should they support in such a situation? Should they endorse the claims of their local lord, often a petty tyrant, or try to remain spiritually aloof?

Rivalry and hostility were common fare in the Italian city states. Armed encounters between one duchy and another, or one prince's retainers and those of another was almost *de rigueur*. Sometimes these conflicts were about trade, or about land and power-seeking in general, as was the case with the Borgias. Not unusually, there were also squabbles within states between the signorial families themselves which resulted in blood-letting. Factional brawls were commonplace, and vendettas of one kind or another were not entirely exceptional. In July 1500, for example, there took place a bloodbath that would not have disgraced a modern Mafia scenario. Known cynically as the Red Wedding, it involved a feud in which half the Baglioni family of Perugia murdered the other half in their beds (Bradford, 1981: 2). The use of assassins was well recognized, and poison as an instrument of policy is well attested. For example, an eminent member of the Milanese nobility, Francesco Sforza, while still quite young, had married a Calabrian heiress, Polissena Russa, the Countess of Montalto, who bore him a daughter. A disgruntled aunt poisoned both mother and child and seized the inheritance. The Spanish were reputed to be particularly adept with poisons, and it is suggested that Cesare Borgia – himself of Spanish descent – had his own personal poisoner as he also had his own hangman (Burckhardt, 1958: 127).

The Italian states, then, 'coexisted in an uneasy balance of power maintained by mutual jealousy rather than common interest' (Bradford, 1981: 6). Venice and Milan were the most powerful states in financial and military terms, and were consequently distrustful of each other. Venice, in particular, had a modest overseas empire, although this was in the process of being slowly diminished by the depredations of the Ottoman Turks. Milan, on the other hand, another great trading state, had long been ruled by the Visconti family, but from 1447 had passed into the control of the Sforzas whose senior member, Ludovico Sforza – an inordinately ambitious man – had seized power from his nephew in 1480. Some of the other Italian states (other than the Papal States), such as Genoa, Savoy and Sienna, can be largely discounted for our purposes, but the lesser, though important, states of Florence and Naples are certainly relevant to our discussion. Florence, as we have seen, was very much the province of the Medici family, and the death of perhaps its most successful ruler Lorenzo d'Medici ('Lorenzo the Magnificent') in the same year that Rodrigo Borgia became Pope almost certainly had an unsettling effect on Italian politics. The kingdom of Naples to the south, ruled by another dominant character, in this case the unpopular Ferrante II, was a subject of dispute between France and Spain, both of whom laid claim to its territories. In these circumstances, one can appreciate that there were often more or less successful attempts to secure some kind of hegemony in Italy. The story of the Borgias is the account of perhaps the most notorious of these, which finally ended in disaster.

The Borgias came originally from Spain, and claimed descent from the kings of Aragon. Alfonso Borgia actually came to Naples in the service of Aragon, and later became a cardinal. Spain at the time sought a dominant role in Europe and very much wanted – perhaps *needed* – a Spanish Pope in the Vatican; its hopes were realized when Alfonso Borgia eventually became Calixtus III in 1455. The popes – certainly at this time – were not above a little nepotism, especially if it was kept within the family. So Calixtus took two of his nephews into his charge, Rodrigo and Pedro Luis, and determined to shape their future careers. The boys became his heirs, and Calixtus made Pedro Luis a dignitary of the Church, and similarly Rodrigo, whose accelerated promotion meant that he became a cardinal when only 26. Understandably, this caused trouble among the prelates who objected to foreigners being given plum positions, especially very young foreigners at that. After Calixtus died, Pedro Luis was driven from the city and died soon afterwards, but Rodrigo survived the protests and went on to serve the next Pope, Pius II, and, as his brother's heir, became one of the richest men in Rome.

Rodrigo was still only 30, and was already establishing a reputation as a well-placed womaniser; on at least one occasion, the Pope had to reprimand him and remind him that his activities were not conducive to his 'high office'. One writer says of him that he was 'handsome, of a most glad countenance and joyous aspect, gifted with honeyed words and choice eloquence. The beautiful women on whom he casts his eyes he lures to love him and moves them in a wondrous way' (Gaspare da Verona quoted by Plaidy, 1958: 15). And although he later became fat and bald, he had a number of mistresses, among them Vannozza Cattanei who was probably a high-class courtesan. She had two boys, Juan and Cesare, who were almost certainly his (one can never be too sure in these cases), and a girl, Lucrezia, born in 1480, who probably was. Two years later Vannozza had another son, Joffre, who may not have been his, but Rodrigo appears to have treated the boy as though he was his natural father. He also had children by other women, but Vannozza and her offspring obviously merited special attention and they were installed in a house close to the cardinal's palace. This was naturally very handy for the odd, discreet visit. Not that Rodrigo needed to be particularly covert about his sexual proclivities or indeed his occasional lapses into domesticity; other prelates – including popes – had maintained ladies for their extracurricular activities, and others had their complement of 'nephews' and 'nieces' to whom they were prone to give preferential treatment. In fact, Rodrigo was so solicitous for the welfare of his 'family' that over time he arranged two separate marriages for Vannozza with suitably accommodating gentlemen, presumably to maintain the polite fiction of ecclesiastical rectitude.

In 1484, Pope Sixtus IV died and there was intense rivalry over the succession. Hopes were raised and expectations increased; after all, Popes could do a great deal for those they favoured. As for Rodrigo, he wanted to perpetuate an even more powerful Borgia dynasty which might actually unite the warring states in Italy under one all-embracing banner. His goal was the Papacy but, for a while, he had to be patient. Innocent VIII was elected, but frictions were such that before very long the Papal States were at war with Naples. To make matters worse, the Neopolitans had influential sympathizers in Rome itself, and soon there was bitter fighting in the streets of the city among rival factions. There was the usual agenda of death and mutilation, looting and unashamed public rape, scenes which probably horrified yet fascinated the young Borgias, yet scenes that were tragically not that unfamiliar in inter-state conflicts. There was a truce of sorts, and again the rulers settled down and waited – or plotted – for the next opportunity. Meanwhile, Rodrigo bided his time and continued to plan for the future. His wealth ensured that he would not be disappointed.

Cynics might contend that 1492 was an unpropitious year. It was the year that Lorenzo d'Medici died and the year that, yet again, Milan and Naples were at daggers drawn. It was, of course, also the year that Columbus discovered what he thought was the Indies – but this was all of little concern to the pater familias of the Borgias. Innocent VIII had died, and this time with a generous distribution of bribes Rodrigo made sure of his election; he was installed as Alexander VI at the age of 61. He could certainly afford to be generous to those who were prepared to support his claims to the papacy. While still a cardinal it was said that 'his revenues from his papal offices, his abbeys in Italy and Spain, and his bishoprics are vast. His office of Vice-Chancellor alone yields him 8,000 gold ducats annually. His plate, his pearls, his stuffs embroidered with silk and gold, his books are of such a quality as would befit a king or a Pope. Altogether it is believed that he possesses more gold and riches of every sort than all the other cardinals put together' (quoted by Chamberlain, 1969: 2).

Rodrigo set about establishing a future for his children, Juan, Cesare, Lucrezia and Joffre. Other Popes had secured positions of wealth and responsibility for their offspring – after all, Rodrigo's immediate predecessor had married his children into Italian royal families – so why shouldn't he do likewise? For her part, their mother was extremely flattered. She seems to have demanded little from her patron except due recognition for her children. Even when he turned to a young and apparently very beautiful new mistress, Guilia Farnese, she was forbearing. As well she might be because she probably felt that the new affair couldn't last; not only was the age difference exceptional, it was also well known that Guilia Farnese, who had been married at 15, had something of a reputation and had made a notorious cuckold of her husband, who had died suspiciously at the house of her then current lover.

In 1492, Cesare was 16 or 17 (there seems to be some uncertainty about this), just one year younger than Juan with whom he always seems to have had ambivalent relations. This was reflected somewhat in his attitude towards his father who appears to have favoured his brothers and especially his sister to his own cost. Certainly, his father's ecclesiastical plans for him were not the plans he had for himself. Whether – as Jean Plaidy suggests in her somewhat sensationalized interpretation – the Borgias lived in a hot-house atmosphere of incest and intrigue, we are unsure; it seems to be without real evidential support. On the other hand, it was well known that Cesare doted on his sister in ways that aroused gossip, and that he was not exactly overjoyed when she was married into the Sforza family. If the incest allegation is true, he may have been temporarily comforted by the knowledge that as Lucrezia was only 13 at her marriage, it was agreed that there should be no consummation – at least, for a while.

Within three months of Lucrezia's wedding, perhaps as some kind of consolation, the 18-year-old Cesare was proclaimed a cardinal, although his was perhaps no great prize because so also proclaimed was the profligate brother of Guilia Farnese (the Farneses were to do rather well out of Guilia's association with the Pope). The Borgia family was now pretty well set up. Even the 13-year-old Joffre was betrothed to the daughter of the king of Naples.

It was just at this point that Rodrigo suddenly found himself in a precarious situation. Charles VIII of France decided to invade Italy, at the instigation of the Borgias' enemies, and annex those territories to which he felt he had an ancient right and subdue the others. It meant that he first had to come to terms with the Sforzas of Milan; this proved to be no problem despite the fact that one of them was now married into the Borgia family. A little incidental treachery was par for the course in current Italian politics; indeed, some may have regarded it as poetic justice that later the Sforza in question was forced to divorce Lucrezia on the humiliating grounds of impotence. Things went well for Charles at first, but the demands of an invading army did not go down too well with the bulk of the Italian populace; combine this with the wily machinations of Rodrigo who so manipulated his alliances that the French got little cooperation from other states, and the whole thing adds up to failure. Charles abandoned the project, and the army, unaccompanied by the elusive Cesare who was supposed to be Charles' hostage, returned to France with little to show for its trouble. The Pope then turned on those states that had resisted his wishes by sending his own forces against them commanded by his eldest son, Juan, who had been called back from Spain for the purpose. He and Cesare went out to celebrate his appointment – and he was never seen alive again.

When Juan's body was eventually dredged out of a river, it bore all the marks of an assassination, though not a particularly professional one. Rumours abounded as to who the culprits were and, more especially, who had ordered the murder. There were just to too many suspects. The

Borgias had many enemies, particularly those who regarded them as unscrupulous, upstart foreigners. But as more investigations took place, the more it was felt that the solution might lie nearer home. And who better than Cesare? There was never much love lost between the brothers and Roman gossip had it that they had vied with each other for the favours of Joffre's wife, who was known to be generously inclined and certainly not averse to mild sexual diversions. Worst of all there were the whispered suggestions that the brothers and the father were all rivals for Lucrezia's affections, no doubt the kind of allegation that many wished to hear but which has never been substantiated.

Cesare now took on the mantle of his dead brother, and leading a small army set out to implement his father's wishes in punishing the recalcitrant states. This really meant dealing with their leaders, which he did quite successfully, especially considering his relative lack of experience in military matters. These operations obviously gave him the feeling that he had discovered his true metier. From this point, events moved rapidly, Lucrezia, once again available after her divorce, was betrothed to the nephew of the king of Naples, and a marriage was arranged between Cesare and the French king's daughter. Coincidentally, the new king of France, Louis XII, who wanted a papal dispensation to annul his present marriage, agreed to give Cesare a French dukedom providing he renounced his office as cardinal – the source of his income – in exchange for papal favours.

The matter was duly agreed, and Cesare went to France with his entourage all expensively bedecked in colourful velvets and jewels, a spectacle that went down well with the crowds but not with the French royals, who were unimpressed and felt that it was simply vulgar ostentation. The king's daughter, who had never been too enthusiastic about the betrothal, now declared adamantly that the marriage was off. But Louis, equal to the occasion, found a substitute bride, a 17-year-old princess in his court who was actually the sister of the king of Navarre. Her avaricious father, taking cynical advantage of the Borgias' embarrassment, set a high price of 100,000 ducats on his daughter *and* demanded, in addition, a cardinal's hat for his son. The Borgia-Louis deal was so imperative that terms were quickly agreed and within two days the marriage – a modest affair – took place in May 1499. Within weeks, Cesare was again on campaign, and his pregnant young wife never saw him again.

What was particularly critical for Italy were the *post*-nuptial arrangements, made between Cesare and Louis effectively to carve up Italy between them. Louis was already allied to Venice and Florence and intended to invade Italy to claim Milan and Naples for himself. Cesare (later supported by his father) agreed providing that he could play a key role in the military operations and use French troops to enable him to 'create' a principality for himself. He reasoned that the Italian states were so hopelessly divided among themselves, that in this disunited condition they were no match for his combined force. The French took Milan without any difficulty and Cesare then led his units to wrest the cities in the northern coastal province of Romagna from their rulers and create a fief of his own. Nominally these were under the direct jurisdiction of the Pope, but in practice the links had become tenuous, and they were run as semi-independent mini-states by rulers who had become rather lax about paying their Papal dues. Cesare needed to deal with them without unduly antagonizing the more powerful Italian states which might suspect – rightly – that he had more ambitious designs further afield.

The campaign began well. Cesare took possession of two cities with the customary attendant carnage, both of which were under the control of the formidable tyrant Caterina Sforza, whose ruthlessness certainly matched that of the Borgias. It still remains a matter of speculation whether Caterina was literally treated as one of Cesare's legitimate spoils of war; he repudiated the charge of rape, insisting that it was unnecessary because women usually surrendered to him quite voluntarily. However, he disengaged the army when the Milanese threatened to march against him; most of the troops were not really his, so he was unable to commit them to a large-scale battle, which he wanted to avoid anyway.

Cesare returned to Rome and became ruler there, though still under the acquiescent eye of his ageing father. There he raised money to continue his military exploits, partly by selling offices to would-be higher prelates. The arrangement with Louis was renewed as the king was still intent on adding Naples to his domains. Cesare now needed his sister to sever her marriage ties to further his political plans. Later, she might be needed for another dynastic marriage. But this time she was unwilling to be a pawn in the game. She obviously cared for her present husband and had no intention of divorcing him to please her brother or to accommodate the exigencies of state. She should have known better. Cesare was not the kind of person to be thwarted by sentiment. The young husband was promptly found seriously wounded by an unknown assassin, whose work was again not up to the trade's usual professional standards. But although the wounded man was guarded on the Pope's orders, the soldiers still weren't diligent enough to prevent him from being strangled in his bed after Cesare had ordered the women who nursed him to leave the room. Again, the evidence against Cesare is not conclusive, but it is very persuasive.

Not all the cities that fell in Cesare's triumphant progress through Romagna were brutally treated. Some, exasperated with their current rulers, welcomed him enthusiastically as their new overlord and others actually asked to become members of his growing domain. By all accounts, even to those that despised him, Cesare brought improved government to the cities he now possessed, often reducing taxation, controlling prices and bringing law and order to the countryside which had previously been the playground of bandits. But these benefits were always bought at a price. Many of these cities had been inefficiently governed by minor nobility who exploited and oppressed the people in order to maintain their positions, and with the takeovers these were either ousted or bought off. By either accepting or choosing Cesare the citizens were merely replacing one form of despotism with another, perhaps on the assumption that it couldn't be any worse, and just might be a great deal better.

Trouble came when he had to tackle the well-fortified city of Faenza which, although traditionally supporting a despotism, was run almost as a republic by its 16-year-old ruler, Astorre Manfredi, and his Council. Faenza decided to resist, and Cesare didn't take too kindly to those who did not comply with his wishes. Furthermore, successful resistance, even serious hesitancy, played havoc with his timetable, and did nothing for this reputation. The siege was begun somewhat unusually in inclement weather in the winter of 1500, but had to be broken off during the worst months and resumed again the following spring. Neither side was prepared to budge from its chosen position. In the city itself supplies were running very low, but morale was still surprisingly high. Faenza's troops fought with great tenacity, much to Cesare's admiration, but eventually the wall was breached and Astorre and his Council sued for terms. By and large, the people were unharmed. Astorre and his half-brother were treated with respect, and after a short time with Cesare were packed off to a castle for 'safe keeping' in Rome. Cesare was all honeyed words and glib assurances. It did not always pay to divulge one's true feelings in these situations and working on the assumption that popular princes are the most dangerous to have around, he made the necessary arrangements. He obviously knew his Tacitus and the expediencies practised in Imperial Rome. The next that anyone knew of the two boys was when their bodies were found floating in the Tiber.

After making a foray into the state of Florence, being careful not to touch the city itself, Cesare made his way back to Rome. Meanwhile, Louis of France had come to an understanding both with Ferdinand of Spain (who was related to the royal family of Naples) and with the Pope (who had to give the necessary imprimatur) that Naples would be invaded and that they would divide the spoils between them. The campaign that followed hardly involved warfare, as such. Naples surrendered almost immediately, and nearby Capua likewise, much to the Pope's delight. (At Capua occurred one of those rare instances that we know of when Cesare entered the battle himself.) The capitulation was followed by extensive carnage in which about 6,000 people were killed. It was not Cesare's normal practice to turn his army loose on an enemy population, although when he felt that he needed to punish or intimidate he was quite prepared to do so. In fact, it is reported that generally he had remarkable control of his troops, especially when so many of them were either borrowed from others (the French king, for instance) or were mercenaries (condottieri). These latter were adventurers who were there as much for the excitement as for the loot. Some actually came from noble families. Oliverotto da Fermo, perhaps a somewhat atypical condottiero, was the nephew of the ruler of the city of Fermo who had treated him like his own son. After spending some time learning the military trade as a 'hired gun' he returned to his home where his uncle prepared an expensive reception for him. Oliverotto repaid his care and generosity by slaughtering him and his whole family, and made himself the new Lord of Fermo (Machiavelli 1513, trans. Rioci, 1935: 38–39).

The next phase of Cesare's plans for a personal kingdom involved rather more subtlety. It was here that he required his sister's cooperation. Negotiations were opened with the important d'Este family for their son, Alphonso, to marry Lucrezia, and a huge dowry – in actuality, a heavy bribe was promised with the bride. Cesare intended to add Ferrara to his 'list', as a powerful buffer city on his northern flank. Initially, Alphonso was extremely reluctant; after all, to be that close to the Borgias could be an unhealthy prospect. But after considerable pressure from his widowed father (who threatened to marry the girl himself if Alphonso refused), he agreed and the contract was signed. The marriage actually turned out to be more successful than any of the d'Estes anticipated. Affairs of state obviously sometimes had their advantages.

Cesare was now established. His fame and his power were generally recognized – and feared – throughout the Italian states. His court became the focus of cultural activities; writers and artists found their way there, although it is doubtful whether Cesare himself had any scholarly aspirations. Presumably he liked to give the right impression when it mattered. Even Leonardo da Vinci, who was naturally open for employment by any generous patron and was an engineer as well as an artist, was engaged for a while, mainly for his fortress designing and fabricating skills. While he was there, though, he took time to make some of the few contemporary sketches of Cesare that we now possess.

By 1502, Cesare felt strong enough militarily to put the pressure on Florence, and as part of his overall strategy he borrowed troops from a long-time friend, the Lord of Urbino, a city near Florence, and then treacherously attacked and occupied it while it was unprotected. As Cesare went on his victorious way in central Italy relations between the co-conspirators, the kings of Spain and France, began to deteriorate to the point where war was imminent. Louis again brought his army to Italy, and was there regaled by complaints from those who had suffered at the hands of his Borgia ally. He responded by outwardly affirming his loyalty to Cesare, but inwardly harbouring serious reservations. Was it possible that Cesare, being of Spanish blood, would desert him and commit himself instead to the cause of the Spanish king? And what would be the reaction of the condottieri, most of whom where in some way connected with the Italian nobility? Would they support Louis and – what proved to be particularly important – would they continue to fight for Cesare who was now beginning to threaten their own kith and kin? It looked now as though Cesare was going to be outmanoeuvred. The whole scene suddenly changed. Members of the Italian nobility, including some condottieri that had fought alongside Cesare, called a conference which presaged revolt. Florence had decided that enough was enough, and applied political counter-pressure; and Louis, despite his protestations of friendship to Cesare, remained an uncertain quantity. So for the would-be conqueror, it all became a precarious balancing act.

Cesare proved equal to the task. Almost inevitably, the nobles fell out among themselves, and after one or two minor engagements the revolt fizzled out. Most implored Cesare for reinstatement, which he granted with apparent good grace, but as usual he was just biding his time in order to deal with them when the opportunity arose. He didn't have to wait long. Some were invited to a banquet – an age-old strategem – and disposed of without further ado; a rebel ecclesiastic, Cardinal Orsini, was likewise dispatched by Rodrigo in Rome and his property confiscated; and those that hadn't been caught in the lethal net, fled (as they hoped) out of harm's way. With this Cesare returned to Rome, consolidating his gains as he went. But from this point onwards, though seemingly at the height of their powers, the invincible Borgia fortunes began to decline.

Shortly after Cesare's return, both he and his father fell dangerously ill, apparently from a fever (though poison was rumoured), from which his father died (1503). It may be that Cesare's condition was exacerbated by his generally low state of health. It seems to be reasonably well established that some time before this, possibly as early as 1497, he had contracted the 'French disease' (syphilis) about which very little was known at the time. He had also taken to wearing a mask in public, though hardly because he wanted to remain incognito. He is known to have looked blotchy for some time (Bradford, 1981: 290–91), and it has been plausibly suggested that the disease had now resulted in some form of unsightly disfigurement. Being weak from illness, he was not able to take charge of the fluctuating military and ecclesiastical situation as he wished. He needed a new Pope who sympathized with his own designs, but the prospects were slim. Furthermore, what could he possibly achieve without armed support? The Spanish were now in the ascendant in Italy, and his ally Louis had largely withdrawn his forces from the country. Cesare still thought he had enough influence to affect the papal elections, and he decided to support the cardinal who afterwards became Julius II in exchange for papal recognition of his position as Duke of Romagna. The ambassador from Florence, the political theorist Niccolo Machievelli, who normally had a high regard for Cesare's political acumen, regarded this as his greatest mistake. There was just no way that Cesare could hold Julius to his promise once the Pope was established in office, and sure enough he reneged and wanted the territories that Cesare had annexed to be returned to the direct auspices of the Papacy. The young fox was now outfoxed. Julius appeared to go along with the original plan, and Cesare was lured out of his Roman fortress under a pledge of safe conduct but, once outside the protection of his castle, he was arrested and his bodyguard destroyed.

By all accounts he now gave every appearance of being a broken man. Former friends did not come to his aid, and former enemies – at least, those who had survived – were quick to look for revenge. The once cold-eyed despot now became a cowering invalid. He was made to sign away his ill-gotten possessions, although he still retained the title of Duke of Valentinois conferred upon him by Louis of France. He was released from prison in January 1504, presumably on the assumption that he could now do very little harm. But he was not exactly powerless. His health was now certainly better, but being without financial or military support he knew that he would have to hitch his political wagon to someone else's particular star. But whose? He made a cynical, self-serving appraisal of the critical Spanish-French conflict and made his choice. The Cesare-Louis relationship was now one of mutual disenchantment, so it had to be the Spanish. In effect, he was hiring out as a highly placed mercenary. But his optimism was short-lived. Again, he had jumped the wrong way. The long-arm of the Papacy reached out to frustrate his ambitions. Julius gave what amounted to a directive to Ferdinand, the king of Spain, not to have any dealings with Cesare, and the king, over and above the call of duty, actually had him arrested once again.

After several unsuccessful attempts to secure his release, mainly by his sister, Cesare finally escaped after two years in custody, possibly with the connivance of his captors. Bribery lubricates many doors. He fled to his brother-in-law in the tiny kingdom of Navarre, which itself was threatened with a takeover, and was given a small force to command. But in carrying out siege operations for his new master in 1507, he was caught in an ambush, killed and – as tradition has it – cut into nine pieces, 'richly deserving death for all the evils he had wrought in Italy' (quoted by Chamberlain, 1969: 79). After this, the Borgias faded into obscurity; but the Papacy continued to support new ecclesiastical dynasties, though rarely of such uncertain provenance.

CHAPTER TWELVE

Enlightened Despotism: an Eighteenth-century European Phenomenon

In some ways the eighteenth century could be looked upon as a kind of codicil to the Middle Ages, although actually it might be more accurate to depict it as an age of transition between Medievalism and what we broadly call modern society. The main bastions of medieval European civilization, feudalism and the unifying influence of Catholicism, were both still in place but had been seriously questioned. Medieval institutions were by no means defunct. Where change was not actually taking place, in Tsarist Russia, for instance, it was being talked about. Systems were being challenged in theory by growing numbers of social philosophers, and in practice by a variety of abortive uprisings, some of which achieved – at most – a temporary success. Catholicism had lost much ground to Protestantism, especially in its Puritan forms. Protestants had contested the authority of Rome as the repository of all truth, yet at the same time had unwittingly acted as agents of demystification. It may therefore be, as Peter Berger has suggested, that Protestantism became its own 'gravedigger'. The Papacy had ceased to play such a prominent part in politics, and the ardent orthodoxy of both communions in the seventeenth century had given way in many places to a spirit of tolerance and scepticism (Revill, 1962: 418). In the economic sphere too, we find that with the rise of entrepreneurial activity and the new wealth that it generated there began a corresponding weakening of the power of the old nobility and a transfer to the crown, the merchants and to the lesser landed gentry who often owed their position to the favour of the king. The phenomenon we know as 'enlightened despotism' may well have developed in Europe partly out of genuine concern for the mass of poor peasantry and partly as a form of populist rebuff to the old established nobility.

In Russia, for instance, Peter (the Great), who could hardly be accused of undue benevolence, showed himself to be an intelligent, tough-minded and – where necessary – quite brutal ruler. He shared the throne with his half-brother from 1682, and succeeded as tsar in 1689. He determined to westernize Russia, and spent a preliminary year travelling and working in Germany, Holland and England to learn how things were done there. In an edict of 1702, he then tried to enforce Western habits of dress, dancing, and so on, on a resistant aristocracy. He was particularly interested in ship-building technology and naval affairs generally, and took a number of specialists with him when he returned home; one, a Scot, Alexander Gordon, became one of his chief military advisers. He also aimed at extending the Russian dominions so that she would have greater access to the sea both in the Baltic and to the south in the region of the Black Sea. Like Ivan the Terrible before him, he waged a constant internal vendetta against the nobles (boyars) who, if they had their way, would have tried to restrict his powers and – in his view – keep Russia in a kind of cultural 'Dark Ages' indefinitely.

Peter's military exploits, particularly against the Turks who contested his Balkan ambitions, met with varying success. On the other hand, he had greater fortune against Sweden with whom he had ambivalent relations. He remodelled his own administration along Swedish lines, but his admiration for such models did not prevent him from engaging in a long and difficult war with Sweden (1700–21), with an army that was largely his own personal creation. But all this cost money – money which he often didn't have. So he had to pay for his expansionist policies by debasing the coinage, initiating a number of new indirect taxes (for instance, on such peripheral practices as bee-keeping, knife-grinding and even beard-growing), and by confiscating some of the wealth of the Church which he sought to control.

Yet Peter did grant some exemptions, and encouraged industrial enterprise so that Russia could compete on even terms with the West. To this extent, he probably deserved the description 'enlightened', but in order to realize his dreams he had necessarily to resort to despotism. Russia was going to be modernized whether the people liked it or not; his vaunting ambition, perhaps laudable in itself, had to be paid for. So for this already overtaxed people a form of poll-tax was decreed in 1718 and introduced in 1724, which caused considerable disquiet. The rumbles of dissention were monitored by a growing army of spies and informers. Furthermore, the system of national service – itself a type of tax – was refined and in-tensified. This and the poll-tax were extended to more social categories. National service could include not just military obligations, but also levies of labourers for work in the mines and other projects. It is estimated that eventually serfs and slaves comprised about 90 per cent of the population. Their expendability can be seen in the building of the tsar's new capital, St Petersburg, which was constructed in an area of swampland and alone cost the lives of thousands of workers (Kochan, 1967: 110).

Peter had come to the throne at a time of bloody political feuding in which a number of his family were hacked to death. The lesson he learned very early was that factions must not be allowed to develop and he was convinced that autocracy was the only answer. If confirmation were needed, no one had to look any further than the 'time of troubles' that had followed upon the death of Ivan the Terrible. Peter was sure that what he wanted for Russia was right, whether it was a cultural whim such as a ban on beards, or whether it was experiments in what, for those times, was mass education. Many of these began with some promise, but failed in the longer term.

A man of gross appetites for sex and drink, Peter could be very brutal when thwarted, and savage in his punishments. When there was a revolt by some of his militia units on one occasion when he was away from Moscow, the rebels met with ferocious reprisals on his return. Their companies were reduced by some 2,000 executions (Red Square was decorated by a display of mutilated bodies) and innumerable banishments to Siberia. Similar atrocities followed in the wake of another failed rebellion of Ukrainian Cossacks in 1707. This was put down just as mercilessly by methods that would not have disgraced Ivan the Terrible.

Peter's despotism, in highly qualified forms, even extended to his own family. He dispensed with his wife, kept his son and subjected him to an educational and disciplinary regime which the boy hated. He married a servant girl who had been his mistress (and the mistress of one of his most trusted administrators before that), by whom he had many children, only two of whom survived to adulthood. His hopes for the succession rested on his son, Alexis, who, to his great disappointment, sided with the distrusted boyars. So Peter gave him the choice of giving up his support for the nobility – which Peter saw as a kind of disloyalty – or giving up the succession. Alexis chose to break with his father and left Russia for Austria. He was later induced to return, whereupon he was charged with treason, tortured, convicted and sentenced to death. Whether the sentence was or would have been carried out nobody knows, but two days after the sentence was passed he was found dead in his cell from uncertain causes (1718). Perhaps Peter just could not face the prospect of a public execution. In future, it was decreed that the succession was going to be entirely within the gift of the reigning monarch. In practice, however, this became the prerogative of the Guards, another of Peter's creations who, acting like the old Praetorian Guard of Roman times, came to make and unmake their own rulers.

Whatever Peter wasn't, he was an *effective* ruler, an autocrat of the traditional type who, nevertheless, by his innovations made an indelible cultural mark on Russian society. Certainly Russia was a European power to be reckoned with by the time he died in 1725, still dreaming of further conquests. When one considers what he did to both the nobility and the peasantry, one wonders if the appelation 'Great' is entirely appropriate. Perhaps he should be judged in terms of his intentions and achievements rather than his methods, which for an '*enlightened* despot' were really the well-tried brutalities of old.

It is interesting to compare Peter with a later ruler, Frederick the Great of Prussia, who is also regarded as an enlightened despot. The eighteenth century was a turbulent one as far as Europe was concerned. It was a time of power struggles, shifting allegiances and seemingly constant war between the Great Powers. The foundations for later Prussian achievements were really laid by Frederick William, the Great Elector, who ruled from 1640 to 1688. From relatively inauspicious Hohenzollern family beginnings, he gradually built up the Prussian state after the drastic experiences of the Thirty Years' War when the country, especially Brandenburg, had been repeatedly devastated by Prussia's enemies. By stringent economies and strict discipline, he slowly welded his diverse territories into a manageable centralized state which by the following century had established its hegemonic supremacy in Germany. The main instrument of the Elector's success was his highly trained standing army which had been enlarged from its modest militia-like proportions in earlier days. His Assemblies (Diets) were apparently happy to leave matters of state to the Elector, and many tasks were slowly taken over by a carefully graded bureaucracy that was answerable to the Elector himself.

Frederick's policies have been generally regarded as progressive. He was not a 'career' militarist; he encouraged the development of the arts and sciences, and was one of the first to welcome the Protestant refugees from France after the Revocation of the Edict of Nantes by Louis XIV in 1685. The Elector died in 1688, and it was left to one of his successors, Frederick William I (1713–40), to consolidate his work, especially in terms of military development. He was much less of an aesthete, let alone a scholar. He was also somewhat impatient with political diplomacy; when he had to negotiate he liked to back it where necessary with the implied threat of force. He trebled the size of the army, and spent something in the order of 70 per cent of his revenue in training and supplying it with the very latest equipment. Militarism (that is, military activity as a way of life) was now to become a critical factor in Prussian society, the ideology of a Junker élite, the aristocracy of the new martial mentality.

Frederick William's son, however, was to be rather a disappointment to his father. In fact, the young Frederick turned out to be something of a throwback to the Great Elector. Not that he was a pacifist or disparaged the idea of military conquest, but, where possible, he definitely preferred political solutions. He was, too, a man of what was known as cultural taste. He had literary and artistic interests which his father regarded as vaguely effeminate and not really suitable preoccupations for a prospective monarch. But despite misunderstanding and often harsh treatment from his father, the young man did not deviate from his self-appointed path.

He succeeded his father in 1740 as Frederick II, afterwards known as the Great. Almost his first act as ruler clearly demonstrated that he was not averse to war, especially if he felt that it would give him a decisive advantage. He invaded Silesia, then part of the Austrian empire which had recently become the responsibility of a young and politically untried empress, Marie Theresa. The Austrians were easy meat. Within a month it was virtually all over, but the incident – if such it can be called – had a political knock-on effect throughout much of Europe. Its repercussions both directly and indirectly sparked off conflicts elsewhere; but then many European states hardly needed either excuses or encouragement to wage war. Leagues were formed, alliances were made and unmade, and those who could were only too ready to take advantage of the weakness of those who couldn't.

Frederick continued on his victorious way fully exploiting the fact that the Great Powers were locked in on-off territorial struggles elsewhere. Italy was at war, Russia was sending troops to help the Austrians, the French were fighting in the Netherlands and were also engaged in colonial wars with England in Canada and India. England was also in conflict with Spain and trying to stem a rebellion in Scotland, which was really indirectly related to her continuing conflict with the French, who, to strengthen their hand, concluded an alliance with Austria. It was all a rather cynical political merry-go-round; a vast expenditure of guile and ingenuity which got nobody very far. Few of these wars produced any lasting results, they left only acrimony and suspicion which in some cases (for example, Canada) have still not been thoroughly resolved even today.

Frederick had benefited financially from the English who were prepared to pay subsidies so as not to get directly involved in Europe's affairs any more than they had to. But by 1756 this convenient vicarious arrangement came to an end and England were once again engaged in a continental war with France. Frederick, ever the opportunist, invaded Saxony, and thus began the exhausting Seven Years' War with Austria and Russia. It was a back and forth affair, with success going first to one side and then the other, with something of a Pyrrhic victory for the Prussians and their allies. It was in this protracted conflict that Frederick displayed – perhaps even discovered – a gift for military leadership. The odds were stacked against Prussia numerically, and she could not have won had it not been that the Russians decided to withdraw from the struggle on the death of their tsarina.

Prussia's losses in men were so great that Frederick recruited officers from abroad, although it was thought essential that they were members of the nobility. He also encouraged foreigners to join the ranks. In Prussia itself, both nobles and commoners were confirmed in their land holdings, and conscription was introduced which, in principle, was somewhat like the ancient Spartan system insofar as only younger members of families were recruited. In this way, agricultural production did not suffer unduly; after all, the army had to be fed. Frederick was opposed to the usual practice of armies living off the land, an uncertain policy which further impoverished the peasants – enemy or otherwise – who had little enough as it was, so great were the quasi-feudal demands made upon them. He seems to have been genuinely concerned for the welfare of his own citizens, but in his reforms there is no hint of future democratization. The changes he initiated in the legal system, the administration and the economy may have been enlightened, but they bore the taint of autocracy. The state was administered by a systematically graded hierarchy of officials, from the king's General Directory down to those operating at the local level, who were responsible for ensuring that the laws were observed. This many-tiered bureaucracy circumvented any attempts by petty nobility to usurp government endorsed prerogatives. In short, it was a system of near-enough absolute uniformity that was enforced by central control. Only the king's decisions had final validity. He approved the budgets and issued the necessary instructions to his departments. This was mostly done in written form as the administration was located in Berlin and the king lived in Potsdam where no minister visited him without a personal invitation. Frederick was something of a workaholic; he took no holidays, held no court, and communicated only through his five secretaries who went with him when he annually toured his domains. There was certainly nothing in Prussia which compared with the French work-cum-leisure set-up at Versailles (Beloff, 1963: 112).

But the system had its problems. Despotisms are notoriously subject to the machinations of ministers who wish to curry favour, and who need to cover their tracks when they have been guilty of some misdemeanour or have made some concealable misjudgment. Frederick was obviously very suspicious about these possibilities, and took steps to check out such matters where he could and, as is so typical of despotism, instituted an informal intelligence system to apprise him of what was going on at every level. Reports were made to him personally and only he could decree punishments, order dismissals, and – if merited – arrange promotions. However, it would appear that there were some limits to Frederick's power. Sometimes when he wanted to alleviate the lot of the peasant he found that he could be frustrated by the self-serving interests of the nobility.

In order to finance his schemes, Frederick instituted a system of tax-farming known as the regie, which was not within the brief of the General Directory. This proved to be extremely profitable for both the government and for those who collected the excise duties. No doubt the agents added a percentage over and above that required by the king, and it is estimated that the average impoverished peasant who was already paying dues to his local lord was parting with another 40 per cent to the state. Centralization of other facets of government economic organization meant that such things as mining, forestry, banking and the tobacco 'industry' (which was a government monopoly) had their own departments which, although imperfectly coordinated, functioned to increase state revenues. The civil service which administered the government machine was open to those of different social strata, though most officials were drawn from the nobility and especially the bourgeoisie. Training, possibly at university, was required, especially by those who wanted to be considered for higher government posts. By about 1790 this bureaucracy, which may have numbered as many as 14,000, reserved many of its positions for ex-army officers; the question of how to settle war veterans has always been a particular problem for militaristic societies.

It may be that the closest thing to a true enlightened despot was to be found in contemporary Austria. The Emperor Joseph II, after a 15-year co-regency with his mother, Marie Theresa, came to exercise sole power in 1780. From the time of his accession, he was obviously determined to initiate a whole variety of reforms. It is generally agreed that he was literate, cultured and industrious. From his extensive travels and discussions, he seems to have been well-acquainted with the problems that he would have to face in trying to realize his humanitarian ambitions. Unlike so many of his royal counterparts, he foresaw real advantages in promoting greater liberty, especially for the serfs who he felt would become more highly motivated if they were free to choose their employers. Furthermore, it would bring about greater equality within the current rigid class hierarchy. Unsurprisingly, however, society was not ready for these progressive ideas, and he found considerable resistance among the great landowners who knew that such reforms were hardly calculated to increase their wealth and prestige. The Church also had serious reservations. The doctrine of the divine right of kings had by this time lost much of its potency. Monarchs were increasingly judged in terms of achievement rather than ascription: subjects were more interested in their policies and practices rather than the unsubstantiated spiritual claims which validated their right to rule. This reflected directly on the Church itself. Any undermining of the authority of the monarch was automatically a reflection on those ecclesiastical authorities who upheld such royal presumptions (and in some cases, vice-versa). They stood or fell together. There was also disquiet among the lower orders, especially artisans and the free poor, who anticipated that they would have to compete with an influx of emancipated labour which in the short term would affect their social status, and in the long term possibly their livelihoods as well.

Joseph also had to face the perennial dilemma of all those who want to introduce truly radical reforms that affect all sections of society. In the end, they so often please nobody, least of all those they are trying to help. It is well attested that once those whom the reforms are intended to benefit become unsettled by promises and unrealized aspirations, all the ingredients are present for possible revolutionary action. Other countries didn't have the contemporary French experience, although some peasant revolts did break out in Austria and Joseph, much to his dislike, found himself having to suppress them with considerable military force – an expedient which did nothing for his humanitarian reputation.

In certain specific areas, Joseph was more successful. There were extensive reforms in the administrative bureaucracy. Yet again, as in Prussia, it was found necessary to have agents (really a euphemism for spies) to ensure that its procedures were not open to peculation or exploitation by officials. Surveys were carried out as a basis for reforms of policy, and in 1786 a new civil code was initiated. This led to the promulgation of a new Penal Code in 1787, and a year later the courts too were reformed so that justice was more equably administered – the class factor was given less importance and the law was applied more impartially.

The Church too was reluctant to admit certain changes, particularly when the higher clergy felt that these diminished their authority. Institutes that had once been the monopoly of the Church passed over to the state. Education, for example, became increasingly secularized particularly in the universities. A Patent of Toleration in 1781 still gave pride of place to Catholicism as far as public worship was concerned, but Protestants, Greek Orthodox adherents and Jews (who hitherto had been largely excluded from public life) were allowed to worship in private, which presumably meant that they were not allowed to proselytize. This was somewhat remarkable for the time, although the standards had already been set in parts of the developing United States, especially in Rhode Island. The minor Protestant sects which had sprung up after the Reformation and which often enjoyed only an ephemeral existence in any one form were still persecuted and excluded from these liberal reforms. Joseph particularly resented the Church's involvement – or as he saw it, interference – in secular matters (divorce, for example), and although he recognized its ecclesiastical authority he saw fit to clip its wings by dissolving some of its monasteries and confiscating its lands, which were estimated to comprise 35–40 per cent of all lands that were inalienable. Much of the wealth that was released by these measures was used to endow socially beneficial causes, although some lands were sold off simply to enhance the Exchequer.

These multifarious schemes, imaginative and progressive as they were, proved to have an unsettling effect on the economy. Some admittedly were profitable, but others, especially those which involved give-away incentives and tax concessions, became quite costly. The Treasury was certainly not as healthy at the close of Joseph's reign as it had been at the beginning. The reforms were not an unmitigated failure, but neither were they a conspicuous success, something which became more obvious in other parts of the empire. Opposition was not long in forthcoming for those with vested interests. In Belgium and Hungary especially there was considerable resistance, most notably from the Church and those of the landed aristocracy who had much to lose by the changes. In the end, Joseph had to compromise on all sides and, by the time of his death in 1790, most of the administrative changes (over which one suspects there had been considerable foot-dragging) were withdrawn in Hungary, where the decree proclaiming the emancipation of the serfs never actually went into effect. Indeed, this reform which Joseph tried to implement throughout his domains and which was the most startling of all his innovations, caused as much trouble for the serfs as it did for their erstwhile masters. In many ways, it actually encouraged discontentment. What is more, its timing was unfortuitous. Revolution was in the air. France was in ferment. And the very idea of liberty and participatory democracy was a heady concoction for those who had lived in poverty and bondage but could now live in poverty *and* freedom.

The disenchantment of Joseph's subjects grew, and he was forced to question his own good intentions when he had ruthlessly to crush potential rebellion in the interests of stability – and, of course, the preservation of the monarchy. In a sense, even his reforms, well meaning as they obviously were, were arguably the act of a despot: people were going to change whether they wanted to or not. And when they resisted, there was always coercion. But then circumstances may demand undesirable expedients.

In some ways, the most interesting of the enlightened despots was Catherine II of Russia, also known as the Great. Catherine began life as Sophia Augusta of Anhalt Zerbst, a rather obscure German princess. She was renamed Ekaterina in 1745 on her Orthodox marriage to the Grand Duke Peter, nephew of the Tsaritza Elizabeth, daughter of Peter the Great. She has been variously described as dissolute and licentious mainly because she is known to have had a number of lovers (estimates vary from 12 to 21) whom she called her 'pupils'. Each had to be medically examined by her doctor before being permitted to commence his royal 'duties', which usually took place after she had lunched at 1.00 p.m. – Catherine obviously didn't relish sex on an empty stomach. Her current favourite was usually allowed two hours, after which it was back to business. Only one of them was ever known to perish *in flagrante delicto*. Lovers were discarded when they had served their purpose, which was by no means only sexual. But when this happened – as it so frequently did – we are assured that they were usually treated with generosity, and that some actually rose to political eminence. As far as we are aware, her lovers never caused her to deviate from her overall aims, which were to retain wealth and power and to enlarge her domain at the least possible expense. But they did sometimes influence her, though more in terms of *means* rather than ends.

Whether she is to be considered dissolute or not she was certainly quite as despotic as any male. In fact, her sexual behaviour would be considered only just about par for the course if we had been talking about a tsar. She was without doubt a determined woman and, when she deemed it expedient, unrepentantly ruthless in achieving her ends. This is clearly evidenced by her coup d'état and subsequent usurpation of the throne once Elizabeth had died. Within six months, in collaboration with her current lover, Gregory Orlov, and the support of the Guard, she had her weak-minded husband, whom she despised, spirited away and murdered. She then seized power for herself (1762).

For some time, her position remained precarious. Gradually, by thoughtful diplomacy and the astute cultivation of the right friends, she was able to consolidate her power. This was accomplished because she was said to be 'devoid of the extravagant ideals and impatience of Joseph II, and ... avoided offending the susceptibilities of the nobility' (Revill, 1962: 433). She needed the close support of the nobility and this, in turn, meant complying with their expectations and ensuring their privileges.

It remains questionable whether she was a practical and pragmatic ruler with a keen sense of what was achievable and what wasn't, or whether she was a not very able person who was at the mercy of her lovers and advisers. Certainly on some issues she was quite clear: for example, she was going to have no truck with the idea of serf emancipation. She was not infected with the 'virus' of radical social reform and did not want Russia contaminated with the kind of revolutionary fervour that was brewing in France. Indeed, in order to conciliate the gentry she actually introduced legislation which meant even further degradation for the serfs on the vast estates. They became little more than chattels and were no longer allowed to petition the monarch against their owners, and were liable to be sold, banished or given or gambled away on the whim of their masters.

Catherine appears to have displayed some political acumen in her choice of competent subordinates through whom she implemented a number of measures, some of which were recommended by her consultative committee. These included internal changes to the law code, and an improvement in the still-unenviable working conditions of the *state peasants*. Externally, she tried to maintain the kind of foreign policy that was generally profitable to Russia. She made useful alliances, particularly with the Western powers where possible, and notably with Frederick of Prussia.

This was all part of her attempt to avoid large-scale wars, although she did become involved in a protracted struggle with the Ottoman empire of Turkey. The first Turkish war won her much of the Crimea and the Black Sea coast (1768–74), and included a notable naval victory over the Turks in the Aegean. In order to pacify her silent partners (Prussia and Austria) who did not want to become embroiled in the war, the ever-vulnerable Poland was cynically divided between them (1772) so that everyone – except Poland – came away with something.

In one sense this arrangement was convenient for Catherine whose ravenous eyes were on the Balkans rather than on Poland where the Prussians had obvious designs. And yet there was a certain irony here because not long before, in 1764, Catherine had had one of her former lovers installed in Poland as king. It could be argued that Poland was something of a danger to neighbouring states, but in certain senses its partition was both militarily and politically disadvantageous to those who had so greedily swallowed the extra territory that they hardly needed. Within 20 years, the rest of the country was taken over by Russia and Prussia, and Poland no longer existed as a separate buffer state. This made the borders of neighbours contiguous, rarely a state of affairs that makes for political harmony among competitors.

It was while Russia was preoccupied with the Turkish war that an illiterate but tough peasant Cossack named Ivanovich Pugachev took advantage of the situation to raise a revolt among his fellow peasants in the Urals (1773). As an ex-soldier with considerable campaign experience he commanded a certain respect, and his ranks were soon joined by the disenchanted from adjacent territories, some in the belief that he was, as he claimed, really Peter III, Catherine's 'late' husband. Pugachev incited his comrades to kill the landlords who had kept them poor, and to confiscate their lands for themselves.

The revolt followed the familiar pattern of the great slave revolts that had once taken place in Classical society. For a time, the rebels had things pretty much their own way. Their numbers swelled to about 30,000, they captured outposts and confiscated weapons, and generally created havoc in the countryside. Many families of the gentry were massacred, and the peasant army, ramshackle as it was, actually threatened Moscow itself (1774). Eventually, this undisciplined but determined horde proved no match for the regular army; they were defeated by the troops and the remnants hunted down mercilessly. Pugachev and some of his men avoided the dragnet and managed to elude their would-be captors for several months. They moved from place to place, sometimes at the rate of 60 miles a day, but after a number of very narrow escapes, Pugachev was betrayed by some of his erstwhile comrades and taken back to Moscow in an iron cage. There, in January 1775, along with others, he was publicly beheaded and quartered as a warning to other malcontents who might be tempted to follow his example. We are told that 'the executioners entertained the crowd with a truly splendid show ... the executions began shortly after eleven [and] it was evening by the time they were finished' (Bowle, 1980: 502). Catherine's regime treated those who questioned its authority with ruthless disregard for their often genuine grievances.

Pugachev's rebellion and its repressive aftermath, in which whole villages were levelled and hangings were commonplace, left an abiding legacy of hatred among the serfs, and it should have made clear to the nobility that serfdom as an institution had only a limited time to run. It had already existed too long, yet in its final throes on its last century in Russia it became more widespread and inhuman than ever. Serfs on both private estates and state lands may have constituted as much as 90 per cent of the total population. They paid their dues in cash and in kind, labour dues usually amounting to three days' service a week, although in some cases it was more than this. Most estates might have anything between 100 and 1,000 serfs working on them, although some fabulously rich nobles had very many more than this. Living conditions were notoriously poor, and punishments for misdemeanors – usually by flogging – were common. Serf rights were minimal; they could even be bought and sold at auction. The system was really just a form of economic slavery. It extended throughout the country, especially the Ukraine and large areas of the Caucasus where the practice came with the grants of state land that Catherine was prone to bestow upon her favourites. It was not, however, properly developed in Siberia even though this was the main settlement area of the government's forced colonization programme. Perhaps this was because the enormous distances involved precluded the operation of adequate control procedures; Siberia was an awfully long way from the locus of power, and its raw living conditions gave it something of a frontier character which supported few local gentry.

The lessons of the rebellion were not entirely lost on Catherine. Russia was a large, virtually unmanageable country, and she decided on a radical policy of decentralization which would give vast tracts of territory their own governments. Towards the end of the century, some 50 such provinces had been formed with their own governors and separate administrators. Governor-generals were appointed over small groups of provinces, and they were directly answerable to the central government. It was not a federal arrangement, but a carefully graded system of control with dele-gated authority encompassing provinces, districts and sub-districts, all in the interests of the despot. This was organized in parallel with the estates of the land-owning aristocracy who were confirmed in their holdings and granted exemption from taxation and compulsory service, as well as from loss of rank or property. A lord was expected to confer with the relevant governor in the administration of local affairs, although it is thought that this did not always work out well in practice. Towns too had their respective charters, but industry and manufacture – which was just beginning to take off in the West – remained at an undeveloped level in most of Russia.

Catherine still had dreams of foreign conquests, which again brought Russia into conflict with the Turks. She was urged on in her ambitions by her then lover, Potemkin, and between 1788 and 1792 her armies achieved success after success. But victory was only bought at a very high cost in human lives. Russia and Austria sustained terrible losses in the assaults, and the Turks lost frightful numbers in the terrible revenge wreaked on the defenders once their cities and fortresses had fallen. And all for very little. When a treaty was concluded in 1792, Russia had not really gained much more than she had before.

In her declining years, Catherine became involved with a 22-year-old officer (much less than half her age), who again encouraged her expansionist tendencies – this time in central Europe. During the Turkish war, Polish nationalism had reasserted itself mainly at the instigation of members of the émigré Polish aristocracy. Being preoccupied at the time, the Russians did little about it. But once the Turkish problem was settled, Russia and Prussia again exerted pressure on the Poles. For a short while the Poles put up a spirited resistance, but when the Russians and Prussians were joined by the Austrians their situation became hopeless. Warsaw itself was besieged, and there was a dreadful slaughter of the civilian population in the suburbs by Russian troops. Poland was re-partitioned, with Russia taking the lion's share.

The age of Catherine the Great has been described as a time of incomparable splendour, 'the golden age of the nobility, the legendary age of Russian opulence and glitter' (Charques, 1959: 108). But for all that, it was an *outward* display of wealth and magnificence; a time of ostentation and extravagance. The style was set by the royal family in St Petersburg, and duplicated on a more modest scale in the mansions of the aristocracy. The court also appears to have been a centre of superficial intellectualism and pretension; one of its minor conceits was that members were expected to speak French, the language of the current philosophers, such as Voltaire, with whom Catherine carried on some correspondence. But, as we have seen, it was all paid for by the grey masses who were beginning to question their own miserable existence.

From a rational point of view, it must be said that it was also an age of considerable expansion. Russia dominated the eastern Baltic, possessed much of Poland, occupied the Crimea, and controlled areas of the Black Sea and with it the grain trade. She also acquired vast expanses of Siberia and Asia, especially in the Caucasus, and by the end of the century was actually contesting territorial rights with Persia (Iran). Needless to say, tribute was exacted from these various populations, which not only swelled the royal coffers but also enabled the state to finance projects elsewhere.

The 'enlightened despots' – not least of all, Catherine – were enlightened only in relative terms. They were primarily concerned that any proposals for reform came from themselves alone. Government was to be *for* the people, but not *by* the people. 'Enlightened' policies should benefit the individual, but more importantly they should be to the advantage of the state and its ruler.

CHAPTER THIRTEEN

Revolutionary Despotism: the French Revolution and its Aftermath

Revolution, in one form or another, seems to be as old as society. But, yet again, much depends on definitions. Should revolution be defined in terms of *form, scale,* or simply *intention?* In the pre-modern world, revolts or coups d'état were usually relatively small-scale affairs, often no more than palace coups to overthrow the existing regime. They were commonly power struggles within the governing elite, perhaps between rival claimants to the throne egged on by their respective, equally ambitious supporters. Or they might be conflicts between governments and the rising class of the aspiring bourgeoisie. Occasionally, they were the result of ideological (frequently religious) differences which generated frictions that were thought incapable of resolution by peaceful means. These ideological conflicts, however, should not be confused with so-called religious wars which really require their own special kind of analysis. Rarely – except in city-states – did such revolts involve the concerted participation of the masses, who were often uninformed and apathetic because they knew only too well that whatever faction or party triumphed it would almost certainly make very little difference to them (see Greig, 1973: 1). Perhaps, instead, we should reserve the term revolution to denote large-scale mass movements which are intended to bring about the *restructuring of society.* Certainly, the French Revolution in the later eighteenth century would be a prime example of this type of movement.

Revolution is but one aspect of social change, albeit rapid and often violent social change. And it follows that revolution, like the much-vexed question of social change itself, needs a theory to try to explain it. As one might expect in the human sciences, there is, in fact, a surfeit of theories, none of them wholly satisfactory but each adding something to our understanding of this phenomenon which is largely a feature of modern society characterized by mass communications.

Theories of revolution can be somewhat simplistically divided into *psychological* and *sociological* theories which inevitably have relevant historical implications or at least contain some important historical elements. Indeed, it is difficult to see how this could possibly be otherwise given that all theories need some kind of historical exemplification.

Psychological explanations often centre on the personality of the revolutionary leader or leaders. What was their background? What were the formative influences in their upbringing? How did they come to endorse these revolutionary ideologies, and what 'flaws' in their characters predisposed them to violence? The main snag with this kind of analysis is that it presents us with the perennial chicken-and-egg problem of whether society makes man or man makes society. If a particular individual becomes a revolutionary leader, is it the result of a collocation of factors in his immediate (early?) environment? If so, why did these same factors not make revolutionary leaders of his school friends who turned out to be lawyers, bankers, priests, and so on? Was early nineteenth-century France shaped by Napoleon or was a Napoleon-type person merely generated by pressures of French society? Did Stalin determine the nature of mid-twentieth-century Russia, or was he a product of a revolutionary state? Is society therefore at the mercy of the personality traits of its leaders?

Sociological theories are likewise both stimulating and frustrating because they tend to be descriptive rather than explanatory. Marx, for instance, maintained that revolutions are really generated by the need to resolve the basic contradictions in the power structures of societies. Fundamentally, Marx and those of his school argue that revolutions are really about the conflict between the haves and the have-nots. Their critics, on the other hand, insist that although societies possess many features that make for disequilibrium, these are not to be seen as basic contradictions. Indeed, functionalist theorists would argue that the very term society implies stability; societies are fundamentally harmonious and that if this were not so, they could not exist. Revolutions, therefore, are mere temporary perturbations that disturb the equilibrium; in the longer term the dust settles and the balance is restored. Perhaps, as Parsons has argued, we will never have a really adequate theory of social change, not least because we need to understand better what is meant by a social system before we can satisfactorily explain its dysfunctional aspects (see Cohan, 1975).

One of the most useful approaches to the phenomenon of revolution was advanced by Alexis de Tocqueville in the last century. On the basis of his analysis of the French Revolution, de Tocqueville suggested that revolutions occur not when the masses are thoroughly repressed, but when the dominant regime is beginning to relax its grip and possibly grant more benefits and privileges. This promotes a sense of optimism and rising expectation which the regime is either unable or unwilling to fulfil; this, in turn, generates such acute frustration and anger that revolution ensues. This theory, which is particularly cogent to any consideration of revolutionary despotism, has been refined and developed by more recent theorists, and it will underlie much of our discussion.

There is no simple way of explaining the French Revolution. It is true that the antecedent historical causes can be traced with reasonable accuracy, but it is not easy to account for the forms that the Revolution eventually took. We can say that while Prussia and Austria were busy partitioning Poland, and Russia was preoccupied with her Balkan adventures and in colonizing the bleak areas of Siberia, France was convulsed with a series of 'democratic' experiments that nearly brought her to disaster. There was actually more than one revolution or, more precisely, the Revolution started out as one thing and evolved into something different. It began with the protests of a disenchanted elite which percolated down to the stratum of middle-class intellectuals who became its spokesmen and ideologues. It was then 'hijacked' by a vociferous proletariat and became a vehicle for anarchy and terror which was only finally brought under control by a military dictator.

The French nobility comprised about 5 per cent of the total population and were a very influential minority, but, by and large, they were not a terribly prosperous minority, at least, not as prosperous as they thought they should be. The people who were making money in French society were the merchants, especially those engaged in the export trade of luxury items such as fine wines. Certain of the more articulate members of the nobility had also long inveighed against the wealth of the Church and the extravagance and inefficiencies of the monarchy. Yet however much they criticized the king they were still dependent on him for favours, and as members of his court they were expected to entertain lavishly, albeit with money they hadn't got. The very highest of the nobility, who were also the principal landowners, had substantial incomes; all the minor nobility had was status. This highly inflammable mixture of mounting debt and the discontentment that existed at every level of society needed very little to spark off a conflagration.

The French state was highly centralized; only in a few recently acquired territories were provincial assemblies allowed. It was government by a hierarchy of government officials (intendents) who were appointed by the Crown and who were directly responsible to the king. There were no elections; even the mayors of local communities were state appointed. This obviously had certain administrative advantages, but it had disadvantages too. Because citizens' lives were so closely controlled by the state, it was the state that also became the focus of citizens' complaints. If, for example, food was short – and this was one of the precipitating factors of the Revolution – it was the state machinery and its principal ministers that shouldered the blame. Actually conditions in France were notably better than in the serf-based systems of Russia or Prussia, but this as de Tocqueville noted, together with the fact that France had a relatively flourishing lower middle class of artisans and traders with increased hopes and expectations, actually made matters worse.

This whole situation was exacerbated by the inequalities of the class system which, as we have seen, greatly favoured the nobility and the clergy – who enjoyed the privileges of various exemptions, such as the capitation tax – while the lower and middle classes bore the brunt of high taxation. There were local as well as state taxes; direct taxes had recently been doubled and indirect taxes, which on food was felt to be especially unfair, were all aggravated by the iniquitous overcharging of the tax farmers, that is, those to whom the tax-collecting concessions were leased by the state. Such exactions all had their supportive sanctions. There were harsh penalties for those who contravened the laws, many of which were framed in favour of the privileged classes. Not all nobles, of course, were social parasites. Many held responsible posts in the government administration, but an unspecified and unhealthy proportion was made up of the frivolous and idle rich. The Church too was afflicted by dissension. Here the cleavage was between the higher, wealthy clergy and the poorly paid priests who found their loyalties divided. In such circumstances, it is little wonder that the lower classes, especially the ill-educated, low paid townspeople, became increasingly volatile.

There was also the intellectual challenge to the prevailing absolutism of the monarchy. Some members of the French literati disputed the whole idea of divine right and, in theory, 'transferred' authority to the will of the people (the 'general will'). Voltaire, for example, could be caustic about current institutions but would probably have settled for some form of enlightened despotism. Montesquieu too, although himself a noble, became very impressed by the institutional arrangements he had seen in England which he felt were a considerable improvement on the French system, and would like to have seen them operating in his own country. At the other extreme of the protest spectrum were the Encyclopaedists who looked for radical change and a structural alteration to society. And then there was Rousseau – sometimes dubbed the 'father of the French Revolution' – who laid the philosophical foundations for a more equal society in his *Social Contract* (1763), although some think it a pity he didn't extend his concern for the underprivileged to his five children who were all consigned to a foundling's home on the rather flimsy and suspicious pretext that he had no money to keep them. Rousseau appears to have been the prototypical 'New Age' Enlightenment figure, a Bohemian by nature who abhorred the coercive power of the state, but whose eloquent diatribes were not matched by his own disorganized and somewhat profligate private life.

The government, well aware that the general tide of public opinion was running against them, felt that a few conciliatory reforms were in order and they commissioned a moderate, Turgot, to carry out some modest changes. But Turgot proved more ardent than they had bargained for. He wanted reforms that ran counter to the vested interests of the privileged, and the king, Louis XVI, and his even more reactionary queen, Marie Antoinette, would not support him, so the Paris parliament refused to register his edicts. With such formidable opposition, the reforms were doomed, and Turgot was dismissed from office (1776).

Things now went from bad to worse. Extra monies were required to finance France's questionable aid to the American colonies in their war with England. Other ministers tried where Turgot had failed, but the task that faced them was so daunting that their enthusiasm was sapped from the start and their half-hearted attempts at satisfying everyone actually satisfied no one. Their efforts were necessarily short-term, almost ad hoc, and involved taking out loans which did no more than ease the immediate situation and store up trouble for the future. Eventually by May 1789 matters had become so bad that it was decided to summon the States-General, in theory representing all three Estates, which had not met since 1614. Needless to say, the Third Estate, the commoners, despite their superior numbers, were initially almost disregarded, but after some dispute a National Assembly was declared and their grievances were given a hearing. By this time, mobs were forming throughout the country demanding various kinds of redress. On 14 July, one mob successfully took over the Bastille, a fourteenth-century fortress which had been converted into a state prison (Voltaire had done time there in 1717–18). This 'storming of the Bastille' has assumed a somewhat inflated role in the mythology of republicanism; actually the prison only housed seven inmates, some of whom were living comfortably with their own food prepared by their own servants. But this relatively minor incident did have a certain detonative force – of symbolic rather than political significance. By showing that this fortress was not impregnable, the Paris crowd had demonstrated that the state machinery was not without its weaknesses.

The tide was now running very strongly in favour of some form of republicanism and desperate attempts were made to find a compromise that would suit all parties. They culminated in the Declaration of the Rights of Man. All citizens were to be regarded as equal, thus undermining some of the inherited privileges of the nobility. The economic system was to be reorganized (among other innovations there was a special issue of paper money). The Church was to come under the aegis of the state; and the army was to be reformed, pay increased, and commissions made available to men of all classes. However, the radicals quickly detected a catch in the system. The new constitution involved an unwelcome separation of powers: there was to be a complete separation of the legislature and the executive, and, perhaps most critical of all, the king was to be given a suspensive veto.

With revolutionary fervour building up, there was no way that this system – reasonable though it seemed to many – was going to work. Two elements, which superficially had little in common, were gradually coming together in an uneasy alliance. The Paris mob, which was fast becoming the role model for the wider French proletariat, shared certain basic aspirations with the intellectuals of the various radical clubs, especially the influential Jacobin club of which Robespierre was a leading figure. The royal family, realizing too late the precariousness of their position, tried to flee in June 1791 but were apprehended before they could reach the border and were brought back to Paris. Austria and Prussia, quickly sensing that revolutionary republicanism was like an invasive disease that might easily spread to other European states, threatened dire penalties unless the king was restored to the throne. Largely at the instigation of the Girondin party who were seeking power for themselves, France declared war on Austria in April 1792, the ostensible reason being that Austria was harbouring refugees who had escaped from possible persecution in France.

Events now began to move very swiftly. While various radicals were falling out among themselves, a mob attacked the Tuileries where the king and his family were housed and massacred a Swiss unit that was on guard there (10 August 1792). By the 20th of September, the king had been suspended from office and a republic had at last been declared. A very serious state of affairs had now become a crisis. France was beset by problems both at home and abroad. There was a royalist revolt, and an invasion by a combination of Prussians and Sardinians. With the enemy forces nearing Paris, there were frantic appeals for volunteers to augment the inadequate force that was trying to defend the capital. At the same time, Paris was rife with rumours of treason and counter-plots by those who it was felt were intent on betraying the revolution. In an atmosphere of suspicion and frenzy, mobs dragged people out of prison and murdered them. Possibly as many as 1,100 people died in this massacre, mainly members of the nobility and the clergy who were under arrest.

Meanwhile, the ragtag-and-bobtail French army – composed of tried professionals and raw recruits – though having some setbacks, also met with some surprising successes against the invaders. It is difficult to explain the victories of such an ill-equipped and, to a large extent, ill-trained army except in terms of revolutionary zeal. Ideological commitment can sometimes work wonders. The intention, however, which some certainly had, of carrying the revolution to other countries did not succeed. Enthusiasm alone was not enough. A coalition was formed of most of the other powerful European states once Louis had been found guilty and executed for conspiring with outside powers to overthrow the revolution in January

1793 (the queen suffered the same fate the following October). The coalition was too much for the revolutionary army. There were defeats and even defections, and very soon France's enemies were again at the frontiers.

Regardless of external threats – or perhaps, indeed, because of them – in Paris and many other districts the revolution was gathering pace. The peoples' Convention had now replaced the Assembly as the effective government of France. The once powerful Girondin faction was thoroughly discredited because of the failure of its military policy. Its leaders were removed from positions of authority and subsequently executed, and power passed to the Jacobins (June 1793). These events may be said to have initiated the revolutionary phase that has come to be known as the Terror. Paris was now in ferment. Dangers were seen just about everywhere, and where they were not seen they were often manufactured. The Terror spread to other cities, especially in the south, where there were also extensive atrocities and mass executions. Anyone thought guilty of treason or conspiracy – an idle word was often enough – was liable to be reported to the newly formed Committee of Public Safety. Legal niceties and moral scruples went by the board. The evidence might be flimsy and the denunciations unsubstantiated but if the Revolutionary Tribunal condemned anyone, there was no further court of appeal.

In following the pattern of so many revolutions in its violence and criminal excesses, it generated the kind of hatred and antagonism that could only be curbed by a repressive police system. The official intelligence service collapsed and was completely replaced by a new formation organized by the revolutionaries. Its task was to root out counter-revolutionaries and those it saw as traitors, especially if they were in the ranks of the revolutionaries themselves. This atmosphere of uncertainty provided just the right climate for the double agent, men like Heron, who, although a paid official of the Committee of General Security, was also paid by the Committee of Public Safety to spy on his employers. He denounced people to both Committees, as it suited his purpose, and became the principal spymaster of the Terror. Others, such as Baron Jean de Batz, ran what can only be described as personal spy networks – an extremely risky undertaking – primarily to further their own careers. Yet Batz survived. Such people can hardly be applauded, but they were certainly masters of deception and the techniques of disinformation (see Deacon, 1990: 44–46).

Inevitably, those who had set themselves up as arbiters of who was or who was not a traitor, counter-revolutionary, or whatever, turned on one another, and one by one these revolutionary despots, including the one-time co-conspirators Danton and Robespierre, fell beneath the knife. There were still one or two old scores to be settled, but by July 1794 the worst was over.

It is questionable whether the Revolution was ever really about the sovereignty of the people. The avowed aim of the Revolution was to grant citizens their 'inalienable rights', but it was rather selective about exactly which citizens were to enjoy such rights; labourers and domestic servants, for example, were not included, and similar rights were certainly not extended to the indigenes in France's overseas colonies. In reality, the Revolution abrogated special powers to those who purported to represent the 'general will'. Indeed, it is arguable whether the 'general will' was any more than a convenient fiction to justify a particular kind of tyranny. In giving the nation a system of distinct representation which ostensibly meant more local autonomy, the new Republic abolished the administrative muddle of the *ancien regime*, and instituted a rationalized, hierarchical system in which everyone was answerable to the central government.

The Republic was, in fact, riddled with contradictions. It abolished some of the more objectionable taxes, but monies were still raised in ways that affected the poor most. Superficially, the new regime could have been construed as some form of socialism, but this would be a mistake. Its interests were really capitalistic. It was keen to protect the right of private property, and encouraged free trade and private enterprise. It extended the franchise to Jews, a long overdue reform, but it declared trade unions and strikes to be illegal. Church lands were confiscated, and the clergy were ordered to take a special oath to the civil authority; some did, but many refused and were evicted from their livings.

With the fall of the Jacobins, more moderate opinion prevailed. Some of the more extreme policies of the Convention were repealed; a certain amount of decentralization took place, restrictions on religion were lifted, and numbers of political prisoners released. A new government, the Directory, was set up in 1795 that was reminiscent of classical Athens. There were two legislative bodies, the Council of the Ancients (roughly equivalent to the Greek Archonate) and the Council of the Five Hundred (almost exactly the same as the Greek Boulé). But the system failed, again to use Greek similes, because the five-man Directorate (*unlike* the ancient Spartan Ephorate) had very little executive authority to get things done. Thus, there were still acute shortages and rising inflation, evils the new government was supposed to cure.

It is impossible to say how many died under the Terror. The number arrested may have been as high as 300,000 although perhaps 17,000–20,000 were actually executed. As the Terror intensified it became even more mindless, and the more indiscriminate it became the more hatred and suspicion were generated. In the last month of the Terror, just in Paris alone, it is estimated that there were 1,376 victims. The great irony is that of the Third Estate, in whose interests this was all ostensibly taking place. More of them were guillotined than any other section of the community:

of those executed about 85 per cent were of the Third Estate, about 6.5 per cent were clergy, and about 8.5 per cent were of the nobility (Cobban, 1965: 237). And after all the bloodletting, including certain counter-terror measures, it is doubtful whether, on balance, the ordinary people were any better off than they were before.

France was still at war with most of western Europe, and to make matters worse the Terror had precipitated a number of internal royalist revolts. Royalist-held Toulon actually went over to the British, but was recaptured in December 1793 by an enterprising artillery officer, one Capitain Bonaparte. His rise to fame then became rapid. When the Directory that had been set up in the aftermath of the Terror was under attack from extremists and looked in danger of collapsing, Bonaparte – now a general – saved the day. For this he was promoted yet again, and at the age of only 26 became commander of the French army in Italy, an appointment facilitated not only by his military reputation but also possibly by his marriage to the well-placed Josephine Beauharnais. Bonaparte's task was to drive the Austrians out of Italy, which he did with a still ill-equipped and understaffed army (1796). This unbroken series of victories compared favourably with the singular lack of success that the French navy was having at sea against the British, and the misfortune that French armies were having in Germany. Again Bonaparte lent a hand and by threatening an invasion of Austria from the Italian side, forced the Austrians to come to terms which, in different ways, were seen as un-favourable to both sides.

With these setbacks the coalition of states that had been ranged against France virtually ceased to exist. Prussia and Spain made peace in 1795, and the only effective opponent left was Britain, whose navy was to prove such a formidable obstacle to Bonaparte's ambitions. In 1797, the Directory made what even they afterwards saw as a mistake: they brought Bonaparte back from the scene of his triumphs and made him commander of the home army with a view to organizing the invasion of Britain – a scheme that hardly needed a general of Bonaparte's military acumen to see was really a non-starter. Like Hitler after him, he realized that without control of the sea there was very little hope of success. Instead, unlike Hitler, he decided that an indirect assault on British power, though less effective, would have a much greater chance of success. British ships couldn't be everywhere at once, so an attack on some relatively distant part of Britain's empire seemed the obvious strategy. Plans were made to send an army to Egypt with the possibility of eventually attacking India. This suited the Directory, who were probably secretly glad to see a popular would-be dynast preoccupied elsewhere – anywhere, in fact, but France. And it almost certainly suited Bonaparte too, who saw himself as a latter-day Alexander the Great. It could enhance his already unsullied military reputation, and hopefully he could then return to France and take over the reins of power from what was rapidly becoming a very unpopular government.

The campaign was almost entirely successful. Bonaparte took Malta en route, and defeated the Egyptians at the Battle of the Pyramids (1798). But only a month later his fleet was virtually destroyed by Nelson in the Battle of the Nile, and this considerably affected his lines of supply and communication. The army wintered in Egypt and many of the specialists that Bonaparte had farsightedly included among his staff commenced their studies of ancient Egyptian culture, with which they were particularly fascinated. Indeed, it was really their work, culminating in Jean François Champollion's brilliant breakthrough in deciphering the hitherto mysterious hieroglyphics on the Rosetta Stone, that initiated the research in this field which continues to this day. In February of the following year, Bonaparte had further victories in Syria, this time against Turks of the Ottoman empire who were obviously becoming apprehensive about his intentions in the Middle East. He took most of Lebanon and Palestine, and then returned to Egypt in May where again he had to subdue resistance from the Turks and Egyptians.

Meanwhile in France, the situation had deteriorated as Bonaparte had anticipated. Despite being virtually bankrupt, the Directory ordered the occupation of both Switzerland and the rest of Italy, and this so angered other European powers that France, besides having to contend with Britain, found herself by 1799 at war again with Austria, the Turks, and Russia as well – an emergency which required the unpopular introduction of conscription. France was successful in driving British troops out of Holland, but she had her work cut out holding the Russians and preventing the invasion of France itself. It was in this situation that Bonaparte returned to Paris and in a bloodless coup replaced the Directory by a Consulate under his direct control. His authority was confirmed by a plebiscite in 1800 (less than one in 2,000 voted against him), and with this endorsement a new depotism began.

Bonaparte lost no time in reaffirming France's military supremacy. With some difficulty he inflicted yet more defeats on the Austrians, although it has been claimed that his report on the campaign is a tissue of lies, exonerating himself from any mistakes that were made and de-emphasizing the role of his general, Desai, who was killed at the battle of Marengo (Cobban, 1965: 14–15). He then came to an understanding with the Baltic states (later to be undermined by Nelson's destruction of the Danish fleet at Copenhagen), and in 1802 obtained an uneasy truce with Britain after the British had defeated him in Egypt.

Bonaparte was now free to turn his attention to more domestic matters. It was obvious from the beginning that he intended to retain what he regarded as the more beneficial changes wrought by the Revolution. He decided to leave economic arrangements much as they were except for measures to counter the effects of the British blockade. He certainly welcomed the benefits brought by the retention of confiscated Church estates. Politically, Bonaparte proved to be reasonably traditionalist; it was in legal and administrative matters that his legacy is most enduring, and here he drew heavily on the Roman example. The legal codes were revised, education was centralized and the tax system – the subject of so much previous disquiet – was rationalized. He also devised the Legion of Honour as a democratic way of rewarding any citizen who had rendered special services to the state.

In order to preserve this new social order, which for a while enjoyed an overwhelming consensus, Bonaparte found that at the margins he still had to resort to coercion. Various attempts were made to assassinate him, so secret police units – the prerequisite of any dictatorship – were formed, and the press – always a virulent agent of dissent – was vigorously censored. While Bonaparte was making his way in the world, attempts had been made by members of the earlier revolutionary intelligence services to secure their own positions and even, like François Babeuf, to try to revive something of the old regime. These obviously did not succeed; Babeuf, for example, was executed in 1797, but Bonaparte learned from these failed practitioners and set up quite a sophisticated service of his own. Its principal architect was Joseph Fouché who had judiciously switched sides more than once; his ability brought him to the attention of Bonaparte, who appointed him Minister of Police in 1799. He not only completely reorganized the internal intelligences, he also built up a network of agents overseas and was particularly adept – both at home and abroad – at uncovering plots to kill or unseat his leader. Fouché was given a large budget. He doubled the number of agents, who included people from all walks of life, not least of all women – something of an innovation – who ranged from useful household servants to ladies in court circles. His opportunism, wealth and knowledge-is-power policy eventually caused even Bonaparte to worry and he was dismissed in 1802, but reinstated in 1804 when the consul became emperor.

A new monarchy was something of a volte-face for French society, yet despite the murmurings and the half-hearted plots, Bonaparte still enjoyed general acceptance and even a certain measure of popularity. He agreed that Catholicism should remain the supreme ecclesiastical system, and he settled matters with the Pope by a Concordat which stipulated that control of the Church in France should become the prerogative of the state and that religious toleration should be exercised in relation to Protestants. Equality before the law was to be a cornerstone of the new constitution, with careers open to those who had the necessary talents.

Not only was Bonaparte's elevation to the monarchy as Napoleon I received with approval by the majority of his own people, other European rulers too greeted it with acclaim, possibly because it reaffirmed their faith in the innate subservience of the masses. By crowning Napoleon the people were acknowledging that their experiment with radical republicanism had failed. Europe could hopefully settle down now to the old ways with increased confidence. But Napoleon's royal peers didn't really bargain for his inordinate ambitions. What were these ambitions? It is reasonable to assume that the new emperor really did want to bring peace to a people who had been devastated by the turbulence of the Revolution. Yet herein lies an inner contradiction. His idea was that peace and prosperity were the outcome of national strength and international respect, and that these could only be gained by war. One senses in Napoleon something of the *pothos* of Alexander, that agonized ambition – almost a desperate yearning – to fulfil what he saw as his destiny, a goal only to be achieved by conquest. After all, his very reputation was based upon his success as a military commander. And this is the way history has remembered him.

The treaty with Britain lasted only a year. Perhaps nobody really expected anything else. Certainly Napoleon saw Britain as the ultimate enemy, yet one with whom he could not directly come to grips. Despite his earlier reservations, the invasion plan was revived. The French army was supremely self-confident and in better shape than it had ever been. There appears to have been a general public enthusiasm for such a venture, and the prospect of success seemed good. There had never been a better chance of success since the unlikely conquest by Duke William of Normandy. So elaborate preparations were made. The landing craft, flat-bottomed boats, were assembled, and everyone was ready for embarkation. But at the height of these preparations, several things happened which caused Napoleon to put off the invasion yet again. These preparations had not gone unnoticed by the British and their government hurriedly stitched up yet another coalition of European states to help thwart Napoleon's intentions. Some states were only too willing, after all if Napoleon succeeded they might be next on the list. His strategy was to lure the bulk of the British fleet to the West Indies, and thus denude the English Channel of enemy ships, but the British didn't take the bait. He was also forced to abandon his plans in order to meet an impending threat from Austria. And if any lingering doubt remained about the advisability of invading Britain, they were dispelled by Nelson's famous victory over the French and Spanish fleets at Trafalgar in October 1805.

However, Napoleon's supremacy on the Continent seemed unassailable. He defeated one Austrian army at Ulm, just a day before Trafalgar, and in December of the same year he had one of his most brilliant victories over a combined Austrian and Russian force at Austerlitz. With yet further losses in Italy, Austria sued for peace, and had to surrender some of her most valuable territories in Italy, Dalmatia and Bavaria. Napoleon then shrewdly dealt with the other members of the coalition in turn. He engineered a tentative, informal peace with Britain by promising her territory, and then turned on Russia and Prussia who were now determined that Napoleon must be stopped. He quickly overwhelmed the Prussian army at Jena (1806) before the Russians even arrived, and it is arguable that without the eventual diplomatic intervention of the tsar, the Prussian state would have become extinct. At the peace of Tilsit (1807) Prussia was forced to cede some of her most important territories to Napoleon who, as a divide-and-rule expert, enjoyed reassigning them to various new confederations. Not only was he a state maker, he was also a king maker; he was refashioning Europe to his own design. He gave kingdoms to his three brothers, and rewarded some of those who had either assisted him or had remained neutral during his European wars.

Napoleon was now the sole arbiter of Europe's fortunes except for his failure to subdue Britain or to mount a decisive campaign against Russia. His military genius is beyond doubt, yet it was not just superior tactics that usually won the day. His army was numerically stronger than those of his adversaries, was more liberally equipped with artillery, and possessed the kind of confidence that made them virtually unconquerable. He controlled the Low Countries, most of Central Europe, Italy and Dalmatia, and part of the Baltic coastline. But he could not match the British at sea, and their command of the oceans made his attempted tit-for-tat blockade of Britain impossible to sustain, especially as the Portuguese, Britain's old allies, who had been overrun by a combined Spanish-French force, refused to cooperate fully in implementing Napoleon's policy. The Spanish, who had given Napoleon considerable support, became incensed when he set up his brother, Joseph, as their king (1808) and they appealed to Britain for help. The British saw that here was an ideal opportunity for a 'second front', and sent money, arms, and what we now euphemistically term 'advisers' to assist with Spanish resistance. To complement this, the British also sent an appreciable force to Portugal under the command of Sir Arthur Wellesley, who later became the Duke of Wellington. This campaign had considerable initial success. The French were driven out of Portugal and a treaty was made, but as far as the French were concerned – and possibly the British also – it was just a means of buying time. Wellesley handed over command to Sir John Moore, whereas on the French side Napoleon took charge of operations personally. He quickly dealt with the Spanish troops and occupied Madrid, and then turned his attention to the British who conducted a skilful rearguard action in which Moore himself was killed. They embarked at Corunna (1809), and the first stage of the Spanish insurrection was at an end.

The British, now well aware that there was a great deal of opposition to Napoleonic rule in parts of Western Europe, at least, decided to follow up their limited success by reappointing Wellesley to the command of a much larger force which could use Portugal as a springboard for further operations in Spain (1809). This campaign, which became known as the Peninsular War, was very much a back-and-forth affair. The French forces, in charge of Napoleon's subordinates, had the greatest difficulty in pinning down their enemies who were carrying out an elaborate guerrilla campaign across the Spanish/Portuguese border. With every British success, Wellesley's army was joined by more and more partisans, until eventually the French were forced out of Spain and retreated back into France (1813).

In the meantime, a resurgent Austria, anxious for revenge, again declared war on France (1809), and yet again were humiliated by French forces and had to cede even more territory. Napoleon, in order to legitimize his claims on Austria, neutralize the intransigence, and possibly also to gain greater acceptance among the other nation states, then made a particularly astute move. He divorced his wife and contrived a marriage with the young Hapsburg Archduchess Marie Louise who then became his empress (1810). However, the wedding can hardly have been conducted in the most auspicious religious climate as Napoleon had been excommunicated by the pope when he had annexed the Papal States. To make matters worse, Napoleon – no great respecter of ecclesiastical authority – had the Pope deported from Rome, although he continued to recognize Catholicism itself as a social necessity.

By this time the Russians were also refusing to enforce the continental ban on British goods that Napoleon had decreed. They were not seeking to antagonize him, but saw no reason why they should obey a foreign despot even at the risk of further war. For his part, Napoleon felt that he could not be defied, even by those who had a perfect right to do so. Although he needed all the help he could muster to deal with the un-get-at-able British, he raised the largest army Europe had ever seen, a half a million men, in order to settle the Russian issue once and for all. His original intention was not necessarily to invade Russia, but to bring the enemy to battle nearer home, possibly in Lithuania (1811). What then ensued is rather a matter of interpretation. Did the Russians cunningly lure the French deeper and deeper into their own territory so as to stretch their lines of communication and cut them off from the possibility of reinforcements? Or were they so disorganized, without any unified command, that all they could do was to retreat with the French following hard on their heels? At Borodino, just 70 miles from Moscow, the Russians made a fruitless stand against the French, but in doing so they inflicted appalling losses on the Grande Armee, which it could ill-afford; and it was here that Napoleon, viewing the battlefield afterwards, is reputed to have observed rather cynically that such losses could be made up by just one night in Paris (1812).

Moscow was undefended, and when Napoleon's troops arrived they found the city virtually deserted. It was then set ablaze, possibly to bring the tsar to the negotiating table. But Napoleon waited in vain. The only news he received was about how badly things were going in Spain, and what disquiet this was causing in Paris. By mid-October, just when the roads and tracks in Russia were becoming rivers of mud and the first snows were about to fall, he decided that enough was enough and that the occupation was to no one's advantage. He ordered a retreat and the long trek back across the frozen wastes has become one of the epics of history. In biting cold, the ill-prepared French troops were constantly harried by guerrillas and remnants of the Russian forces. Hunger and frostbite added to their troubles, and probably caused as many casualties as the enemy attacks. By the time they reached Minsk, only a fraction of the original force was left. At this point, Napoleon, knowing that he must go back to Paris as soon as possible to take control of the situation there, left those that remained in charge of his generals, and with a few companions hurried on to Paris while his tattered remnant struggled home.

The destruction of his forces now encouraged his enemies to try again. The Prussians were called to arms (1813) but were held by Napoleon who, almost unbelievably, had raised another army of inexperienced French troops and levies of foreign allies. But when the Prussians were joined by the Austrians, he was defeated at the battle of Leipsig (October 1813). The omens were now quite clear for all to see, except presumably Napoleon himself, who out of personal conviction or overweening self-confidence refused to give up. The coalition armies invaded France (1814) with overwhelmingly superior forces, and after a fighting retreat Napoleon was compelled to abdicate once they had entered Paris. He went into exile on the island of Elba, still dreaming of a possible come-back. This was tantalizingly and temporarily realized the following year. He escaped from Elba and returned to France where, despite his failures, he was given a rapturous welcome by the people. Then came the final defeat at Waterloo by the British under Wellington; a victory that was clinched by the arrival of the Prussians commanded by Marshal Blucher who had already beaten him at Leipsig. Napoleon was banished to the comfortless island of St Helena, there to meditate – apparently conscienceless – about what might have been, if only ...

Napoleon's prominence must, in the last analysis, rest upon his undoubted military genius. Yet if we confine our judgments to his reputation as a conqueror, we have to take into consideration the untold hardship he brought upon Europe in an almost unrelieved period of warfare and the unprecedented misery that he inflicted upon his own people who were just trying to recover from the ravages of the Revolution. Like so many despots, he was popular while he was winning. But unlike so many despots, his memory is still not reviled, probably because he once brought France her most memorable but fleeting moments of greatness.

CHAPTER FOURTEEN

'Proletarian' Despotism:
Stalin and the Great Terror

Marx contended that the revolutionary force in a capitalist society is the proletariat, the people who have to earn wages in order to live. It is the industrial working class in capitalist society that is deprived and oppressed, but which has the potential – if properly led and educated – to emancipate itself from capitalist domination to become the creators of 'true' socialism. The proletariat, therefore, is not to be equated with the 'People', a term which can include all ranks and classes and factions within the state; it is meant rather to denote – as in popular usage – the ordinary people, the proletariat, as opposed to, say, the aristocracy or the nobility. For Marx, the proletariat were the *creators* of wealth as opposed to those who were the recipients of wealth. But in the hypothetical classless society, presumably ushered in by revolutionary structural change, there would be an abolition of privilege, and society would be subject to the will of the working classes. Critics argue that this 'dictatorship of the proletariat' is to be identified with the rule of the Common Man or Mass Man or what has been more starkly called the 'tyrant from below' (Llewellyn, 1957: 3), a pejorative term suggesting the subservience of those who know best to those who know least.

How accurate is this Marxian analysis? Can revolutions really bring about democracy, or do they merely exchange one form of domination based on an oligarchy of wealth for another based on the monopolization of power? Or is the will of the people or the dictatorship of the proletariat simply an attractive but convenient fiction to 'explain', or disguise, a concentration of control in the hands of an autocrat? This has certainly been the case in some societies, and there is probably no more salutary example than that of Stalinist Russia, where a particular theory of the state was reinterpreted – or manipulated – in order to justify a singular form of despotism. It was not only used to uphold one-man rule, it also served to endorse his attack on the state *in the name of the people*. Stalin created what has been called an 'empire of fear' (Petrov and Petrov, 1956), yet, paradoxically, an empire based on a fawning adulation of the leader, or at least the leader-image.

The early days of the Soviet regime were marked by real uncertainty. No one, including the Soviets, was quite sure if it was really going to endure. The virtually bloodless revolution of November 1917 had succeeded – to just about everyone's surprise. The problem was, could it last? At one of those interminable debates at the Smolny Institute while the revolution was in progress, one of its principal architects and leading theorists, Leon Trotsky (later to be murdered on Stalin's orders), argued that there were only two alternatives: either the revolution was going to create a general revolutionary movement in Europe, or the European powers were going to crush the revolution. He wasn't far off the mark because in the next three years or so, the European powers tried to do just that. They thought that the Soviets would be overthrown in any one of the many civil wars they had either fomented or supported. These effectively coalesced into two main confrontations – that against the White armies (aided by British, French and American allies) in northern and southern Russia, and that against the Poles to the west. Theoretically, White (anti-Soviet) armies should have overwhelmed the Red (Soviet) forces, but they were disunited and not agreed on their ultimate objectives, whereas their ill-equipped opponents were quite sure about theirs. Lacking allies, but possessed of a fanatical zeal somewhat reminiscent of the French Revolutionary armies many years before and good – if ruthless – leadership, they won through, and by 1923 Europe had to recognize that Lenin and his Bolsheviks were there to stay.

The civil war left the country in a parlous condition. When peace came in 1920, Russia had lost her Baltic provinces and Poland, but the rest of the country was under tight Communist control. There were the usual recriminations, and many of those who opposed the regime were either liquidated or exiled. To make matters very much worse, transport was disorganized, the economy was in ruins, and there were such acute shortages that many thousands died of hunger. Indeed, the famine was so bad that it almost succeeded where the foreign expeditionary forces had failed.

From 1917 to 1922, when the USSR was officially formed, the country was run on a strict 'socialist' basis where private property and private trading were disallowed. In theory, the system was supposed to work, but things were no better in practice. The peasants reacted unfavourably and Lenin was forced to introduce the New Economic Policy in 1923. Doctrinaire socialism, as it had been generally understood, was 'reinterpreted' to meet the exigencies of the current situation. A qualified amount of private enterprise was reintroduced into the system. Individual traders were once again allowed to carry on their commerce, and peasants were again permitted to sell at least some of their produce for profit. But all this entrepreneurial activity could only take place under licence from the government, and every precaution was taken to ensure that vested interests would not develop to challenge the prerogatives of the state which still controlled the main economic agencies: banks, foreign trade, and so on.

Lenin did not live to see these economic innovations materialize. He died in 1924, and many expected him to be succeeded by Trosky, who had done so much to ensure the military success of the Red army. But by cunning manoeuvrings, Trotsky was ousted by Josef Stalin who eventually drove him into exile. Stalin, until this time very much a background figure, held the influential position of secretary of the Communist Party which dominated every aspect of the machinery of government. In effect, he had been a kind of understudy to Lenin and, as such, had immediate access to the Council of People's Commissars. At no time was there really any question of a dictatorship of the proletariat, only a dictatorship *over* the proletariat nominally by the Party. In reality, this meant a small oligarchy of the political elite, but even this did not last for long. Stalin saw to that. The New Economic Policy was abandoned, private enterprise was again largely forbidden, and plans were made to more than double industrial output within the next five years. Trotsky's idea of extending socialism everywhere was jettisoned for the more manageable and realistic objective of achieving 'true' socialism in one country only: Soviet Russia.

This concentration on development both in industry and in agriculture was to prove a qualified success. There is no doubt that the results in certain areas were truly impressive and contrasted favourably – or so many felt – with the difficult conditions being experienced in the capitalist West which was in the midst of the Depression. But this success was bought at an enormous cost in human suffering. Nowhere can this be better seen than in the enforced collectivization of agriculture where peasants, especially those with larger holdings (the Kulaks), were forced to merge, and sacrifice their livelihoods in order to meet government targets. A great many objected, and consequently paid – often with their lives – for their stubborn resistance (Carlton, 1994). In industry the situation was different. Here, the results were most evident. There was a rapid expansion of the facilities for technical education because, by and large, Russia was trying to develop without a properly skilled work force. So even industry had its problems. More managers were introduced to discipline the workers, and sanctions in terms of reduced pensions were imposed for those without a satisfactory employment record (Kochan, 1967: 292–93). Although blessed with plentiful supplies of raw materials, Russia required machines to take advantage of these vast resources. She needed machines to make machines. These had to be brought in from abroad, especially from the old enemy, Germany, and it was agricultural exports that had to pay for them, to the detriment of the peasants, who suffered another terrible famine. This was conveniently attributed to peasant ignorance and the evil machinations of class enemies, and was so successfully disguised from the outside world that a number of influential but gullible Westerners were fooled into thinking that a famine which killed some seven million people didn't actually exist.

By 1934, with all effective opposition ostensibly crushed, the Soviet Union had become more or less respectable in the eyes of the world. She was recognized by other European states with whom she joined in the League of Nations, despite the fact that she had begun feverishly to rearm. However, there were still some internal matters to be dealt with: real and imagined factional disputes which Stalin saw as dangerously subversive. Curiously, what dissent there was did not come primarily from the new intelligentsia; the young Communists tended to accept their social and political values ready-made. It came from the old brigade, those who knew Stalin once as a comrade and who had braved the oppression of tsarism and the struggles of the revolution with him. People who referred to him in intimate terms as 'Koba', and who – when the storm came – found it incomprehensible that their one-time friend had turned against them. In the middle of 1925 his close associates Zinoviev and Kamenev had disagreed with him and were removed from office. Then it was Trotsky's turn; and in 1927 all three, together with some 75 of their supporters, were expelled from the Party. Stalin (unlike Hitler in this respect) felt no loyalty to these men. Rather he saw them as something of an embarrassment; people who did not afford him the respect – almost worship – that he had begun to enjoy from the new generation of believers. He no longer wanted questioning or criticism, only adulation and implicit obedience. The cult of the leader was enhanced at every opportunity. In 1934, for instance, when three members of a balloon crew died while setting a high altitude record, it was asserted that their dying gasps included the words 'Stalin ... Stalin ... Stalin' in recognition of the one who had inspired their achievement (McNeal, 1989: 187). The purges of the 1930s were to eradicate every member of Lenin's Politburo except Trotsky, who was not murdered until 1940. It probably paid Stalin to keep Trotsky and his mythical movement alive for a while as a symbol of the external threat to Soviet socialism, and as a prime subject for Soviet vilification.

The Sixth Congress in 1928 was the last at which any variety of opinion was permitted. The Seventh Congress in 1935 did not allow any public participation in the formulation of policy. The 'socialism in one country' was strictly adhered to, the theory being that once Russia had built up her resources, she would eventually be strong enough to direct world revolution instead of being dependent upon it. But, as an interim measure, revolutionary movements in other countries were initiated and supported or not, as it suited Soviet purposes. And these purposes often changed, much to the consternation of the foreign Communist parties who were expected to fall into line, the classic examples being Soviet policy changes during the Spanish Civil War (1936–39), and pre-eminently with regard to Germany in the Stalin–Hitler pact in 1939.

The critical factor in determining relations between Stalin and those often termed 'the old Bolsheviks' rested on their different approaches to the theory of the state. Both Marx and Lenin had taught that the state would still persist in the hypothesized transition from capitalism to socialism, but they regarded this as a temporary phenomenon, though just how temporary could not be specified. These ideas were still upheld in the 1930s by one of the leading and influential Soviet theorists, Nicholai Bukharin, who continued to insist that eventually the state would (should?) 'wither away', and that good Communists should regard all states, including their own, as essentially repressive and inimical to the freedom of the individual. But when Stalin introduced the new constitution in 1936, he attacked this thesis, arguing that the Soviet state was unique and must develop in a particular way, something that Marx could not have foreseen, and Lenin had not anticipated. He insisted that the old doctrine might still apply in the non-Communist world, but not in Soviet Russia which was no longer dominated by a particular class or section of society. He argued that in Russia the state must actually become stronger, if anything, in order to withstand the hostility of surrounding capitalist societies. Russia must not dissipate its resources, but conserve them so as to become a formidable force in the world. This would eventually lead to external respect, and internally to a higher (purified?) form of communism. In the Eighteenth Congress of 1939, he was still reiterating this theme, presumably to justify the elitist nature of the Party with its restricted membership, and his own continued hold on power. He insisted that the state must exist until capitalist encirclement was liquidated and the danger of foreign military attack had disappeared (Carew-Hunt, 1962: 204–06).

It is common to date Stalin's brutal, repressive activities from the late 1920s, but the witch-hunt mentality had existed ever since the Bolshevik takeover. Executions of class enemies had been a common feature of Lenin's regime, especially in the early days when the Bolsheviks were trying to consolidate their rule. In 1926, Dzerzhinsky, the original head of the Cheka (one of the forerunners of the later KGB), died after declaring that he never spared himself in the interests of the state. This becomes understandable when one considers that between 1917 and 1921, the Cheka carried out an estimated 250,000 executions (Andrew and Gordievsky, 1990: 41). It would seem hardly possible that things could get worse, yet under Stalin the death toll ran into millions. Periodically, there would be minor purges of dissidents, 'traitors and wreckers', those who were deemed guilty of economic as well as political subversion. The condemned were sent to one of the numerous labour camps that had been set up in the extreme north, or they disappeared altogether. Sometimes the accused were accorded the privilege – or indignity – of a trial, and often the whole procedure would be hopelessly prejudiced by deliberately drummed-up public indignation, with parades of people demanding death to 'imperialist agents'. When the socialist experiment went wrong, either through accident, inefficiency or downright bad planning, it could not be allowed that it was socialism itself that was at fault. It had to be the work of outside agencies that were anxious to bring about the collapse of the regime. Conspiracies were seen everywhere. The then Secret Police (OGPU) had a seeming addiction for counter-revolutionary plots, and this was not helped by Stalin's incurably suspicious nature.

In 1934 the OGPU was reconstituted as the NKVD (People's Commissariat for Internal Affairs) under the leadership of one of the more unsavoury members of the Soviet hierarchy, Genrikh Yagoda. Although, terminologically, NKVD referred to the political police, the expression was used generally to denote a powerful force that combined regular police, the criminal investigation branch, border police and – most sinister of all – the political police themselves. As is common in autocratic societies, this force was answerable directly to the leader himself, in this case to Stalin (still simply referred to as the Secretary) via his personal secretariat. In this same year, one of Stalin's main rivals, the Leningrad Party boss, Sergai Kirov, was assassinated, almost certainly on Stalin's orders, though the blame was carefully deflected elsewhere. The officials who 'facilitated' Kirov's death were not punished at the time, but they were quietly shot in the purges three years later, possibly so that nothing could ever incriminate the real culprits. Complementarily, during those same purges, the murder of Kirov served as a convenient excuse to accuse others who had nothing to do with the crime of complicity (as Stalin himself put it, 'the evil murder of Comrade Kirov' has revealed 'many suspect elements within the Party' quoted by Andrew and Gordievsky, 1990: 101). It also precipitated new legislation which gave the NKVD effective power of life and death over all those who were broadly classified as 'terrorists', or even suspected of any kind of so-called subversive activity.

It has already been observed that those who are closest to despots have most to fear from them. Stalin exemplifies this perfectly. It is clear from the evidence that he planned to get rid of many of the associates that he either didn't quite trust or who might oppose his policies; Yagoda is a case in point. After two years in office, he and his organization were accused of dragging their feet in the pursuit and punishment of counter-revolutionaries. Yagoda was dismissed, only to turn up on Stalin's proscription lists several months later. His place was taken by, if anything, an even less endearing character, Nicholai Yezhov, a former factory worker. Yezhov was a very diminutive man (he was less than five feet tall) who had an incomprehensible fondness for oversize overcoats which made him look faintly ridiculous on official occasions. But there was nothing comic about his work as head of the NKVD; in fact, he was to become one of the most feared men in the Soviet Union, and the period of the purges is sometimes known unofficially as Yezhovsheina, the dreaded reign of Yezhov. It was not long before Yezhov was publicly accusing his predecessor of treachery to the state and of setting up spies even within the NKVD itself. One of the more cynical members of his audience observed that the applause which these allegations received was probably largely determined by the audience's wish to live, even if it meant betraying their closest friends.

The hypothesized opposition to the regime took two main forms, though at times these became fused during the trials. There was said to be a conspiracy of the 'left' which was associated with the exiled Trotsky who, together with his supporters and the remnants of the White army and exiled monarchists, was said to be in league with reactionary regimes abroad, such as those of imperialist Japan and Nazi Germany. No matter how unlikely these purported alliances were, they were obviously accepted, either out of conviction or, more probably, out of prudence, by many second-string officials. Whether other members of the Politburo believed this kind of conspiracy theory is a moot point. In addition to these counter-revolutionary forces, there was also said to be the menace of a 'right' opposition, the leaders of which, Bukharin and Rykov were about to be dealt with (a third, Tomsky, having committed suicide).

There was precious little evidence for any of this. The charges against those who were seen variously as wreckers, spies, assassins and deviationists – in short, 'enemies of the people' – were, as far as can be judged, almost entirely without foundation. But they fed the fantasies of those who needed sacrificial victims to assuage their political exasperation and to provide a diversion for those who felt that things were not going as well as they should. It is now known that in the interrogations preceding the most important trials (1936–38) confessions were extracted from the accused which were patently false. The interrogators used a mixture of methods to obtain the responses they required. Some were direct, such as promising the victims their lives and, more importantly, the lives of their families if they complied (promises, certainly in the case of the accused, that were rarely kept). Others preferred a well-tried miscellany of physical torture; in fact, anything that worked. The record shows that although there was some prevarication by the accused under extreme provocation from the bullying State Prosecutor, almost no one ever permanently retracted their confessions. Some not only responded to the charges, but elaborated extensively on their own 'guilt' in the hope of more lenient treatment.

To many outside observers, these false confessions are one of the most incomprehensible features of the whole sorry episode. How was it that threats supplemented by promises were enough to make men deny themselves? The late Arthur Koestler, who himself was once under sentence of death during the Spanish Civil War, suggested that it might be because by keeping silent about their true situation they could do one last service for the party (Koestler, 1941). Another contributory factor may have been that many of the accused had themselves been guilty of condemning others. Many had blood on their hands from earlier days when they participated in, or, at very least, acquiesced in the persecution of other victims, in which case they may not have felt able to judge their own accusers. They may have taken the view that they were all victims of the same corrupt system which was a perversion of their ideal of *The Party*. This is to some extent borne out by those who maintain that although interrogation methods, particularly when applied over months or even years, can break the strongest will, this is not the decisive factor. What mattered at the time was that the majority of Communists had to preserve their faith in the Soviet creed. The system was like a faith. To renounce it would have been impossible for them. This can be seen in the particularly poignant re-evaluation in the last plea of Bukharin, who was not exactly an innocent himself: 'For three months I refused to say anything. Then I began to testify. I asked myself, if you must die, what are you dying for? – an absolutely black vacuity arises before you ... There is nothing to die for, if one wanted to die unrepented ... But suppose you do not die, suppose by some miracle you remain alive, again what for? Isolated from everybody, an enemy of the people ... completely isolated from everything that constitutes the essence of life' (Bukharin Trial, 777–87, quoted in Conquest, 1990: 118).

And how did the relatives of the accused react when they were condemned either to death or to what was often a kind of living death in the Gulag? Understandably, many were entirely distraught; in cases where their loved ones were sentenced to the camps or had simply disappeared, they were often unable to get any news or response from the authorities at all. In some, more bizarre, cases, relatives gave their approval to the purges, even when several members of their family had been executed. Faith demanded that the dictates of the Party must be right. But in very many instances, especially where those concerned were in the upper echelons of the regime, their relatives, wives and children just did not survive. The Party had no compunction about wiping the slate completely clean.

The media were duly harnessed to justify and even applaud the trials and the sentences, although there was much that never became public knowledge at the time. As just one example of how the public (in its ignorance) responded, one could cite a poem published in *Pravda* in 1936 entitled 'No Mercy' which effectively called for the execution of the so-called conspirators. It contained such deathless lines as:

Betrayers of the motherland,
Pseudoparty traitors, liars ...
Underground enemies, fascist agents ...
They were going for Stalin!
But they failed to get ... him!
We have guarded Stalin ...
We guard him as our head
We guard him as our own heart!
              (quoted by McNeal, 1989: 188)

And so it goes on, almost a hymn of adoration of one that must forever remain inviolable, the leader whom it is sacrilege to threaten. The press and the radio only mentioned the main show trials for which the Party mobilized the necessary support. The media were also adept at reporting items which acted as suitable diversions for the public, who were encouraged to focus their attention on the achievements of Soviet culture, most notably those of Soviet sportsmen, aviators and the like, which were contrasted with the perfidiousness of the accused. Stalin's timing on these matters was nothing short of adroit.

Once the near infallibility of the leader had been accepted, he was free to pursue more far-reaching plans to rid the regime of 'plotters' and 'traitors'. The purges extended down through the hierarchy to hosts of lesser officials. It is estimated that some 206 secretaries of regional party organizations down to district level perished (Medvedev, 1979). If Stalin's agents decided that a particular regional boss was an enemy of the people, he was liquidated, together with most if not all of his staff. Under interrogation, a man might incriminate his colleagues, or maybe they would be found guilty simply by association. In such cases, executions were often carried out without the pretence of a trial. It appears that Stalin initialled death lists, often with several hundred names, as a daily routine, although he took care to distance himself from the physical reality of the terror. There is certainly no reliable evidence that he ever attended an interrogation or an execution, although he may have witnessed some trials secretly. One set of lists for 20 August 1938 contained 736 names, of which 200 were military men and 15 were wives (Conquest, 1990: 235). One wonders just how much time was given to studying each individual case. Those who were imprisoned instead may have thought themselves fortunate, but they were by no means safe from death in the camps. There were probably about 125 camp clusters, each comprising about 200 camps, in all containing some 7–8 million people (1938) who might be there for the most trivial reasons or – not unusually – for no clear reason at all. (This should be compared with the pre-Revolutionary period (1912) when there was a total prison population of about 200,000.) Inmates were, of course, likely to die of hunger, cold and disease, but they might well be put to death. A sentence of ten years in a camp 'without correspondence' usually meant death anyway. Periodically, there were calls from the Kremlin to the local NKVD for more executions of those under arrest. Some would be included on the death list just because they had been denounced for complaining about conditions in general. Yezhov is known to have gone personally to the Ukraine to order 30,000 more executions for which the NKVD would be required to submit 'completion' lists.

The purges were not just about political enemies in the narrow sense. The Communist theory of the state demanded the 'correct' interpretation of all aspects of its corporate life, therefore it was thought legitimate for Party leaders to call the nature of the entire Soviet culture into question. The arts and – perhaps more inexplicably – the sciences were subjected to careful scrutiny. Heterodoxy was anathema, deviationism had to be checked, so the Terror was extended to academia. Both students and academics were arrested. At the Kiev Academy of Sciences, for instance, each of its successive secretaries between 1921 and 1938 was arrested, as were also six of the seven Principals of the University. But it was writers, who as a 'class' tend to exhibit a more independent turn of mind, who probably fared worst of all. It is estimated that, for a variety of reasons, of the 700 writers who met at the First Congress of Soviet Writers in 1934, only 50 survived to attend the Second Congress in 1954. The Union of Soviet Writers now estimates that some 2,000 writers were 'repressed', of whom 75 per cent met their deaths in prisons or in camps.

Even more incomprehensible was Stalin's assault on the armed forces, especially the Army. Despite the extensive system of political control carried out by specially appointed commissions in the Army, the NKVD claimed to have uncovered a 'Counter-Revolutionary Military Fascist Organisation' plot in 1937. It is now believed that there is some justification for thinking that the authorities believed that something of the kind really existed. There is also some reason to believe that further 'evidence' for it may actually have been fabricated by the Intelligence Branch of the Nazi SD and fed indirectly (probably via Czechoslovak sources) to the NKVD; but it is doubtful whether this really fooled Soviet Intelligence. The purge of the Army began with the arrest and trial of Marshal Tukhachevsky, by all accounts a brilliant if somewhat insubordinate commander with whom Stalin had not enjoyed the best of relations since the 1920s. He was alleged to have been a key conspirator in a network of traitors in the Army High Command. Tukhachevsky and seven other senior officers were tried in June 1937, quickly convicted and peremptorily shot. For the next year or so the purge continued and was extended to the Navy as well. The number of victims steadily mounted until eventually it affected, according to Soviet sources: 3 of 5 marshals, 13 of 15 army commanders, 8 of 9 fleet admirals, 204 of 243 corps and divisional commanders and 99 of 108 army political commissars (quoted by Conquest, 1990: 450). Besides these, it is estimated that between May 1937 and September 1938, 36,761 Army Officers and over 3,000 Navy Officers were dismissed, though many were re-enrolled at the outset of the 'Great Patriotic War' in 1941. It hardly needs to be stressed that this had a catastrophic effect on Russia's capacity to withstand the initial German assault. The lack of any very clear strategy contributed to the devastating losses of men and material that Russia sustained in 1941–42. Yet this did not stop Stalin executing even more officers (including very senior Air Force personnel) for inefficiency, when the faults were by no means entirely theirs.

It is a feature of contract killing that it is sometimes found expedient to eliminate the killers themselves, presumably in an attempt to cover the tracks of those who order the contract. In this there are some close resemblances to the Stalinist purges. Stalin, who had always been careful not to appear directly involved in the Terror, badly needed someone who could be held responsible for the killings. When most of the dirty work was done, Stalin turned on the agency of death, the NKVD. The secret police had been his instrument of murder not only in the political and military spheres, but also in liquidating undesirable Communists abroad, especially in Spain. By the time the Terror was at its height, Yagoda had already fallen foul of his master. Now came the turn of his principal executioner, Yezhov. Late in 1938, a secret Commission was appointed to look into the affairs of the NKVD and its leader. Yezhov was found wanting and replaced by another very accomplished butcher, Lavrenti Beria. This was an ominous sign, although he was not actually arrested until the following April and charged with being involved in a plan to assassinate his master and seize power – a plot which, in its initial stages, he himself claimed to have uncovered. A combination of Stalin's personal agents and Beria's imported Georgian NKVD set about the task of investigating the investigators. On the basis of such evidence that was presented, Yezhov and some 150 of his collaborators and assistants were found guilty and executed.

At the time, the West found the trials virtually unbelievable. Some rejected their authenticity entirely, others – including many notable left-wing writers and academics – accepted them as necessary. But probably the majority of observers felt that there had to be *something* behind the many accusations, even if they were somewhat exaggerated. There were a few who, not knowing all the facts or the extent of the purges, speculated that maybe it was the price some societies must pay to achieve industrialization and eventual stability and progress. Robert Conquest argues that this is like saying that cannibalism is one way of attaining a high-protein diet; an intolerable price to achieve this particular end. Actually, given the pre-World War I level of technological development in

Russia, it is arguable that despite the legacy of serfdom and the rule of an intransigent monarchy, the requisite standards might well have been reached without the Communist Revolution.

Present-day historians are still not quite sure what to make of the Terror. Material from both Western and Russian sources now give us a fairly clear, if approximate, idea of what sorts of figures were involved in the purges:

Those arrested in the USSR: 8 million
Those in prison (1938):   1 million
Those in camps (1938):   7–8 million
     (NB: Soviet sources give the 1952 figure as 12 million)
Those executed: 1 million

(quoted by Conquest, 1990: 484–89)

These figures are quite apart from the 20 million given in USSR sources for the peasant repression (1929–33), which presumably includes those who died in the great famine. By *why* did it take place. Was Stalin insane? Krushchev in his now famous exposé speech in 1956, three years after Stalin's death, indicated as much and referred to him as being 'sickly' and 'morbid' (quoted by McNeal, 1989: 182). Or were his actions against the Party, as Roy Medvedev claims, carefully planned and premeditated and prompted by his 'inordinate vanity and lust for power ... [his determination] to be in a position of absolute control, ruling as an autocrat with no restraints of any kind'? (Medvedev, 1979: 111). If he was mentally ill he certainly possessed the ability to communicate his own bizarre reality to a great many others. Their conviction was not just born out of fear; they shared Stalin's ideological world-view and sympathized with and actively supported his aims. The Terror had its own strange and perverted kind of rationality. There were further purges, particularly towards the end of Stalin's life, though not on so grand a scale, yet despite everything he was still seen by the public as the 'father of the nation'. Perhaps he could never have become a prophet in his own country if those who had known him as a mere fellow-revolutionary had not been eliminated. As a despot, he no longer wished seriously to discuss, only to dictate. He wanted no opposition from his peers, so they had to go. Only then could the cult of personality find its true uninhibited expression.

Populist Despotism:
Peron of Argentina

Perhaps the most fascinating thing about the particular brand of despotism found in Argentina in the late 1940s under Juan Peron is that its developmental phase coincided exactly with the *decline and destruction* phase of the most notable fascist and totalitarian regimes in Europe. Admittedly, the regimes in Spain and Portugal were not directly affected by World War II, but the war spelled the demise of various fascist or quasi-fascist systems, pre-eminently those of Germany, Hungary, Poland (?) and Italy. Whether Peron's regime can be categorized as fascist is, as we shall see, somewhat disputable; much depends on whether we are prepared to define 'fascist' in functional terms, that is, in terms of how it works and what it does, or in terms of the socio-economic conditions in which it thrives, or in terms of ideology, which can be equally instructive. John Weiss lists the characteristics of fascism as:

1. organicist conceptions of community (e.g. Nazi 'volk')
2. philosophical idealism
3. idealization of what is 'manly', including peasant/village virtues
4. hostility to advanced, corporation or monopoly capitalism
5. resentment of mass democracy
6. elitist conceptions of political and social leadership
7. racism which may or may not take the form of anti-semitism
8. militarism
9. imperialism

All these, Weiss insists, indicate an opposition to liberal values and institutions, and represent a fascist movement when they are combined in an effort to gain mass support, if necessary by violence and thought control (Weiss, 1967: xi–xii). Important as these features are, they must be regarded as a highly generalized set of characteristics. As we noted in the introductory chapters, not every system designated 'fascist' would conform exactly in the sum of its characteristics or in the relative importance of some characteristics compared with others. Furthermore, lists of features of this kind tell us little or nothing about the preconditions which generate such systems and which 'create' a sense of elective affinity among its supporters.

There has also been some controversy as to whether or not fascism is really an anti-modernist movement. This argument seems rather laboured. It is true that all fascist movements contain elements of protest against modernization and urbanization, but they sometimes also contain tendencies towards the restructuring of society in a more futuristic sense. They can also be seen as anti-modernist in that most, if not all, fascist movements – and certainly successful fascist regimes – have been characterized by atavistic ideologies. They have often been concerned to recapture some believed ideals or practices of the past, although the *means* whereby these were to be realized or reactivated were usually decidedly modern. Such parties have been categorized as either pragmatic, particularistic or ideological in type. This is again a rather general non-discrete typology, but it does reflect not so much party organization or recruitment patterns as their value orientations and the ways in which these values inform actual political activity. In Argentina, the Peronistas (unlike the Socialists) while adopting a clear *ideological* stance, were willing to be *pragmatic* and compromise with others in order to strengthen their position.

In some respects the 'implantation' of European-style fascism on Latin American soil in the 1930s was neither a simple nor a natural process. There were too many factors that militated against it. Success was hardly assured for reasons that have been cogently analysed by Alistair Hennessy (Laqueur, 1979: 248–57). Hennessy maintains that the adoption of the European models was limited despite the efforts made by the Germans and Italians to encourage and subsidize their sympathetic minorities in several Latin American countries, especially Argentina. Such ideas had a particular appeal for certain intellectuals, but, by and large, were not taken up generally because the conditions prevailing in Germany and Italy (though to a lesser extent in Spain) which facilitated the development of fascism were not paralleled in the Latin American states. These differences were critical:

1. They had been barely touched by the devastations of World War I and had therefore never experienced the socio-economic and socio-psychological legacies of total war. Their populations had not been decimated; and in the aftermath they had not undergone the horrors of epidemic disease.
2. They had not, therefore, encountered the heart-searching and critical intellectual enquiry that had followed from the war, and the polarization generated by the potent forces of communism and fascism.
3. They had not then passed through a period of debilitating and humiliating economic depression. Poverty is terrible at the best of times, and is endemic in Latin America, but in some ways it is an experience which falls hardest on those who have known better days.

4. They had a strong tradition of what might be termed simple or folk Catholicism. This was also the case in Italy and Spain but these countries also had minority though powerful traditions of anti-clericalism which, at that time, were hardly developed in Latin America.
5. They had an influential but, as yet, inadequately organized labour movement, something which was much more highly developed in Europe. Such socialist-inspired movements also tend to have under-lying anti-clerical orientations. Insofar as these found support in Latin America, that support came largely from the youth organizations and academia, institutions which in Europe often subscribed to fascism.
6. There was no developed racial ideology except where there were substantial indigenous Indian populations. The traditions of the Spanish, in particular, are perhaps best not recalled in this respect, but by the 1930s treatment of the indigenes did not approach the sort of excesses found in Europe. In states such as Argentina, the population mix was such that racism was already largely neutralized.
7. They had a long-established culture of violence, of revolution and counter-revolution, of military takeovers, of restriction of rights and often despotic repression. Such experiences leave the ordinary people numbed. Fascist methods therefore seem no different from any others. There is a pervasive resignation about political change. Whoever is in power, the lot of the masses stays pretty much the same.

Despite these factors, what were arguably forms of fascism did take root in some states, and Argentina is particularly interesting in that it did not conform to any existing pattern, although in its initial phases it was very much influenced by the policies and practices of European fascism.

Argentina was declared independent in 1816, but freedom from foreign rule brought with it all kinds of political problems. None of the aspiring civilian leaders had any significant political experience, and their efforts to organize the new state were frustrated by disunity and their obvious inability to put corporate interests above local concerns (Bruce, 1972: 303). State authority was increasingly questioned by the wealthy, land-owning aristocracy (caudillos) who were also the leaders of the militias which had helped in the battle for independence and were now reluctant to relinquish their power. One of these, Juan de Rozas, became Argentina's first dictator and ruled the country repressively until 1851 when he was deposed by his erstwhile supporters.

In 1853, Argentina was finally unified under a democratic constitution, and under a series of presidencies developed into one of the most economically progressive states in Latin America. In 1916, a Radical party came to power, although the land-owning aristocracy were still extremely influential. Neither groups could do much to save the country from the ravages of the Depression in the late 1920s, and the economy and the reputation of the government were in such a parlous condition that it precipitated a military coup in September 1930 under General Uriburu, in which the young Juan Peron was also implicated. As with so many takeovers of this kind, the intention was to restore order and confidence, but Uriburu, possibly influenced by the Italian model, attempted to turn Argentina into a fascist state. At much the same time as the rise of this intensely nationalistic movement there was a parallel development of organized labour. It was Peron who was able to represent and, to an extent, encapsulate the aspirations of both within his brand of fascism which stressed simultaneously the destiny of the state *and* social justice for the underprivileged classes.

One tends to associate Latin American states with military rule. The support of the military has always been a critical factor in the establishment and maintenance of political dictatorships; better still if the aspiring despot was himself a member of the armed forces. It was not at all unusual in Latin America for young officers to form esoteric cliques or secret organizations which were breeding grounds for possible coups d'état. Argentina was no exception. Its Grupo de Oficiales Unidos (GOU) was just such a fascist oriented set-up of which Peron was a member.

The officer corps of the various states was drawn mainly from the middle classes, and therefore tended to endorse traditional values. In contrast, the rank and file were often party strong-arm men (compare Nazi Germany's early SA) who became part of the National Guard if their party was successful. Interestingly, in 1928 only six Latin American states were ruled by the military, though only a few years later this had changed considerably. After some 50 years of civilian rule, eight out of ten presidents between 1930 and 1957 were either generals or colonels, though one of the most enduring, Batista of Cuba, was only a sergeant (Lieuwen, 1960: chap. 5). Despite their apparent popularity in the presidential stakes, it could be argued that their training as military professionals hardly fitted them for their role as full-time politicians. Peron, for instance, who had little experience of economics, initiated hurried programmes of industrialization when possibly a greater concentration on developing a firm agricultural base would have been a far sounder proposition for the country as a whole. Military leaders also tend to have divided loyalties; allegiance to their fellow officers and adherence to military codes and objectives do not always square with the needs of the people. And even where the objectives are very similar, such as the viable future of the state, the *means* whereby this is achieved may be seen in very different terms (witness the not too distant events in China). On the positive side, one could cite the fact that it often takes the military to oust the military. Revolutionary coups are a military speciality, whether it means installing a military leader or de-throning an unpopular military despot.

But when they do have to go, how much do they take with them? It is estimated that in just five years (1954–59) Latin America's dictators took with them some hundreds of millions of dollars, quite apart from what they had spent on personal and family luxuries while in office (Trujillo's *annual* 'take' in Dominica, for instance, was estimated at about $30 million). It may be that no one got away with as much as Peron, who is said to have 'appropriated' something in the region of $700 million (Lieuwen, 1960: 116). The graft was so vast, and the accounting so imprecise that a hundred million here or there makes no real difference to the estimates or the degree of culpability. Little wonder that one authority has written that military 'parasitic appropriation of the surplus produced by the economically productive civilian sectors of the society was one of the most powerful factors inhibiting technical progress' (Andreski, 1964: 162).

The rise of military governments in so many Latin American states, especially during and since World War II, has been accompanied by a clamour for increased industrialization as the obvious route to prosperity and development. Industry has been mainly concentrated in the large urban areas which are also the centres of power and administrative authority. Various leaders promised that industrialization would lead to more equality in the distribution of rewards and fairer access to highly desired goods and commodities. Governments have usually made signifi-cant contributions to the development of industry, but although, in general, the people have profited, the technological El Dorado has not been realized. Despite the considerable improvements, if anything the gap between the rich and the poor has actually widened.

From the military's point of view, industrialization has also meant the possibility of more sophisticated, up-to-date equipment. (This was par-ticularly evident in the Falklands War in 1982 when Argentina displayed a wealth of advanced – mainly French – weaponry). Notably, arms build-up has not led to interstate warfare on any scale, indeed, such conflicts have been really quite rare. Rather it seems to have been desired for *intra*-state purposes, for control and even intimidation, and, of course, for display and the enhancement of national prestige. The military presence has also served as an expression of national identity. Economic factors have always been of overriding importance as far as political unrest and political change are concerned, but nationalism has been elevated to the status of the major political ideology. It has become the manifest dynamic for many of the most important Latin American revolutions, not least in Argentina.

Some animosity has often existed between the military and the lower orders of society, not least because of the extremely good pay in the services. During the Peron era, in which military numbers were doubled, pay, especially for officers, was more than generous by comparative standards, and their income was increased by fringe benefits. After 30 years' service, they were also entitled to a 100 per cent pension. Besides this civilian hostility, the military were not beyond factional strife within their own ranks, as was evidenced by the executions which accompanied the deposition of Peron. It didn't really pay to be on the wrong side in Latin American politics. The other main instrument of control, the police, have in the past often comprised hastily recruited men of little education and even less intelligence. They were feared but hardly respected. Some were apparently no more than one-time guerrillas who had found themselves suddenly catapulted into positions of legal respectability now that the party they supported had at last been recognized.

The Peron dictatorship followed a rather turbulent period of political comings and goings. As we have noted, General Uriburu took power in a military coup in 1930, but only remained in office for two years. He was a conservative with broadly fascist leanings, and was replaced by another conservative, General Augustin Justo, who commanded a wider spectrum of support. He inherited a difficult economic situation, but continued with varying success until 1938 when he gave way to Roberto Ortiz who did what he could to liberalize election procedures. He too only remained president for two years, when he was succeeded by another conservative, Ramon Castillo (1940–43). At the outbreak of war in 1939, Argentina, despite her relatively strong trade links with Britain, remained neutral. More worrying – especially to the United States – was the fact that when the US entered the war in 1941, Argentina still reaffirmed her neutrality. This issue united the opposition groups. Castillo was ousted in 1943 by his own Minister of War, General Pedro Ramiriz, yet this still did not solve the problem. There followed a very uneasy transition period in which another general, Arturo Rawson, took over as president, but was forced to resign after only two days because of his pro-United States stance. General Ramirez succeeded him, and for a while neutrality was maintained. Shortly afterwards opposition increased, possibly in the wake of the Allied victories. There was press censorship and the dissolution of all political parties. But pressure from the US eventually forced Argentina to break off relations with Germany, a move naturally opposed by fascist sympathizers. With further agitation, this time within the ranks of the military, Ramirez turned over the presidency to General Edelmino Farrell in 1944.

Meanwhile, Colonel Juan Peron had been slowly developing political stature by using the labour unions as his power base. He began with a modest position in the government's labour department in 1943, and his reputation with the unions was established when he helped them to secure increased welfare benefits for their members including better vacations and retirement conditions. Within two years, his success brought him the vice-presidency and the post of minister of war. Despite what many regard as fascist tendencies, he was instrumental in securing a belated declaration of war against Germany. This may well have been an act of sheer political opportunism, but it did render Argentina *persona grata* with the United States, and enabled her to become a member of the United Nations. He also initiated a number of liberal policies, including the 'reconstruction' of political parties and the granting of autonomy to the universities (an interesting – and risky – move considering that students in Latin America have been traditionally associated with the Left, unlike those in Nazi Germany who were largely supporters of the Right). Unsurprisingly, these innovations generated demands for yet more liberalization. There were mass demonstrations, and the inevitable emergency measures were taken by the government. The military were necessarily involved, and a power struggle ensued. Peron's enemies secured both his removal from office and his arrest, but the labour unions came to the rescue and he was released within eight days. Now everything was reversed and his opponents were forced to resign instead. He set up a labour party that was fiercely opposed by the conservatives, and successfully contested the 1946 elections for the presidency. He won by a narrow majority, but significantly enlarged his share of the vote (65 per cent) during the next elections in 1951.

Once in power, Peron became increasingly authoritarian in his style of leadership. 'Unsuitable' people were removed from office and the posts filled with Peron appointees. Orientations changed. Certain areas of free enterprise were curtailed, and public services were nationalized. A greater financial priority was given to urban industrial workers from whom Peron drew his support rather than from the rural proletariat. The public were not greatly perturbed that the remnants of democracy – albeit not very efficient democracy – were gradually reduced, providing that the economy was in reasonably good shape and living standards were improving. But by 1949, the optimum point had been passed. Terms of trade worsened and inflation increased. There were new impositions, and although Peron was re-elected for the term 1952–58, he encountered more and more hostility among the laity. When this spread to the army, a successful coup was organized, and Peron was forced to resign in 1955 and went into exile.

There followed a succession of military and civilian governments which ruled with varying degrees of incompetence. Peron's party was dissolved and the labour unions were put under state control. But the Peronistas were still a force to be reckoned with, and in return for their support a successful radical candidate for the presidency, Arturo Frondizi (1958–62), readmitted them to the political arena. They had mixed fortunes for several years, and by 1970 they were so rent by schism that one group actually resorted to assassinating some of the leading members of another group. They had become divided into right and left wings, one of the key issues being whether they remained under military rule or whether they returned to a constitutional government.

During this whole period, Peron, still in exile, was working clandestinely with the Peronista organization for a possible return to political life. All sorts – perhaps any sort – of coalition or compromise were considered possible providing they enabled the Peronistas to get back into power. Their connivings finally paid off after they had managed to effect a deal with – of all people – the Radicals, in the 1973 elections. Once the coalition was in power, friction again inevitably developed between left and right. A left-wing president held office for only two months, and after a brief interim period, Peron was again elected president and took office together with his new wife, Isabel Martinez de Peron, in October 1973. He continued his purge of the left, with the police taking a heavy toll of its supporters, especially among highly politicized groups such as the unions and the students. Peron's new reign was, from the opposition's point of view, mercifully brief. He died in July 1974 and was succeeded by his wife with whom he shared the presidential ticket. The unrest and factional strife still did not cease; the economic situation was desperate, with inflation running riot at 600 per cent. The air force eventually became involved, and in 1976 yet another military government was installed. The economy was stabilized, inflation fell quite dramatically, foreign trade improved, but not without continued factional violence, in which some thousands were killed, imprisoned or just conveniently disappeared.

It has been argued that conservative governments such as Peron's depended on simple electoral fraud to give them a semblance of democracy (Silvert, 1963: 353–72) and that this was necessary where the bulk of the population was so ignorant that it was likely to vote against its own best interests. In totalitarian systems generally, leaders do tend to see themselves as vessels of superior truth and their parties merely as the agencies whereby they can gain power. Frondizi, for example, once in office, did an almost complete volte-face by abandoning his anti-clerical, anti-American stance despite his promises and his party's avowed policies. Really, the intention of totalitarian leaders is to do away with political parties in the commonly understood sense of the term because they cannot countenance any kind of effective opposition. Peron's government, like so many Latin American governments, was based on a combination of economic and military power. It was certainly a form of authoritarianism, but was it fascist? Or was it really a type of syndicalism consisting of a powerful ruling oligarchy legitimized by religious sanctions? It cannot be said that Peron was the complete revolutionary leader because he did not escape – if indeed he wanted to – from the limitations imposed by traditional cultural values.

The Argentinian situation differs significantly in emphasis from other recognized European fascist systems in that:

1. Its class support came from the lowest classes as opposed to the middle-class base, as in Italy, for example. Peron had his most serious tussles with the upper-middle-class land owners, industrialists and leaders of commerce. His appeal was of the populist variety.
2. Peron's power largely derived from the unions, whereas in European fascism attempts were made to reduce union influence or eradicate it altogether.
3. Disputably it did not rely as much on charismatic leadership, regardless of the considerable appeal of Juan and Eva Peron.
4. The ideology was there mainly to justify the leadership principle. When it was intellectualized as a grounding for the party's policies, it was seen to contravene traditional – especially religious – values, which eventually resulted in its breakdown.
5. Peron's government was largely based on militarism, whereas that of, say, Hitler, was established *despite* the full support of the military, which he always distrusted.
6. Race was not a factor of any importance to the state, although it was of some concern to members of the upper classes.

Peron's rule was certainly authoritarian and it employed something of the ideology and *style* of fascism, but arguably it was not fascist in the sense that it was not revolutionary in either the cultural or structural sense. It was unable to maintain unquestioned supremacy, because although it succeeded initially, perhaps due to its legacy of wartime prosperity, it just could not maintain the economic momentum. It was unable to go on producing the goods – the cardinal sin as far as the people were concerned. It eventually succumbed to a coup organized by yet another military junta which was supported by a good deal of public sentiment.

It remains to be asked to what extent Eva Peron was really influential during Juan Peron's first presidency. In recent years there has been a tendency to rewrite history and possibly give 'Evita' a more prominent place than she really deserves. Perhaps, in part, this is due to the disillusionment with Peron's second presidency, which was characterized by a much more aggressive conservatism. In contrast, Eva Peron's proclaimed concern for the poorest classes is rather simplistically reinterpreted as the only really worthwhile feature of Peronism. Add to this her rags to riches experience and her poignantly early death, and we have all the ingredients for a new cult of 'madonnaism'. But the myth is not the reality. When Peron was ousted for the first time three years after her death, the very people that had idolized her were shocked to discover the unbelievable wealth she had amassed at their expense. Tier after tier of shelves in the undamaged part of Peron's 'Pink Palace' were laden with millions of pounds' worth of jewels. Still in storage were 600 hats, 800 pairs of shoes (some hand-made from lizard and snakeskin, others studded with gems), 400 gowns (many of which were encrusted with diamonds), over a hundred fur coats of every description and hundreds of handbags. Much of it was presumably paid for by 'voluntary' contributions to the Eva Peron Social Aid Foundation, which she promised in her autobiography to keep in 'a crystal, transparent cash box, so that this clean money ... that comes from the hands of the workers, should never be tainted with the faintest shadow of suspicion' (Bruce, 1977: x, 238–40). As with the unlamented Marcos regime in the Philippines, the people had to be fleeced to pay for the senseless extravagances of the ruling family. The Perons had done much for the people: the ordinary worker had a better deal than before; women were enfranchised; the homeless were, on balance, better cared for; and public health – Eva Peron's special concern – was significantly improved. But as rulers they were ruthless, corrupt and vain. They had suppressed political liberty, put opponents in jail where they faced torture, robbed the poor of their money, and generally ruined the state – all, ostensibly, in the interests of reform and greater liberty for the people.

CHAPTER SIXTEEN

Religious Despotism: Messianism and Fundamentalism Islam

Messianism, the expectation of a chosen or appointed 'Deliverer' or 'Saviour', is by no means a new phenomenon. It can certainly be traced to the early history of Judaism, and possibly even further back to the idea of divine kingship which, in one form or another, was characteristic of many pre-industrial societies. It can still be seen today in certain kinds of political leader, and among various types of Adventist groups. Messianic expectation is usually most evident where the established values of a group or people are being threatened, or where a group or people need either to be reminded – about the singularity of their culture, as in the case of certain Semitic societies, or reassured about the purpose of their existence. The authority of the messiah, it is believed, will be based on charismatic appeal and on revelation as a fulfilment of the known tradition. It is when human aid fails that people tend to turn to the past for inspiration, and on this basis begin to imagine the possibilities of a utopian future. Discontentment gives way to longings for something better and the belief that this cannot actually happen unless it is initiated from a supernatural source. Even those leaders of avowed materialist intentions often claim (as Hitler) that they have providential support.

In many ways, the mission of the messiah is much like that of the prophet, and the conditions in which they appear are often very similar, but there are a number of features which distinguish them. Messiahs are less common than prophets, and tend to make their appearance not so much when the values of the group need to be reaffirmed as when the group itself faces the possibility of actual extinction. The threat of disintegration to certain Melanesian societies earlier this century, and especially in the aftermath of World War II, gave rise to a whole miscellany of prophet/messiah-based movements commonly known as Cargo Cults (Worsley, 1970). But the critical distinction between prophets and messiahs is that whereas the prophet claims to speak for the god(s), the messiah, by definition, claims to be a personal representative of the god(s), or may even purport to be a god himself, as, for example, Father Divine, who flourished among the Negro fraternity in the United States in the 1920s and 1930s.

Under what specific conditions, then, can the appearance of a prophet/messiah be expected?

1. *At times of religious innovation.* When, for example, in a conquest situation one people threatens to impose new patterns of belief and ritual on another, the prophet/messiah may appear to call the nation back to the old ways and remind them of their traditional beliefs. So Jeremiah in the sixth century BC feared that the Babylonian exile for many Jews after their defeat (586) would mean that they would adopt the new culture (which many of them did) and forget the customs of their forefathers. We are left with the impression that only a remnant kept the faith and returned to rebuild Jerusalem under their leaders Ezra and Nehemiah after the defeat of the Babylonians by the Persians in 539.

2. *At times of spiritual declension.* Religious decline is usually a situation which calls for a forceful reminder that it will not pay to go 'whoring after strange gods'. Again, the Hebrew prophets are a good example: Elijah, for instance, tried to persuade his countrymen not to be seduced by the attractions of the foreign cults that had been imported by Israel's King Ahab after his marriage to the Phoenician princess, Jezebel.

3. *At times of rapid social change.* This may be occasioned, as in (1), by the imposition of alien cultures. For example, it is rather interesting that although medicine men and shamen (holy men) were well known in American Indian cultures before the days of colonization, there were no religious practitioners of the prophet/messiah type until the arrival of the Europeans. Or, again, in the 1930s and 1940s with the development of the car industry in the US, southern Negroes, most of whom were simple Baptists by persuasion, found themselves in conflict with the ideas of those in the secularized north when they moved to Detroit in search of work. In these conditions, they 'produced' prophet-type people.

4. *At times of political instability and unrest.* Not uncommonly situations which threaten to cause the disintegration of a group or people will call for prophet/messiahs such as those which existed, for instance, in sixteenth- and seventeenth-century Europe in the post-Reformation period.

5. *At times of politico-religious persecution.* This follows naturally from (4), as instability gives rise to new movements of the initiated who are often led by a type of prophet/messiah. One has only to think of the many Jewish groups that grew up in the Middle Ages in Europe as forms of organized and sometimes disorganized protest against ill-treatment by the authorities.

6. *At times of nationalist resurgence.* There is little doubt that nationalism provides people with a sense of identity, and provides both inspiration and impetus for its search for goals.

7. *At times of economic depression.* This may not be a determinant, but it is often a *concomitant* of messianism. The Father Divine movement, at its height, claimed millions of adherents and flourished so well that eventually it owned millions of dollars of real estate and formed cooperatives ('heavens') for the deprived in the black communities of the United States.

8. *At times of racial conflict.* If we look at South Africa we find that not only have there been Bantu prophets, but that in more recent days the mantle of the messiah has passed to those with a strong politico-religious message. It is these people who have appealed to the masses and urged them to claim what they feel to be their rightful inheritance. Complementarily, leaders have emerged on the extreme Boer right who make similar claims, again in terms of a religious ideology.

We can see from this outline analysis that prophet/messiahs can appear on the social scene under all sorts of circumstances, although usually when there is a special need of some kind. The categories we have looked at obviously overlap in various ways, and it is evident from other sections of our discussion that many, if not most, of the despots we are considering have risen to prominence in circumstances which fall into one or more of these categories. Hitler, for instance, a messiah-type figure, would be a typical case in point.

Before we go on to explore our own particular interest here, perhaps we should look briefly at the messiah as a type. As we have already seen, the prophet/messiah has a *charismatic personality*. This much used – and abused – term usually denotes a kind of magnetism and the capacity to attract and retain followers. Contrary to some common beliefs, it is a non-moral quality and may be used for good or evil purposes. It is this quality which gives authentication to his *message*; this may not be original, but is part of a tradition which is revivified and proclaimed by the leader with renewed vigour. The prophet/messiah will be convinced that he has a *mandate* to declare these 'truths', and it is this that gives his message its unique *authority* (see Wach, 1945: 354). If this can be further validated in religious terms, it may be regarded as incontrovertible and therefore uncontestable by believers. An important point that needs to be made, however, is that the same conditions, the same focus of protest, may generate quite different kinds of response. It may be militant, as with, say, the Black Muslim movement in the United States popularly led by Malcolm X, who was later assassinated. Or it may be non-violent as with the contemporary Civil Rights movement originally led by the equally charismatic Martin Luther King, who was also assassinated. It should also be noted that the message may be concerned with the here and now, with urgent demands for radical change, or it may be otherworldly in that it anticipates some future spiritual state. The emphasis may be chiliastic insofar as demands the repudiation, even destruction, of the old order and the imposition of a new order (note the 1970s regime of Pol Pot in Cambodia). On the other hand, it may be eschatological, concentrating on eternal retribution for the wicked and the future rewards of the 'faithful'. In the words of Eric Hoffer, 'He [the prophet/messiah] articulates and justifies the resentment dammed up in the souls of the frustrated. He kindles the vision of a breathtaking future so as to justify the sacrifice of a transitory present' (Hoffer, 1960: 105).

Islam provides us with an excellent example of a politico-religious messianic movement, 'born of the desert' and founded in the classic charismatic tradition. Islamic lore has it that Mohammed was born about AD 570 in Mecca (Arabia) and raised by near relatives, his parents having died while he was still a child. As a young man he worked on the caravan routes, and is said to have married an older, wealthy woman who employed him. It may be that during his journeys to Damascus he could well have encountered various, possibly debased, forms of Judaeistic monotheism which influenced his later ideas. The history is a little hazy, and it is therefore difficult to know to what extent Mohammed, like so many other people whose early lives are little known but who became famous afterwards, such as, say, Gautama Buddha, has had certain biographical details 'supplied' for him. The story goes that he claimed to have had psychic experiences while still a young man, but that it wasn't until he was 40 when he repaired to a cave at Hira, near Mecca, where he habitually went for meditation, that he is said to have been visited by an angel in a dream who commanded him to proclaim the kindness of Allah. He convinced his family and friends of his 'call' to be a prophet, and their support sustained him when he went through an agonizing period of doubt and depression when the angelic visitations ceased. However, once they resumed, he was instructed to tell the people that they should abandon their animistic beliefs and practices because idolatory was iniquitous, and assure them that Allah (the all powerful) was the absolute sovereign deity. He was also to warn the people that hell was a reality but that the faithful would eventually be rewarded in paradise.

At first there was a very limited response, and Mohammed was only able to recruit a small body of believers who were largely ignored, even ridiculed, in Mecca. Hostility increased and he had to leave the area; he tried to set up in another town but, again, without success. It was at this very low point in his career that his fortunes began to change. He was now 50, his wife had died but he was hardly without marital comforts; he married another widow, and subsequently had seven other wives. In 622, he was able to establish a small religious community run on embryonic Islamic lines. Other monotheists could see nothing essentially new in his message, and some regarded him as something between an unprincipled charlatan and a misguided crank. However, he was gradually able to build up a thriving movement among what were originally polytheistic Arabs in the town of Medina, afterwards known as the 'city of the prophet'.

Strictly speaking, Islam was not a new religion; other contemporary monotheistic systems acknowledged this, and originally Mohammed recognized it too. It was really a sacred community dedicated to the will of Allah, and controlled by the authority of the chosen *interpreter* of that will, the Prophet himself. The problem with all revelation-based systems, is that they are always susceptible to greater or higher revelations, and this worked to the advantage of Islam. The early community developed as a kind of autocracy, and with the years this inevitably led to disputes about the matter of succession. Was it to be open to any possible candidates, and if so what criteria would determine the choice? Or should it be kept within the ruling hierarchy? Or, more restricting still, should it be confined to the leading family, that of the Prophet himself? It was this last dynastic solution which was finally settled upon, yet it cannot be said to have succeeded in averting future conflicts. The movement faced the further problem of just how it was going to be defended and extended. Thus, Islam took up the idea of the jihad, or holy war, which had already been a feature of earlier societies, especially Israel. In the very early days its policy was that conversion was to be by persuasion, but further (appropriate?) revelations condoned and even encouraged proselytization by violence. Hostile tribesmen who refused the opportunity to 'submit', first had to be subdued. As part of this policy an attack on the recalcitrant city of Mecca was planned especially to capture the sacred enclosure which housed the Black Stone (Ka'ba) that was believed to have important symbolic (magical?) properties. This stone, which was probably an ancient meteorite, was originally associated with idolatory but later became incorporated into the sacred impedimenta of Islam. Once Mecca was taken and its 360 idols of the Ka'ba destroyed, its townspeople surrendered to the Prophet and joined his forces. A law was then promulgated that never again should an unbeliever enter the Holy City now that it was consecrated to Islam.

The army of Islam was commanded by Mohammed's adopted son, Ali, and it was commissioned to go forth and make war on all unbelievers who were to be offered the choice between receiving Islam with the certain prospect of Paradise in the next life, or death by sword in this world and hell in the next. This understandably proved to be a potent recipe for making converts of conquered people who felt that they really had little alternative but to accept. Actually death did not necessarily follow refusal, and some conquered states, Egypt for example (639–42), were given extremely liberal terms. Instead, the non-Muslim inhabitants were required to pay a special tax which usually went to defray the costs of administering these new territories.

There were further battles, and every success was attributed to divine intervention. Where others would not heed the message, they had to be punished. Any thought guilty of obstruction or duplicity were summarily dealt with. So the Beni Koraidha, a Jewish tribe, were duly massacred after surrendering at their discretion. Seven hundred died under the eyes of the Prophet and their goods confiscated as the spoils of war. All this was believed to be in keeping with the new revelation which promised that just one night spent in arms availed more than two months of prayer and fasting. Sins would be forgiven, and at the Day of Judgment even lost limbs would be restored to those who had fought for the cause. This conception of jihad was wedded to a radical doctrine of predestination. The cause was a crusade, and whatever happened was fated to happen – it could not be avoided.

By 631, the entire Arabian peninsula was under Mohammed's control. Deputations came from outside the area for instruction in what many saw as a new and dynamic faith, and the Prophet sent missions to Egypt, Ethiopia and Persia (Iran) urging their conversion to Islam. He died in 632 having enfranchised his slaves and built the Great Mosque at Medina, and in general leaving a powerful organization that was determined to promote the interests of the faith. Mohammed did not leave any personal testimony; the holy book of Islam, the Qur'an (Koran), was put together after his death, and is purportedly based on his teaching.

The speed with which the Islamic empire was established was impressive. Within a hundred years of Mohammed's death most of the Near and Middle East had succumbed to the Muslim armies. The invasion of Europe (Spain) began in 711, and threatened to engulf France as well until the Muslims were repulsed by Charles Martel at Tours (732). This rapid expansion was not really facilitated by voluntary ideological conversion but by force of arms. Whether this meant that the Muslims were militarily superior, or whether it was that Islam imposed a greater discipline and therefore closer unity on its troops, is difficult to know. What is certain is that although expansion brought its own problems, it also brought many achievements, for wherever Islam triumphed it also developed particular cultural styles. This can be seen pre-eminently in architecture which, although influenced by the cultural conditions of the societies in question, displayed certain unique features. For example, one might compare the style that characterized the fabled 'golden age' of the Abbasid Harum-al-Rachid (785–809) and that found in Mogul India in the sixteenth and seventeenth centuries, exemplified by the Taj Mahal at Agra, built of white marble in the early seventeenth century by the ruthless Shah Jahan in memory of his dead wife. (Note that aesthetic taste and ruthlessness may go together – Shah Jahan killed his relatives at his accession.) In the sciences too, Islam showed the way in medicine and mathematics while Europe was still struggling out of the Dark Ages. It has to be admitted, however, that much had been anticipated by the Greeks, and even earlier by the Babylonians, and that Islam was to be overtaken by Europeans from the fifteenth century onwards.

Islam had its periods of retreat and resurgence: revival in the eleventh century with the successful battles of the Saracens against the Crusaders, but devastating defeats by the Mongols in the thirteenth century when the armies of Chingis Khan emerged from the Asian steppes to bring havoc and indescribable slaughter to the Muslim world. Then again revival, especially with the rise of the Ottoman empire of the Turks and their final subjugation of the remnants of the Eastern Roman empire situated at Byzantium (modern Istanbul) in 1453.

Inevitable power struggles arose between nationalist factions within Islam. (The main Muslims unaffected by these were those of the pietistic – almost monastic – sect of the Sufis which began with the ascetic Hassan al Basri in the eighth century, and still enjoys a limited popularity.) Sometimes power resided with the Caliphate in Baghdad (Iraq), sometimes with the Caliphate in Cairo (Egypt), and sometimes in Persia (Iran) depending upon which was the dominant dynasty at the time. These 'transfers' of authority were sometimes accompanied by assassinations (Ali himself was killed in a dispute over the succession) and even civil war. One of the main causes of friction was the division which existed between those who enjoyed very strict adherence to the teachings of the Qur'an (the Shias) and those whose policies and practices were more liberal (the Sunnis). This, in turn, was reflected in the changes in supremacy of different ruling houses, the Abbasids at first representing fundamentalist principles, and the Ummayads the more liberal position. But, with time, the Abbasids moved closer to the more relaxed interpretations of the Ummayads, allowing the Shias to become the main and most vigorous proponents of a fundamentalist Islam, a reputation which, despite varying fortunes, they retain to this day.

Any consideration of fundamentalism and what might broadly be called liberalism must rest on the interpretation of the traditional beliefs and practices of Islam. The basic institutional imperatives are neatly summarized in what are known as the 'five pillars of wisdom':

1. *The recital of the creed* (Kalima) is a confession of faith which in Islamic states has been traditionally proclaimed from the minaret by the Muezzin five times a day.
2. *The call to prayer*, which all Muslims are supposed to observe, is the recitation of verses from the Qur'an on the Holy Day (Friday), as well

as the prayer the Imam usually preaches at the local mosque at noon and at sunset. Attendance for males is obligatory; traditionally women were supposed to pray at home.

3. *Fasting* takes place especially during the month of Ramadan (that is, the ninth month of the lunar year) and is usually observed during the hours of daylight.

4. *Almsgiving*, which the law books specify should be 1/40th of annual revenue in money or in kind, is *not* to be seen as a tax but as a loan to Allah who will repay manyfold in good time. Other free-will offerings are regarded as a means of expiating offences, the money being customarily given to the needy and the destitute.

5. *Pilgrimage* (Haj) to Mecca is expected of the faithful at least once in a lifetime, finances and health permitting. The worshipper is expected to be in a state of ritual cleanliness, and to abstain from certain proscribed activities (sexual relations, for example) during the prescribed period.

To these might be added:

6. *Jihad* (holy war): here the distinction historically between pagans (polytheists) and other monotheists is not always clear. At times, the injunctions seem to have been addressed generally to unbelievers who must 'submit or die'. Despite the Qur'an's respect for other monotheistic traditions we find, for example, Mohammed's immediate successor, Abu Bekr, on the eve of the conquest of Syria, enjoining his troops to take the land out of the hands of infidels, to spare the women and children, to cut down the palm trees, fruit trees, corn, and so on (which will presumably cause the population to starve), and to cleave the shaven skulls of other (that is, monotheistic) priests. All survivors were to accept Islam or to pay tribute (tax).

    The last formal jihad was declared against the Allies in World War I by the Sultan of Turkey, a war that was notably unsuccessful. The modern activities of the Shia movement, especially in Iran, Israel and the Lebanon, undoubtedly constitute for them a contemporary form of holy war.

7. Certain prohibitions including a variety of *social practices* which are formally out-of-bounds to believers, such as drinking alcohol, gambling, eating pork, usury, and so on, and, of course, homicide, theft, adultery and so forth. It is well known that these prohibitions are not always observed, but much the same can be said of the adherents of other religions.

The military revolutionary nature of Islam has been evident in the various sectarian movements which have formed since its inception. We have only to glance, for example, at the Wahhabiyah Sect founded in the eighteenth century which arose in answer to Turkish oppression. It stressed the need for a 'pure' Muslim state based on a literal interpretation of the Qur'an and the Hadith (the corpus of extra-canonical deeds and sayings attributed to Mohammed which, with the Qur'an, are regarded as authoritative sources of moral and ritual law), and was eventually responsible for creating the kingdom of Saudi Arabia. Notable movements have arisen throughout Islamic history proclaiming the advent or imminent advent of al-Mahdi, the guided one, who would enable Islam to deal with oppressors and restore justice and ritual observance. The Shia movement believes that its 12th Imam (spiritual leader) in the ninth century will return shortly before the end of the world for this very purpose. There have been a number of claimants to the title, perhaps the best known being the Sudanese Mohammed Ahmad who, after a religious experience, led an uprising against the Egyptian government in the last century. He captured Khartoum in 1885 after a long siege, but died the same year.

It should also be stated that there has been a persistent, but less well-known (certainly in the West), strand of pacificism running through Islamic history. It can be seen in the quietism and mysticism of the Sufi movement founded in the eighth century, and in the interestingly heretical Baha'i faith which has been prohibited in some countries, Indonesia, for example, and persecuted by orthodox Muslims in others, Iran, for instance, where it was founded in the last century. Baha'i, which against strong Muslim feeling has its headquarters in Haifa in Israel, teaches world brotherhood and the abolition of all prejudice. The very fact that it calls for a universal faith puts it quite beyond the pale of any kind of fundamentalist or even liberal Islam.

Modern militancy within Islam can probably best be traced to the foundation of the Muslim Brotherhood in 1928 by Hassan al Banna, a teacher from Ismailia, then in the British Suez Canal zone. It began as a youth club with strong Islamic overtones at a time of increasing secularism in Egyptian intellectual circles. It gave its moral support to Egypt in 1936 at the time of militant protests over the Anglo-Egyptian Treaty which coincided – perhaps by design – with an armed Arab uprising in what was then Palestine. In 1939 the Brotherhood formally became a political organization with unambiguous Islamic credentials. It espoused Islam as a total ideology which offered 'an all-powerful system to regulate every detail of the political, economic, social and cultural life of believers' (Hiro, 1988: 61). By 1940, the Brotherhood had 500 branches, each with its own educational centre, with its headquarters in Cairo. Branches also gave military training to prepare its younger members for the jihad that was intended to liberate Egypt and other Islamic states from Western domination. Hiro (1988: 62) makes the point that Egyptians were made particularly aware of their subservience in 1940–42 when British and Commonwealth troops were in their country in force preparing to counter the threat from Rommel's Afrika Corps. Indeed, it could be inferred that some Egyptians, at least, looked forward to an Allied defeat, a fact confirmed by post-war indications that some Nazis made their way to Egypt as a haven of anti-British and anti-Semitic sentiment. However, it should not be overlooked that although the British had extensive interests in the Middle East at this time – in Egypt (and Suez), Israel, the Gulf and Iran in particular – there was also the domination of the French Vichy regime in Muslim Syria, Tunisia and Algeria, and the none-too-liberal Italian fascist regime in Muslim Libya (Mack Smith, 1979).

The Brotherhood drew people of all classes and professions into its ranks, and it was especially well supported by students. Members were encouraged to become more fervent Muslims, to conduct their lives in keeping with the teaching of the Qur'an, and to raise the Islamic consciousness of their fellows in order to reawaken their sense of nationhood. Their ranks swelled, and by 1946 they had some half million members in 5,000 branches, all ostensibly dedicated to the cause, and all – according to their slogan – prepared to die for the faith. After the war, anti-British sentiment became more pronounced. Some members joined their compatriots in the fateful Arab-Israeli war. (Hiro, somewhat one-sidedly, blames lack of essential supplies, obsolete British equipment and upper echelon corruption for this defeat, but fails to give due recognition to the skill of the numerically disadvantaged Israeli forces who were not particularly well equipped at this time themselves.)

It was not long before the Brotherhood outgrew its official acceptability. Its continuing agitation against the Egyptian government and its recourse to terror and subversion led to its proscription, whereupon a member assassinated the prime minister. The government countered by becoming more oppressive, and arranging for its agents to kill the Brotherhood's leader. The Brotherhood was still seen as a predominantly religious organization, and the ban on its activities was rescinded in 1950. But once free from official disapprobation, it resumed its political stance and, together with a number of Army officers, played a significant part in organizing anti-British riots and later the coup that overthrew the Egyptian monarchy in 1952. This brought the military to power, firstly under Brigadier Neguib and then his much better-known successor, Colonel Abdul Nasser (1953).

From now on all political parties were banned, but the Brotherhood, again because it was regarded as first and foremost a religious 'club' and no doubt because of its valuable contribution to the coup, was allowed to continue and even offered seats in the cabinet, which it declined. Once in power, however, the military junta were slow to implement the Sharia (divine law) which was the aim of the Brotherhood. They were quick to introduce changes, but not the kind of changes that the Brotherhood had in mind. It was not looking for rapid modernization, it did not want to ape the industrialized nations, and it certainly did not approve of Nasser's cupboard-love courtship of the Soviet Union whose materialist ideology was anathema to its religious principles. The Brotherhood looked for an Islamic theocracy, but it was obviously not going to be realized in the current, increasingly secularized, Egyptian society. As far as the Brotherhood were concerned, the revolution had betrayed its promise, so subversive activity started all over again.

Assassination attempts were met with harsh government reprisals. Some members were executed and more than 4,000 were imprisoned; others escaped the proscriptions by seeking refuge in neighbouring Arab states (1954). Some diversion was supplied by the Suez crisis two years later from which Nasser, whom the West saw as a kind of petty Hitler, emerged with increased authority in the Middle East. This was not to the Brotherhood's advantage, and its fortunes began to fluctuate considerably. There was an amnesty in 1964, perhaps because Nasser wanted its cooperation now that he had fallen out with the Soviets. But it was only a temporary respite. It resumed its anti-government subversion, and there were more executions among its leaders and more imprisonments among the rank and file (1966). Such punitive measures were acceptable by society at large because the public were not primarily worried about ideology, they were more concerned about poor material conditions. So as long as Nasser continued to produce the goods, whatever he did was optimistically regarded as necessary. But the situation changed after the disastrous defeat in the Arab-Israeli war (1967). This brought total humiliation to the military which this time was well supplied with modern equipment, and severe embarrassment to a government which had promised the extinction of its enemies. A year later, Nasser again released his Brotherhood prisoners; he now needed all the help he could get.

After Nasser's death in 1970, the presidency passed to Anwar Sadat who had maintained strong links with the Brotherhood for many years. There is every reason to believe that Sadat was personally devout, and that he intended to apply Islamic ideals to the government of the country. There was an amnesty for Brotherhood prisoners and the issuing of clear directives that Islamic practices would be encouraged and Islamic associations established wherever possible. Yet another holy war was initiated against Israel by Egypt and Syria in 1973 in which the coalition if not actually successful, nevertheless acquitted itself well enough to force a stalemate. The fundamentalists saw this as evidence of divine blessing, and some felt inspired to take the matter further. More extreme groups wanted actually to overthrow the already strongly oriented Islamic regime and set up a 'true' Islamic state. Their initial efforts at a coup proved to be abortive, but they still survived as underground organizations. One such group, the Muslim Society, founded by Shukri Mustafa, actually advocated both military and spatial separation from what it saw as an infidel-influenced society. Its secret cells engaged in numerous acts of violence. When there was a concerted clampdown by the security forces, some hundreds were arrested and tried by military courts and five of its leaders, including Shukri, were executed (1977).

The Brotherhood, now divided into moderate and extremist factions, continued to flourish, especially as a bastion against what it saw as atheistic Marxism on the one hand and Western secularism on the other. The truth is that the Arab states affected to despise Western materialism while welcoming Western aid and technological know-how. The presence of atheistic elements, especially in the administration, caused profound disquiet in government circles, and this, combined with the desire to conciliate the fundamentalists, prompted serious discussion about new legislation which would bring the government fully into line with the Shira (divine law), even to the point of considering a presidential decree in 1977 specifying the death penalty for those who renounced Islam. Such ideas were only abandoned after serious protests from the Coptic Church.

Economic conditions in Egypt deteriorated under Sadat's rule. The rich became richer and, if anything, the poor were worse off than ever. This alienated the general public, but the crisis that gave added impetus to Islamic fundamentalism was undoubtedly President Sadat's rapprochement with Israel. For many Muslims, this was a denial of everything they had worked for and everything they hoped to achieve and inspired vociferous demonstrations when the peace treaty was finally signed in 1979. The Brotherhood took on a new lease of life, especially among the more idealistic student fraternity, and by the late 1970s had taken control of most Islamic Associations. Despite Sadat's attempts to pacify the fundamentalists, for instance by making religious instruction compulsory in the universities, his position became increasingly insecure, particularly when he failed to respond to the plight of the Lebanese who were now locked in a seemingly intractable internecine struggle. In 1982, in desperation, he ordered the arrest of some 2,000 dissidents and instructed that all religious organizations (including the mosques) together with their functionaries must register with the state. The military was purged of suspected dissidents and councils were set up to ensure that disciplinary action would be taken against any students or government officials who were regarded as subversive.

It is perhaps unsurprising that in this volatile climate Sadat and seven of his subordinates were assassinated during a military parade by the very soldiers he trusted to help stabilize the situation. The murder was carried out by extreme Islamic fundamentalists of the Al Jihad organization. There were other eruptions of Islamic discontentment elsewhere, but none of these – not even the assassinations – was enough to arouse public sentiment in the way that the perpetrators had hoped. A new moderate president, Mubarak, was sworn in, and within a few days he had imprisoned some 3,000 extremists. Many recanted and were eventually released, although Mubarak had the assassins executed, an act which caused some disquiet in parts of the Arab world. Al Jihad, which had not come to light until 1978, believed that it had the necessary spiritual imprimatur for its actions; it taught that armed struggle was the true vocation of the earnest Muslim whose solemn task was to rid Arab lands of infidels and compromised rulers. The ideology of Al Jihad was particularly worrying to the authorities because it enjoined not only a return to the 'purity' of Islamic traditions but also encouraged a *permanent* holy war until this task was accomplished – a policy which implied ongoing instability for the states concerned.

Despite – or perhaps because of – the fairly relaxed regime in Egypt, fundamentalism flourished, presumably inspired by the extremist takeover in Iran. By 1986, the universities, which in the West tend to be havens of liberal tradition, were in the grip of fundamentalist student unions who were 'pressuring [the] university authorities to bring the curricula and textbooks into line with Islamic precepts and enforce sexual segregation' (Hiro, 1988: 83). Fundamentalism also permeated certain commercial organizations, giving it an independent economic base. Legal institutions were also influenced and – most distressing for the authorities – the intelligence services and the military as well. The police, the bulwark of any authoritarian regime, also appear to have been affected. In 1986, the Brotherhood rioted, ostensibly against corruption and luxury, causing damage estimated at some half a billion dollars. Such violence did the Brotherhood's image little harm as far as the people themselves were concerned. Persecution by the authorities generates sympathy and is regarded as the typical response of an unheeding, repressive regime. The Brotherhood is still a potent force in the Islamic world and, if anything, fundamentalism is on the increase in its clamour for the institutionalization of the Sharia (see World News, *Sunday Times*, 27 June 1993).

The failure of the Egyptian government to control inflation, check unemployment, and reduce the enormous national debt, has forced more and more people to look for other solutions to their problems. Disillusionment with Western models and uncertain dependence on Western money, have encouraged them to trace an atavistic path back to the old and trusted ideology, Islam. Similar patterns can be seen in other Muslim countries, where in one form or another (clandestine or otherwise) the fundamentalists form various organizations and have their own particular 'creative interpretation' (ijtihad) of the divine law. Nowhere is this better seen than in Iran, the Islamic state *par excellence*. Here, in the 1970s, was the ideal combination for a dynamic form of the traditional ideology: a charismatic leader, Khomeini, who directed the people from his sanctuary abroad with the promise of a messianic return; an independent economic base (oil) which freed the country from Western domination; and a clear objective, the overthrow of the despised, westernized regime of the Shah and the transformation of Iran into the idealized, theocratic state. Such a state, in order to achieve the correct degree of 'purity', is itself necessarily repressive – at least by Western standards. In addition to a whole host of restrictions, any attempt to undermine the state or 'spread corruption' is likely to merit capital punishment, and several thousand deaths have been reported of those hostile to the regime. Nevertheless, Iranian revolutionary practice is undoubtedly proving to be the inspiration for similar movements throughout the Islamic world. But how they will successfully settle their own internal, sectarian differences, especially the aims of humanitarian Sufism with the claims of secularized Sunnism and the militant clamour of the Shias, remains to be seen.

CHAPTER SEVENTEEN

Military Despotism: Uganda and the Rule of Idi Amin

It is something of a truism to say that a great many despots have emanated from the ranks of the military. It is already evident from our foregoing discussion that it is pre-eminently the military and its leaders who have the means at hand to effect the necessary takeovers of power and establish control of an autocratic or oligarchic kind. Nowhere in the modern world can this be seen more clearly than in some of the decolonized states in Africa. We need only think of the experiences of Nigeria, Ghana, Malawi and the Central African Republic under Bokassa; but perhaps the most tragic case of all is that of Uganda during the 'reign' of its self-styled liberator, Idi Amin Dada, from 1971 until 1979.

Despotism in developed societies such as Italy and Germany in the 1930s ran a quite different course from the decolonized territories after World War II. In some respects, European fascism was an attempt to put the clock back; an experiment in de-modernization − not technologically, of course, but in terms of its social ideologies and institutional arrangements. In contrast, the decolonized states were in their own ways attempting to adopt Western ways while at the same time trying to retain certain aspects of their traditional cultures. This desire to reconcile modernity and traditionalism often created insuperable problems. The right balance was difficult to achieve, and this asymmetricality became one of the necessary pre-conditions for the emergence of autocracy.

Pre-colonial Uganda had a well-established tradition of despotism (Chapter 3). The Kabaka, the tribal head of the Baganda, Mutesa I, shocked early explorers (already quite used to human brutality) by his many acts of calculated cruelty. At his accession, his brothers − his rivals − were burned to death, and many slaves were ceremonially mutilated. He deployed a huge army for slave-raiding forays to satisfy the demands of Arab traders, and at his court at Rubaga death was a daily occurrence. Everyone was at the mercy of his arbitrary whims, and even courtiers and headmen went in fear of his displeasure. His control was so absolute that chaos and civil war reigned when he died. The hegemony of the Baganda over the neighbouring tribes was challenged, especially by the Bunyoro and the Acholi, a situation that is now more-or-less resolved but which was still a key issue during the Amin era. The territory of the Baganda became a British Protectorate in 1894, and gradually the British also took over other Nilotic tribes to the north, vying with the Germans and the French who were also seizing lands in East and Central Africa. Missions were opened, enslaving was prohibited, industries were developed to exploit the country's natural resources, particularly cotton, coffee and copper, and a vital railway was built using imported Asian workers.

This slow process of westernization had mixed results. The growers of the cotton and coffee had little control over its production and distribution; this was left largely to the government, which worked mainly through Asian middlemen who became disproportionately represented in the retail trade. Their prosperity increased relative to that of the native Ugandans, a disparity that eventually made for considerable ill-feeling. An uneasy unity was established, and in 1962 Uganda became an independent state within the British Commonwealth. In the following year, as was perhaps to be expected, Uganda was declared a republic under the premiership of Milton Obote of the Acholi. This resulted in the anomalous situation of a republic which also had a king – a situation that was made for difficulties. In 1958, Obote had formed the Uganda People's Congress, which opposed both the Democratic Party and the supremacy of the Baganda and their king in Ugandan affairs. Consequently, once in power, the friction between Obote's party and the supporters of the current Kabaka, Mutesa II (popularly known as 'King Freddie') came to a head. In 1966 Obote, who held the effective power, overthrew the Kabaka with the aid of the military, and he called on Colonel Idi Amin who had just been appointed Army Chief of Staff to besiege and then shell the Kabaka's palace. Amidst the furore and the bloodshed, the Kabaka escaped to Burundi and then to Britain where he died in near poverty in 1969, possibly of alcoholic poisoning.

Obote took the Kabaka's place as president of the republic, and thence began a regime of 'moderate' repression; arrests were ordered, and from 1969 Uganda became a one-party state. For a while at least, Obote – who often went in fear of his life – came to rely on Amin and the military to keep him in power, but he soon came to realize that the servant wanted to become the master. He survived several assassination attempts, in one of which he was seriously wounded. Important people began to ask what Amin was doing about it, and he was accused of neglect and desertion by his deputy, Brigadier Okoya. Amin, typically, could not allow this kind of allegation to reach an enquiry stage, so Okoya was mysteriously murdered on the porch of his house one night, and the assailants then took the added precaution of entering the house and killing his wife.

Under Obote's rule, Uganda's economy began to look up with an increase in GNP of some 10 per cent per year. But at the same time, there was still considerable unemployment, higher taxes, and corruption and exploitation in high places. As people became increasingly disillusioned with the government, so Obote became disillusioned with his protégé. A great deal of money had gone missing from Defence funds, and Okoya's murder had still not been cleared up to the president's satisfaction. Obote began to groom others to take over key places in the Army structure, and planned to replace Amin while he was abroad. But Amin anticipated him. The president had not appreciated the considerable amount of support that Amin had among the soldiers, and before he could effect Amin's arrest, the tables were turned. Amin's troops took over the armouries, rounded up as many of Obote's men as they could find, and encouraged the populace to think that their day of liberation was at hand. Obote fled to Tanzania and vowed one day he would return and deal with the usurper.

Amin began his rule in true despotic fashion. To justify his accession he began a systematic denigration of the previous government in general and Obote in particular. They were accused of wholesale corruption and mismanagement, and he promised that henceforth things were going to be different. There was going to be honest trading, free elections, and a new era of peace and prosperity. He said that he wanted nothing better than a spirit of international brotherhood both within the Ugandan federation of tribes and with the world at large. As a sign of goodwill, the body of the old Kabaka was brought back for a ceremonial burial and the Kabaka's young son, Ronnie Mutebe, was also allowed to return to a royal welcome, although later Amin made it quite clear that there was to be no restoration of the monarchy despite a petition from the tribal elders. The people rejoiced, many political prisoners were set free (it was said that in 70 years of colonial rule the British had detained 35; in just nine years Obote had detained 4,000), and Amin pledged that in future Uganda would be subject to the rule of law. However, it was emphasized that these things would take time and that therefore certain freedoms, such as the right to hold rallies and to participate in other political activities, were to be suspended for the time being – just until the new government had got everything under control.

Hardly had these resounding proclamations been made when the purges began. Within three weeks of Amin taking office in January 1971, it is estimated that 70 Army officers and over 2,000 men died; and within three months, elections were cancelled, the prisons were again fully occupied, and some 10,000 civilians were slaughtered, many of them Obote's men (Kamau and Cameron, 1979: 53–54). Troops were empowered to arrest merely on suspicion and any hint of resistance was ruthlessly dealt with by specially recruited extermination squads, known rather ironically as Public Safety Units, who had their HQ just outside Kampala's city centre. Interrogations and torture were carried out at a number of sites, but principally here and at the barracks of the secret police, euphemistically called the State Research Bureau. The killings themselves were often neither quick nor clinical. Victims were either bayoneted or their limbs and skulls were crushed with hammers and old car axles; they were usually only shot when they took too long to die. The corpses were then either buried in forests or, when the killers were not too particular, thrown into the river for the crocodiles. When two Americans tried to investigate the rumours that were current about the killings, they too were murdered by their military escort, their bodies burned and their ashes cast into the river.

Idi Amin had come a long way from the days when he was a dutiful but uninspiring private in the King's African Rifles. He had been rather brutal at times with those he had to punish, and there was, of course, that incident concerning Private Adaka, who was going to report some of Amin's suspect tactics to his superiors but who had died somewhat suspiciously while on patrol ... But that was all in the past. Now, as the military dictator of a Commonwealth state, he was about to be feted by the British (who distrusted Obote but had wanted his cooperation) and by the Israelis from whom he needed arms. He no doubt pondered his good fortune. It had taken seven years for him to make it to Lance Corporal. He was a willing if semi-literate functionary whom one officer described as 'having not much grey matter, but a splendid chap to have about' (Kamau and Cameron, *ibid.*: 31). Promotions had followed, and when he at last became a captain he was sent on a Commanding Officer's course in England and a parachuting course in Israel, neither of which he actually completed; he had learned to kill rustlers and Mau Mau with impunity, but he apparently refused even to make one parachute jump. Did it matter? Now that he was in charge he could assume what rank or what decorations he pleased, so he began to promote his image with a kind of self-conscious theatricality.

On this overseas tour, he gave the impression to the notables he met that Uganda needed a breathing space in which to recover from the ravages of the previous regime – which, in part, was true – and that it would therefore be helpful if the payment of any outstanding debts could be accordingly delayed. Uganda, he stressed, was surrounded by actual and potential enemies who wished her harm – which, at first, was patently untrue – and that security, recuperation and development were his main aims. So if his hosts could spare more armaments and perhaps extend the loans, he would be most grateful. They might well have guessed that it was all an act. Actually, the potential aggressor was Amin himself. His neighbours, Kenya and Tanzania, had adopted a watching brief policy; true, they were apprehensive, but they were prepared to wait and see just how Amin's rule would affect them. Generally speaking, this was also the attitude of other interested parties such as the British and the Soviets; for the time being, they were prepared to give Amin the benefit of the doubt. Certainly for the first year, the Europeans seemed to have no idea what was actually taking place in Uganda.

Uganda's economy, ostensibly one of the dictator's priorities, began to suffer. Exports of cotton and coffee declined, the lucrative tourist industry all but dried up, although government spending on such items as a new conference centre and luxury hotels still went ahead. Amin had to keep the Army sweet, and the military budget increased five-fold to $100 million, a vast drain on an already depleted treasury. The economy was not helped by Amin's policy of Africanization which, to be fair, was not peculiar to Uganda. Getting rid of Europeans, including clergy, and the majority of the Asians was a body blow to the country's commercial activities. The considerable Asian community, which was very much involved in the wholesale and retail trades, found its members subjected to a campaign of vilification and many were accused of business and professional mal-practice. Consequently, their citizenship rights were withdrawn and they were forced to abandon their livelihoods and leave the country within 90 days: an act for which Amin claimed religious sanctions. Not only was the economy affected, the expulsion of the Asians also affected schools (700 Asian teachers left), university staff and hospital staff, and depleted the number of skilled artisans. The victims of this arbitrary, heartless and – as it turned out – imprudent policy, lost many of their possessions and forfeited much of their cash, despite Amin's promises that they would be recompensed. They were also the butt of much physical abuse; before they could get away, numbers of girls were sexually assaulted, and some people were attacked and even killed.

The next object of Amin's attentions was the Israelis; being a Muslim, there was a 'natural' antipathy to Jews. So, in his over-dramatic and oppor-tunistic way, he sought to curry favour with the oil-rich Arabs who could do him and his increasingly bankrupt country a power of good, and it was not long before Arab money was forthcoming and increased Arab trade was promised. Amin accused the Israelis of a plot to invade Uganda and overthrow his regime. He publicly approved Hitler's extermination of most of European Jewry, and commended the Palestinians for their slaughter of Israeli athletes at the 1972 Olympic games. None of this endeared him to the West, of course. In disgust, Britain stopped a £12 million loan, and the United States a $10 million loan. Amin retaliated by seizing British businesses and expelling a number of British subjects. For someone who usually needed all the help he could get, he was doing little to win friends and influence people. Those who at first had seen him as an outsized but amiable buffoon, now began to look at him in a different light, as a pre-tentious and dangerous despot. His many exaggerated speeches, rambling tirades which lacked consistency or any clear strategy, did possess a kind of primitive logic, which did much to influence the unwary.

As his power became more absolute and its exercise more despotic, so his pronouncements became more contradictory and his actions more ludicrous. He threatened to destroy the capital of Rwanda 'in a minute', promised to liberate South Africa, and had ready-made solutions for the struggling Heath government and the Ulster crisis. He did not attend the Commonwealth Conference because Queen Elizabeth II failed to send a jet for him and the Secretary General had not supplied him with a pair of suitable size 13 shoes; then – to top it all – he presented himself with eight medals for very distinguished service which had obviously escaped everyone else's attention. From a Ugandan point of view, his only notable achievement was in ridding the country of 'subversives', both imaginary and actual, such as the ill-trained Obote-sponsored loyalists from Tanzania who carried out an abortive invasion of Uganda. They were stopped in their tracks, and the Ugandan populace was treated to the first public executions for 50 years, a spectacle that would be rarely seen because as much as possible Amin's atrocities were carried out away from the public gaze.

In theory, Uganda was going to be given a semblance of popular government with an executive president as head of state, a prime minister and a deputy (all military appointments), a cabinet representing 21 government ministries, and a national forum. Provincial administration was to be carried out by the traditional array of district commissioners, chiefs and head-men. But it didn't get beyond a plan. In practice, Amin ruled by decree as Head of State, operating through a mainly military Defence Council. The National Forum, which would have introduced at least an element of democracy was judged to be 'superfluous' in the circumstances. Regional administration became the task of senior Army officers aided by additional Army personnel. Amin hired and fired as he pleased, and administrative efficiency became a thing of the past. People of ability who questioned government policy were either summarily dismissed or resigned. Failing this, they just disappeared. No one was safe. Government officials, business executives, media controllers, even the husbands of women whom Amin and his cronies coveted – all were liable to be visited by the executioners. As is so common in autocratically governed states, nepotism was rife. Loyalty to the despot can pay rich dividends, and Uganda was no exception. But, as our discussion has already shown, the extreme capriciousness that attends despotic rule often means that a person could be a friend today and a corpse tomorrow.

Amin's behaviour became ever more erratic. Even his own doctor, Head of the Department of Medicine at Makerere University, had to flee after a tip-off that he was about to be killed. It is possible that his death had been ordered because he knew too much. This might have been related to the fact that he had learned that Amin had been infected with syphilis, a disease that can result in a syndrome of grandiose paranoia. Amin would go through periods of extreme agitation and indecisiveness, even to the point of banishing his doctors and then later wanting to know where they were. To counter this, he was treated with anti-psychotic drugs, but apparently refused to take them regularly, with unpredictable consequences.

For all his abysmal knowledge of economics and social problems generally (he once ordered his finance minister to print more money if there wasn't enough), he knew what power was all about. He knew too that it could be fragile, so he salted away a fortune in Libya for the day when he might be forced to retire. But before this, he milked the state for all he could get – and other states too. He took money from sympathetic Arab countries to 'convert' Uganda into a true Muslim state even though only about 10 per cent of the population were followers of Islam. He saw himself as a kind of black messiah, a delusion no doubt later confirmed when he was successfully able to put down an attempted Army coup led by one of his Brigadiers. His religious 'crusade' resulted in the persecution of both Catholics and Protestants on the grounds that they constituted a kernel of opposition. With this went an attempted control of the legal system and the educational institutions which were largely staffed by non-Muslims. Military tribunals replaced local courts and were given carte blanche to dispense 'justice' as they pleased. Almost invariably this meant torture and often death for those who had the misfortune – and often the courage – to be arraigned before them.

Charges of genocide were brought against Amin's administration at a 1973 meeting of the Organization of African Unity (OAU), mainly by the previous president, Milton Obote. Some thought it was merely sour grapes and all grossly exaggerated, but others were not so sure. Characteristically, nothing was done, and Amin was vigorously supported by a delegation of black Americans who had been promised Ugandan citizenship and the gift of free land as resettlement for those who 'had been kidnapped by whites' – another promise, incidentally, which never materialized. Americans, in general, were less impressed by Amin's extravagant and specious statements, and after some provocation decided to withdraw their embassy. As far as Russia was concerned, Amin took a straightforward instrumental line. Although totally opposed to communism on ideological grounds, he, like so many rulers of self-proclaimed non-aligned states, was quite prepared to accept Soviet aid, especially in the form of armaments and military advisers. The Russians supplied military transport, including light tanks. They also sent MIG jet fighters, and Czechoslovakia provided the necessary pilot training. There was also military aid from China and France, all ostensibly for the 'liberation of Africa', but such a build-up caused understandable consternation among some of Uganda's neighbours.

By 1976, the inconsistent nature of Amin's behaviour became even more obvious. He divorced three of his four wives, one of whom was later killed in an accident, and tried to have another murdered. Meanwhile, the economy of the country was in a desperate state: industrial production had fallen, essential commodities were scarce, there was a serious down-turn in trade, public services had deteriorated, and inflation was running at 85 per cent. Yet Amin was still saying that all his countrymen could be millionaires, and blamed the shortages not on mismanagement but on exploitation and sabotage. With things getting worse by the week, Amin was ostentatiously offering aid to other countries including Britain – a gesture which, needless to say, never bore fruit. He worried about such trivia as the immodesty of girls in mini skirts, and then sensibly harangued students about the dangers of venereal disease, possibly on an unsubstantiated cause-and-effect basis. He outfitted units of his army in Scottish kilts and plastic sporrans (complete with a pipe band) for the benefit of visiting dignitaries. Later, he made a fool of himself at the UN General Assembly when he offered to lead an Egyptian army against Israel and, to show his earnestness, said that he would swim the Suez Canal. Harmlessly ludicrous as all this was, Amin had to be taken seriously, for beneath all the meaningless display was a pathological intent.

The tortures and the murders still went on, and rumours of these atrocities began to percolate to the outside world. Despite official statements and denials suspicions were rife. The media, the UN and even the OAU were becoming alarmed. Amin's reputation was such that when Uganda became the host country for an OAU conference only 19 of the 42 members were represented by their actual heads of state despite the enormous trouble that Amin took to prepare a sumptuous welcome, and for which he had promoted himself to Field-Marshal. There were greetings from the equally oppressive regime in China, and a commendation from the now discredited ex-UN secretary Kurt Waldheim. In the conference speeches there were the obligatory anti-Western diatribes interlaced with promises about the eventual 'liberation' of Africa; a great deal about the injustices of South Africa but nothing about those of Amin, and little about the rivalries within the member states themselves. Jonas Savimbi, the rebel leader of UNITA, was there fresh from his civil war in Angola, so was the ubiquitous Yasser Arafat, the leader of the fractious PLO, and General Gowan of Nigeria, who was actually ousted by a coup d'état while at the conference.

Of all Amin's considerable misjudgments, including demands for territory from Kenya and the Sudan, none was greater than the Entebbe incident. An Air France jet, Flight 139 from Tel Aviv to Paris, was hijacked by terrorists with Palestinian sympathies and diverted to Uganda where its 158 passengers, many of them Israelis, were hustled into an old, disused building and kept as hostages. The captors demanded the release of fellow Palestinians and others who were being held by different governments, many on capital charges. There was close cooperation between the hijackers and the Ugandans, which demonstrated that there had been some collusion between them before the operation had taken place. The terrorists threatened to destroy both the plane and the hostages unless their demands were met. The Israeli government stalled, the deadline was extended, and the terrorists ominously separated Jews from non-Jews and allowed the latter to leave. Meanwhile, the Israelis worked out details of a possible rescue mission on the assumption that the terrorists were in earnest about killing their captives. The Israelis discovered that the terminal building in which the hostages were being kept was not yet wired with explosives; this meant that they had a real chance of getting their fellow Jews out alive. They secured the cooperation of the Americans and the Kenyans, and after careful planning mounted a night-time raid on the airport and freed the hostages. The operation was carried out with daring and panache; the whole thing was over in 50 minutes and was considered an outstanding success, even by a grudging Amin. Only three hostages were killed and another three wounded in the mêlée. The cost to the captors was high. All seven terrorists were killed, together with 20 of the 70 Ugandan guards, and seven precious Ugandan MIGS were destroyed on the ground. The Israelis lost their commander, and five of their number were wounded.

It goes without saying that Amin had his revenge on those whom he held responsible for negligence or betrayal. He also had a 73-year-old sick Jewish woman killed, who had been a passenger but was left behind because she was in a Ugandan hospital. He mustered the support of friends in the OAU who condemned the raid but the UN saw fit not to censure Israel for what was generally regarded as a justifiable operation. Amin also decided to persecute Kenyans living in Uganda because of Kenya's complicity in the Entebbe raid. This was a ruthless and senseless hunting down of people who were in no way implicated in the Israeli attack. About 250 Kenyans were killed indiscriminately, and this heightened the tension between the two states.

Amin's ineptitude and his gratuitous cruelties eventually generated discontent among his own troops and though complaints were met with peremptory punishment, there were still several attempts on his life. Using the national emergency with Kenya as an excuse, he had some 1,200 soldiers and civil servants executed. Protests were quickly dealt with: dozens of students were shot by troops as they held a rally to question current policy. He also vented his spite on the Church because it too found that it had to voice objections to his regime. It is even rumoured that Amin lost his temper and shot the archbishop personally, then arranged for the death to be disguised as a road accident, a strategem which fooled few people, especially other bishops.

The reports of atrocities and the welter of indiscreet bombast that issued from Kampala eventually made Amin an embarrassment to the OAU and began to cause consternation among statesmen abroad. Sanctions were now deemed appropriate. He was told that he would not be welcome at the next Commonwealth Conference, especially when the International Commission of Jurists reported in 1977 that an estimated 80–90,000 people had been killed in Uganda in the first two years of his presidency and that the slaughter was still going on. Amin retaliated by placing restrictions on Britons living in Uganda and by executing one who had taken out Ugandan citizenship, but who admittedly was involved in a corruption scandal. Worst of all for the dictator were uprisings among his own people which were unconvincingly attributed to the subversive activities of Western agents. He took a terrible revenge, and more and more officials were hauled before military tribunals to await execution.

By 1978, Amin's reign was nearing its end. He had been too ruthless and had made too many rash moves to be accepted any longer as a responsible statesman. The Ugandan economy was now deteriorating rapidly, with inflation running at 700 per cent, and the government still continued to spend money it hadn't got. Exports were plummeting and some of Uganda's best customers, especially Britain, were having second thoughts about dealing with a dictator of Amin's kind. Then, as a proverbial last straw, Amin made a classic miscalculation. In October 1978, he ordered a strike force into Tanzania on the pretence that Tanzanian troops had attacked Uganda. At first, it was successful. The Tanzanians were unprepared for the onslaught of killing and looting that followed the invasion. Ugandan troops slaughtered hundreds of villagers and took what belongings they could find. Meanwhile, some home-based units of the Ugandan Army were restless and another revolt broke out, but the rebels were scattered and some 600 were executed. This was more than enough to galvanize Tanzania's president, Julius Nyerere, into action. He called for help from the OAU, but the organization was divided on the issue, and nothing was done. Nevertheless, Nyerere was determined to deal with Amin once and for all. He argued that Amin had murdered more people than the whites in either Rhodesia (Zimbabwe) or South Africa, and maintained that if Amin had been white, the African states would have had no hesitation in condemning him. The Tanzanians went on the offensive, and the exiled Milton Obote, waiting in the wings, implored Ugandans to overthrow their dictator. The following year, Amin canvassed his erstwhile sympathizers, Saudi Arabia and Libya for support; Saudi Arabia was unforthcoming, while Libya sent 3,000 troops but to little avail. By April 1979 it was all over. Resistance quickly crumbled, the people turned out the government, and the dictator fled. The Tanzanians and rebel Ugandans had triumphed against all expectation.

What the liberators found in Uganda was horrifying. Several thousand people were released from Uganda's notorious prisons, but massacres had taken place in anticipation of the arrival of the Tanzanians. Grenades had been thrown into some prisoners' cells; hundreds of other inmates, who were found chained together, had been tortured before they were killed.

The remnants of Amin's army retreated to remote areas of the country in a fruitless bid for freedom, still killing as they went. Their leader, the 'father' of their crimes was more fortunate. He and his family got away just in time and left their associates and rank-and-file perpetrators of those crimes to face the vengeful justice of a new regime. Not that this regime was anything like perfect. Tanzanian troops looted Kampala, and, after rigged elections, Milton Obote was again voted in as president. The result was more regional and tribal civil war, and further terrorism by undisciplined forces (see Johnson, 1983: 533–37).

In general terms, the Baganda had profited from the absorption of Western ideas and culture, but at independence (October 1962), it was the Acholi troops who were used by Obote to keep the Baganda and other Ugandan tribespeople in line, a factor which helped to build up a reservoir of discontentment with the Acholi. At this time the Uganda military was a small force, yet one that had seen service in Kenya during the Mau Mau emergency. It contained only nine Ugandan officers and approximately 1,000 men, all serving under white senior officers. There were problems over pay differentials despite Obote's promises, so that the officer corps was divided within itself. By January 1964 the divisions had become so bad that there were rumblings of mutiny, and British troops were imported from Kenya to deal with the situation. It was then that Amin, at this time a major, helped to quell the uprising (Gutteridge, 1969: 38). He was by now a seasoned campaigner, and his success in this situation may well have confirmed his hankering for power. His cruelty had long been evident, but it was only when he seized control of the military that it was given full rein. Once Amin was in power, his cruelty was directed towards particular categories of people: the Acholi and Lango tribes, some of whom were serving in his own army; Europeans, especially British and Americans; neo-colonial regimes such as South Africa and Rhodesia (a stance which brought him considerable support from the OAU); Catholics and, of course, Jews, whose persecution was calculated to find favour and financial backing from the Arab States. His executioners were largely drawn from his own Kakwa tribe and specially recruited Sudanese mercenaries, whom one-time Ugandan Minister of Justice Lule described as 'more vicious than anything dreamed of by European imperialists' (quoted by Kuper, 1981: 167).

Amin was not exactly atypical but, with the comparable exceptions of Bokassa and Papa Doc Duvalier of Haiti, was about the worst of a bad bunch in Africa. Still, anti-Western prejudice was such that one of the most scandalous aspects of the whole tragic episode was the lack of a timely response by the UN, including the OAU and many non-aligned states in general, even when presented with clear evidence about what was going on in Uganda. And, to date, it is one of these states that is still harbouring the fugitive dictator and his retinue.

Parvenu Despotism: the Case of Saddam Hussein

Since the takeover by the Ba'ath Party in Iraq in 1968 and the 'accession' of Saddam Hussein, the country has been subjected to a form of autocracy reminiscent of the medieval caliphs. In 1989, the US State Department Country Report on Human Rights concluded that execution preceded by torture was now the established Iraqi method of dealing with political and military opponents. And Amnesty International, on the basis of reports from released detainees, documented 30 different types of torture used by Iraqi interrogators, including burning with irons, burning the eyes with ultra-violet rays, mutilation, sanctions involving cutting off the penis, breasts, or hacking off limbs, and facial disfigurement, such as cutting off the nose and gouging out the eyes (*Observer*, 11 March 1990). Added to all this is the not unfamiliar charge of genocide. It is estimated that under Saddam's rule, some 200,000 Kurds have been killed either directly or indirectly through the poisoning of water supplies; this also includes – more ominously – perhaps as many as 4,000 villagers killed by chemical weapons. Yet despite all this, prior to the Gulf War, the Western allies were anxious to court the dictator, possibly because Iraq was the third largest oil exporter in the world. Saddam was offered huge loans by Britain and the US, who were both still pouring armaments into Iraq knowing that she was a menace to stability in the Middle East but hoping that she would remain a bulwark against the Islamic fundamentalism of neighbouring Iran.

Saddam had really come from nowhere. He was born in an obscure village in 1937 to an even more obscure family. His natural father is said to have died before Saddam was born, and it is added – perhaps by way of psychological exculpation – that his mother married again and that his step-father treated him particularly badly. He was brought up as part of a traditional Muslim, Sunni community (Sunnis comprise about 20 per cent of the Iraqi population), but Saddam, although affecting orthodoxy, has seemingly taken a purely instrumental attitude towards religion. When it suited him he could affect the attitudes of a suitably devout believer. But he is no religious idealogue; there is no question of religion taking precedence over political and military exigencies.

It would appear that from his early days he kept very questionable company, and that by the time he was in his teens he was little more than a small-time hoodlum. These things are now difficult to verify, especially as his reputation has gathered so much opprobrium, but some accounts of his formative years suggest that when he was in his early twenties he was already known as a useful assassin in the ranks of the Ba'ath Party, which was totally opposed to the then Iraqi monarchy, itself a legacy of British administration. The Ba'ath movement, which had been founded in 1954 by a Syrian schoolteacher, Michel Aflaq, was an unholy amalgam of socialism and fervent nationalism. Its object was to establish a dominant Arab state somewhat after the fashion of Egypt, whose Colonel Nasser had similar aspirations. And it was fairly obvious that given two states with hegemonic ambitions, the possibility of Arab unity was really a non-starter. The conception was laudable but the reality was a sure recipe for disaster.

The 1950s were a particularly turbulent time in Middle East politics. There were civil conflicts and rumblings of revolution in a number of Arab states and hints of possible Western intervention in the Lebanon, Jordan, and perhaps even Iraq. In 1958 a military coup in Iraq led to the murder of the royal family and the setting up of a republic. This was ruled by a Revolutionary Council under a military leader, Brigadier Qasim, and made all the customary promises about honouring pledges and treaties and working for Arab unity and social betterment. A fundamental problem for the new regime was how to reconcile its own undisguised bourgeois character with the left-wing sentiments of the people. There were stirrings of radicalism among large sections of the community. In less than a year there was an attempt by an army faction to force a union with Egypt, which was successfully thwarted. At the other end of the spectrum there was the unceasing restlessness of the ICP (Iraqi Communist Party). This was systematically suppressed, although there is no clear evidence that the ICP was actually planning a takeover. There seemed to be plots everywhere and the government became ever more suspicious and thus ever more immoderate in its demands. It took control of unions, dismissed 'unsound' employees, and curtailed freedom of assembly. Inevitably, this led to more trouble. The Ba'athists, who had no love whatever for the Communists, supported their efforts for social reform, partly to keep up the pressure on the government. An attempt was made on Qasim's life in which the young Saddam Hussein, who had joined the Ba'athists in 1957, was directly involved. It was incompetently bungled, and the conspirators had to wait until 1963 in order to carry out a successful coup, which in this case was marked by extensive bloodletting.

The Ba'athists set up a para-military National Guard which carried out arbitrary arrests and summary executions including those of Qasim and his aides. It is reported that there were 'at least 1,000 dead in Baghdad alone' (*Le Monde*, 14 February 1963, quoted by CARDRI, 1989: 31). Many of the old republican organizations were proscribed. These included trades unions, republican student organizations, and so on, which were replaced by fascist-type counterparts. Interrogation centres were established to sort out those suspected of anti-Ba'athist activities, and torture was commonplace in order to extract information about possible co-conspirators. It goes without saying that many of those arrested, including the First Secretary of the ICP, just disappeared and were never seen again. The new regime was virulently anti-Communist. Many Communists had suffered under Qasim's rule, and the Ba'athists made it quite clear that their plight could only get worse. They kept their promises, and in February 1963 Baghdad radio – ostensibly in the cause of Islam – called for the annihilation of the enemies of the regime, and perhaps as many as 5,000 Communists died in the purges. Despite this, the surviving members of the ICP still posed a very real threat to the government. This, plus the growing unpopularity of the new regime generally, gradually generated disenchantment even among the military that had helped to bring it to power, and it was toppled later in the year (November 1963) and its leaders arrested.

The new military government also had a strong nationalist flavour and broadly speaking wished to follow much the same lines as Nasser in Egypt, with whom the Ba'athists had come to disagree. Though not as repressive as the Ba'athists, the military still held many political prisoners, and were unsympathetic to the clamour for democratic reforms. Conditions in the country did not improve, and growing unemployment produced more and more discontent among the people. Furthermore the government was determined not to bow to Kurdish demands, which meant that warfare continued in the north against these tribesmen, who by this time had been reinforced with some contingents of refugee Communists. The general situation deteriorated to the point where there was another coup in July 1968 by a reinvigorated Ba'ath party.

The new Ba'ath government was not dissimilar from its 1963 predecessor, but it had learned a few lessons and this time took things a little more cautiously. By continuing its anti-Kurdish, anti-Communist policies it still alienated certain sections of the population, but at the same time it introduced a number of economic reforms which were undoubtedly well received. This way it was able astutely to divide the opposition. Gradually, however, the old leopard's spots began to show. The regime, under the ironic banner of 'popular democracy', suppressed all effective dissent by a combination of terror and intimidation. Yet, despite all this, its measures obviously had support, even to the point where the crowds chanted for more public executions.

Regardless of the running sore of the unresolved Kurdish question and the consequent drain on Iraq's military resources, the huge influx of cash after the oil crisis of 1974, and the rapprochement with Iraq over common borders in 1975 (negotiated by Saddam Hussein, at the time Iraq's vice-president), considerably improved the domestic image of Ba'ath and its leaders. Anything, therefore, that was seen as a threat to the state with its new-found wealth and its singular identity, was deemed worthy of punishment. Thus, the continued persecution of the Communists, 31 of whose members were executed in 1978, and any other bodies who presumed to question Ba'ath authority. In many ways, Ba'athism was the Arab counterpart of 1930s European fascism. It presented a socialist image, but it was a national socialist-type system with its reverence for the great leader, its monolithic structure, and the same atavistic desire to recapture something of the old unity and purpose of – in this case – a dominant, if highly secularized, Islam.

By only 1975 Iraq's annual oil income had risen from $500 million to £8,000 million. With all this wealth, both the public and private sectors expanded rapidly. It is estimated that by 1980 there were some 700 multi-millionaires, most of whom were officials and members of the Ba'ath party (CARDRI, *ibid.*, 47). Lucrative contracts for construction projects were agreed with the West, and luxury goods – so long at a premium in Iraq – began to flow into the country in exchange for oil. Not least of all, the cash surpluses were such that Iraq was able to buy Western technology, especially vast amounts of military hardware.

CARDRI (Committee Against Repression and for Democratic Rights in Iraq) would have us believe that regardless of this wealth the people were really dissatisfied and were still pleading for democratic reforms. It has an understandable antipathy to dictators, capitalists and the like, and obviously wants to believe that the 'people' – as Aristotle once argued – are the best judges of that which affects their own interests. But how true is this of Iraq? The evidence here and elsewhere is that by and large even autocrats are acceptable provided they are bringing home the goods. If anything, the evidence suggests that wealth and the benefits it provides effectively anaesthetizes most people against the demands of despotism, especially if they are largely untouched by its injustices. They can put up with restrictions and may even come to see them as justified. The cult of Saddam the leader and Field-Marshal, though without any army training or appreciable education, seems to bear witness to this. And injustices there are. Take the matter of education. Those who do not support the Party are 'overlooked' by the state if they apply for overseas scholarships; they find that they also fail to get places in Iraqi institutions of higher education. Teachers too who are not Ba'athists have had a difficult time, and a great many have been dismissed from their posts. But the fact that many too have emigrated shows that there is a limit to repression; in a thorough-going despotism such as, say, Stalin's, such a move would not have been allowed.

Iraq is a one-party state; Ba'athism does not permit its people to have any other political affiliations, and any previous ones have to be declared. In other words, the Party and the leader will brook no kind of opposition, all of which is by no means uncommon in autocratic systems. What is much more disturbing is the penalty for breaches of these regulations, which is, quite simply, death. Whether this is absolutely unequivocal and applied in all cases is unknown, but it is clear that a number of people have been executed for contraventions of this kind. Even members of the party have not been safe. When Saddam became president in 1979, the same year that the shah of Iran was deposed, he instituted a reign of terror in the upper echelons of government reminiscent of Stalin's purges in the 1930s, except that Stalin kept very much in the background, while Saddam unashamedly promoted himself as the invincible leader of the Party. At a specially convened meeting, long-standing members of the Party were required to read 'confessions' of how they had supported Syrian-inspired plots against the regime. Saddam is said to have had tears in his eyes as he condemned many of his erstwhile comrades to death (Darwish and Alexander, 1991: 210). Nevertheless, the purges went on for several days. Apparently, Saddam had six members of the Revolutionary Command Council and another six who had been charged with treason to make up a firing squad to execute those of the leadership who had been condemned. All this was done to the acclaim of the rest of those present; a video was made of the proceedings and distributed to those who were not there, just in case they had any ideas of their own. The complete death toll from the purges was something in excess of 500. It did not pay any longer to disagree with Saddam's stated policies. In fact, there were very few actual protests. People kept their heads down. The oil revenues increased, foreign reserves mounted, employment increased, and terrorism continued behind the guise of Big Brotherly munificence.

The war that Saddam unleashed on Iran in 1980 and which dragged on until 1988 was one of the most fiercely fought wars in recent history. The casualties were enormous. It is particularly infamous for Saddam's use of chemical weapons. The Americans had used defoliants in Vietnam, but from 1984 Saddam actually used nerve gas and mustard gas against the Iranians, and later, when the war was nearly over, he again resorted to gas against the Kurds, of whom, 5,000 are said to have died. No one profited from the war with Iran except those that supplied the armaments; from 1980 to 1986, France alone sold weaponry to the Iraqis costing around $16 billion. About a quarter of a million Iraqis were killed and another million wounded, and at the end of this pointless conflict Iraq had exhausted her reserves and was at least $80 billion in debt. Iran fared even worse. Its people had not long replaced one despot with another, this time the fundamentalist Ayatollah Khomeini, who, from the way he squandered Iranian youth, had Muslim martyrs to spare and lost about a million of them in heroic – but fruitless – mass attacks against the invaders.

The war has been described as a Pyrrhic victory for Saddam, but it was really a stalemate for both sides. Frustrated by this set-back, he reversed direction and increased his warring threats against Israel, a strategy that would perhaps reinstate him with the rest of the Arab world. But with the fall in the price of oil, he was forced to settle for smaller fry: Kuwait, the tiny oil-rich state to which he already owed a great deal of money. His invasion went smoothly and he was easily able to exploit a victory that was not to every Arab's liking. After the invasion, he wrote a remonstrative letter to one of his Muslim critics, Hosni Mubarak, the Egyptian president, asserting his superior status. He pointed out that Mubarak came from common stock while he, Saddam, was descended from the Prophet (Bulloch and Morris, 1991: 45) – an unverifiable and presumptuous claim that demonstrated that he had messianic pretensions as well as territorial aspirations. Kuwait really had no defence. It was all too easy for him. But this time he had miscalculated. He underestimated the determination of the Western allies and the coalition of Gulf States to protect their vital oil interests. In order to frustrate them he perpetrated the worst single assault made on the eco-system when in January 1991 he ordered the pumping of crude oil from tankers and the Sea Island terminal to the tune of some 8 million barrels. For Saddam, the war was not just about oil but domination of the Gulf and leadership of the Arab world.

The war was all over in a few days. Incomprehensibly, Saddam survived to vent his ire on the poor, wretched Kurds whom the world seems largely to have forgotten for the time being. Perhaps one day they will have a part to play, but it will only be in a much larger game.

Many people take the view that concessions to would-be dictators are fatal. Appeasement of the Munich variety only means that trouble is being stored up for another time. It is better, if at all possible, to stop despots in their tracks. This policy undoubtedly dictated the Western response to Iraqi aggression, although until the Gulf War the West had pursued an uncertain – arguably contradictory – policy towards Iraq. The Allies, for want of a better term, wanted to maintain a balance in the Middle East and especially to contain a volatile and unpredictable Iran. They also wanted to safeguard their economic interests, not only concerning oil, but also in the promotion of their all-purpose arms bazaar in the Middle East. There were voices in favour of compromise. After all, why jeopardize a very lucrative market? Opinion in the West was also clouded by differing perceptions of Saddam himself. He had taken a relatively inconsequential Arab state, and by manipulation of a small, unrepresentative political party, the Ba'ath, he had built up 'a mass movement which controlled every institution in the state according to his personal bidding' (Bulloch and Morris, *ibid.*, 180–81). He had also created a military and technocratic elite to organize the substantial forces which existed to further his policies. Thus, opinion was divided. Saddam was a good customer; but he was also consumed by an overweening ambition. For everyone's sake, not least the even better customers in the Gulf, he had to be stopped.

To date, he does not appear to have learned the lesson, and it could be argued rightly or wrongly that the Allies failed to carry the task through to its logical conclusion. Saddam is now repairing the harm done to his state and his reputation, and is almost certainly poised for further adventures.

CHAPTER EIGHTEEN

Syndicate Despotism: the Mafia

Despotism should not be regarded as the special preserve of large-scale or developed societies. As we saw in the introductory chapters, in any study of despotism it is important to distinguish between *intensive* and *extensive* factors. We noted too that when despots entertain a policy of untrammelled expansionism and try to exercise their authority over an extensive area, possibly involving many disparate peoples, their actual capacity to control may be considerably weakened. On the other hand, despots who wish to exert intensive control over relatively few people may find their task that much easier. This is the case with the capos (or 'bosses') who are the heads of the respective Mafia families to be found in the United States. In this study, we are going to concentrate on their period of most significant expansion, especially in New York, and try to get some idea of how Mafia 'law' constitutes an intimidating form of despotism when it is put into operation by particularly powerful family heads.

There is considerable doubt as to the origins of the term Mafia. It is almost certainly a Sicilian word which originally denoted someone who displayed the kind of courage and (for males) manliness that generates *respect* – a word much used among the cognoscenti. There are similar doubts about the origins of the movement. Mafia mythology has it that it derives from the resistance activity that developed in thirteenth-century Sicily when the island was ruled repressively by the French. In Palermo, in particular, the population rose against the French garrison and thousands died, including French civilians and even Sicilian women who had married French soldiers. We are just not sure whether a secret society was born at this time or not; some think it almost too romantic to be true. It is more likely that the modern Mafia derives from one or more of the movements that grew up during the time of Bourbon rule in the eighteenth and early nineteenth centuries. For much of their history, Sicilians have been subjected to foreign domination and occupation, and various societies have arisen in the cause of justice and liberation. But most of them always seem to have had some criminal dimension. As one authority put it: 'The societies developed the techniques of rural gangsterism, practised by mountain brigands for centuries, into a continuing system of retributive justice and organised criminal revenue' (Short, 1986: 17).

The particular feature that characterizes the Mafia, and which, in other forms, is also typical of many secret societies elsewhere, is the code of *omerta*, which effectively means silence. No member may admit, on pain of death, either that he belongs to such a society or even that such a society exists. Punishment can be swift and certain, even for such a highly placed mafioso as the late – if not lamented – Willi Moretti, who carelessly threatened to bring the organization to public notice. In the modern Mafia, variously termed the Syndicate, the Organization, the Outfit, the Mob or the Cosa Nostra ('our thing'), punishment has been extended to cover all sorts of other infringements. It is, for instance, a 'capital' crime to interfere with another member's women, including mother, sisters and daughters, besides a wife or mistress. Death will almost certainly result too from any attempt to cheat the organization. In 1947, the Mafia associate Ben (Bugsy) Seigal, who spent millions of dollars of the Mob's money in a prescient though, at the time, unsuccessful attempt to develop the casino industry in Las Vegas, was killed by assassins while sitting on a settee reading a newspaper in the house of his recent girlfriend (wife?). Few tears were shed for Seigal even though he was part of Hollywood's gangster chic. His death had obviously been ordered at the highest levels of the organization, possibly by his one-time equally lethal partner Meyer Lansky, who had become the economic brains behind its operations. As far as the police were concerned, it was good riddance to one more known killer who had already escaped justice more than once.

In its early days in the USA, the Mafia was still composed of Sicilians, and certainly high office in the organization was very strictly confined to those of Sicilian stock. Alphonse (Al) Capone, who was probably the greatest organizer of crime in his or any other era, and who very largely helped to develop and consolidate the organization in the States, particularly in Chicago, always wanted to be a capo mafioso but was ineligible because he was a Neopolitan (Sondern, 1961: 58). Capone arrived in Chicago as a penniless hoodlum and became the protégé of a Mafia boss, Johnny Torrio, who was not at all like the public's impression of a notorious capo. He was not dissolute, he neither drank nor smoked, nor seemed to have any other obvious vices, and to all appearances was an exemplary family man. But he was the Mafia's most thorough organizer of prostitution and liquor distribution in Chicago.

Capone learned quickly; by 1925 he was the millionaire czar of a huge criminal empire largely financed from the proceeds of bootlegging. His position was won at considerable cost: in a period of just five years there were over 500 gangster murders in Chicago alone, and no one was ever convicted of these crimes. If there were any witnesses they were either killed or they unaccountably disappeared. This was often the task of young aspiring mafiosi who became 'made men' by means of a simple blood ritual after they had proved themselves by carrying out one or more of these killings at the behest of their superiors. There were bitter rivalries between gangs, all vying for a more influential slice of the liquor industry.

It was the era of the one-way ride, of tit-for-tat gangland killings; of attacks on rival distilleries and bars with bombs, shotguns and machine guns. This finally culminated in the infamous St Valentine's Day massacre in 1929 – almost certainly engineered by Capone – when executioners posing as policemen lined members of a rival gang against a garage wall and mowed them down with Tommy guns (the Thompson machine gun nicknamed the 'Chicago piano'). This period effectively came to an end with the repeal of Prohibition and the conviction of Capone for income tax evasion – the only crime that could successfully be brought against him.

The Mafia diversified its operations. It still continued with the hijacking of alcohol for cheaper distribution, and with prostitution (which, inconsistently, rival Irish gangs wouldn't touch), and greatly expanded its interests in gambling and into union control and into legitimate businesses such as real estate, cheese and oil, and clothing. Its most controversial venture, with which, of course, it is still identified, was the importation and distribution of drugs – a market even more lucrative than booze. The competition – and therefore the killing – still continued, but not at such a frantic pace. In New York, the most powerful Mafia centre, there were serious differences between the older Mafia leaders who eschewed the drugs trade and wanted to continue with the traditional rackets which still generated considerable revenue, and those who wanted to concentrate on drugs. This was resolved by one of the most notorious capos, Salvatore Lucania (Charlie 'Lucky' Luciano), who after arranging the murder of his immediate superior in 1931 instituted a purge of those who opposed the new thinking within the Mob. He began the reorganization of the Mafia into a coordinated nationwide syndicate in association with other non-Sicilian mobsters. The whole country was effectively divided up and responsibilities allocated according to proven efficiency and Syndicate requirements (Cook, 1973: 69–70). There was to be mutual recognition and respect. All rivalries were to be resolved and random killings were to stop. All disputes were to be settled either by the capos or their deputies, or, in the case of problems arising at the highest levels, by the national commission (or council) of capos that met from time to time. Special personnel were delegated to deal with police and politicians; a huge slush fund was set aside to bribe the necessary officials. More monies were also allocated for the education of young, promising mafiosi as potential leaders of the organization.

In order to enforce its decisions and deal with the necessary elimination of informers, rivals or other sundry undesirables usually within or on the fringes of its own ranks, the organization set up its own rationalized killing machine, which was later dubbed Murder Incorporated, a group of professional executioners who murdered to order. The police had been aware of a spate of slayings for some time, but the public did not realize what was happening until one of the organization's killers, Abe Reles, was apprehended and decided to tell what he knew. This turned out to be a great deal, but Reles knew that once he 'sang', he had to get his superiors convicted or else his life would be worth absolutely nothing. From these interrogations, it transpired that this syndicate agency, which operated from coast to coast, was run by two key figures in the New York Mafia, Joe Adonis and Albert Anastasia, and was officially responsible for 63 homicides, and probably a great many more. Reles was personally involved in many of them. He had a good memory for dates, places and people; he just knew too much to be allowed to live. Consequently, despite what was supposed to be a vigilant round-the-clock police guard, he was found dead one morning in November 1941, having 'fallen' from a sixth floor window – an incident that has never been satisfactorily explained, though later an informer insisted that he had been thrown out. Without this key witness, the state was unable to indict the principals of Murder Incorporated, including Anastasia, its 'Lord High Executioner', although a few underlings were duly sent to the electric chair – possibly thrown to the authorities by the organization itself.

Luciano effectively ran the Syndicate until he was arrested in 1936 and convicted on 62 counts of running prostitutes. He was sent to prison for 30–50 years, which meant that his power was thus considerably reduced, but from his cell he was still able to get orders to his subordinates. Thomas Dewey, the man who had prosecuted him, also when Governor of New York, arranged his parole – yet another incident that has never been fully explained. The story goes that through his criminal connections, Luciano was able to render valuable services to the government during World War II by getting his subordinates to police the docks, presumably for saboteurs but also for hijackers intent on getting goods to the black market. It now seems incredible that the authorities should seek the help of such a notorious racketeer, whose merest word could bring the underworld to the aid of the state. But it happened, and was confirmed after the war by German Abwehr (Military Intelligence Service) agents who insisted that their men could do little at the docks either by way of sabotage (perhaps by American Nazi Bund members) or of gathering information. Furthermore, it is rumoured that Luciano also helped to 'facilitate' the US Army landings in Sicily in 1943 by enlisting the support of the island's mafiosi, though this has been seriously disputed by Mafia-watchers as highly improbable. Help certainly was received from the Sicilian Mafia, which had anyway been depleted by Mussolini's police, but it is hardly likely that the American capos would have been given privileged information about the proposed American invasion plans to the criminal fraternity (Sondern, 1961: 91).

Luciano's release on parole became effective in 1946, when it was decided to deport him to Italy. But barely a year later he was back in Cuba, staying at expensive hotels and tightening his hold on the narcotics trade. It is no coincidence that the first large consignments of drugs to the States were received at about this time. He moved around judiciously, even – so it is said – making clandestine trips to the States. All the time he was in constant touch with his American counterparts. The set-up was simple and carefully organized with the aid of a network of well-paid couriers who transported heroin from Italy, where the pharmaceutical industry was poorly administered, to the United States. With time, the Mafia image began to change. It invested heavily in legitimate businesses, but continued with its covert but highly lucrative extracurricular activities. It was no longer run by hoods with snap-brimmed trilbys and suspiciously bulging armpits, but by genial, middle-aged innocuous-looking gentlemen like Luciano who made it a practice to keep a low profile while making regular contributions to charity. These Mafia chieftains did not want too much attention – they just wanted to be allowed to continue with their profession of making vast profits out of ruined lives while remaining good American citizens.

In 1963, a 30-year veteran of the Mafia turned informer. Joseph Valachi, a self-confessed 'button man' (lower echelon killer) who was serving a 20-year sentence for drugs offences, was convinced that he too was earmarked for death by the Syndicate because they believed he had already given information to the authorities. Another prisoner *had* been ordered to kill him, and Valachi, not knowing who this was, unwittingly clubbed the wrong man to death. Partly out of remorse, and partly to secure protection, he decided to turn state's witness (Maas, 1970). What he told the US Senate Permanent Sub-Committee on Investigations clarified their ideas about Mafia organization and activities. He confirmed that the Mafia (or Cosa Nostra as he preferred to call it) was organized in families, each ruling criminal activities in their respective cities. Only one city, New York, had more than one family, though its five families were often in dispute with each other. Each family was headed by a triumvirate consisting of a 'boss' and his 'underboss', and an assistant-cum-legal adviser known as a 'consigliere'. The remainder of the family comprised its capo-regimes (officers) and soldiers (button men). Coordinating the whole was the National Commission consisting of about ten (the number varied) of the most powerful bosses who settled top level disputes, allocated territories and decided policies. It was later confirmed that there were about 25 such families all told, consisting of a very uncertain number of 'made' members and their associates (Short, 1986: 37).

Valachi has since died, but other mafiosi have come forward (usually out of fear for their own lives) to give information in mitigation of their own sentences. Each has made some addition to our knowledge. For example, Gerry DeNono made it clear that it was no longer *de rigueur* to kill in order to become a 'made man'. The organization was now much more interested in how much money an aspirant could contribute or generate; in its own way, the Mafia has always been an enthusiastic supporter of the enterprise economy. Another of the government's most valuable informants, Jimmy Fratianno – famously pictured on one occasion with other Mafia bosses and Frank Sinatra – admitted that he had taken part in nine gangland killings. He gave some idea of the Mafia attitude to murder when he insisted that he would never kill a woman or a child or, hopefully, an innocent person, only gangsters, killers like himself. He didn't ask why, it was enough that his superiors had ordered the 'hit'. There were no special bonuses for it, it was just part of the job.

The specific concern of this discussion on Syndicate despotism is the kind of man who put out such 'contracts'. In the case of Valachi it was Vito Genovese, who, coincidentally, was also serving a long sentence for drug offences at the same time. Genovese was an archetypal Mafia boss. Born in Italy in 1897, into a family of very modest means, he seems early to have developed a distaste for manual work of any kind. Exasperated, his father, a small contractor, packed him off to relatives in New York while the boy was still in his teens. Here he gravitated to the fringes of the criminal underworld and eventually became a member of the Mafia. He was arrested at different times on various charges, including homicide and felonious assault, but other than a short sentence for carrying a gun he was never convicted. As usual, there was a lack of evidence. A whole procession of witnesses was found, but they were so intimidated that they found themselves unable to recollect what exactly had taken place. Very soon, Genovese graduated to become underboss of one of the New York families, with special responsibility for prostitution. He emerged unscathed from the family feuds of the early 1930s, and then demonstrated his particular penchant for viciousness by ensuring the convenient demise of a young man who happened to have the misfortune to be married to a woman that Genovese coveted. The husband and another unconnected man, who may have accidentally witnessed the crime, were both found bound and strangled with sash cords. Whether the woman was involved is unknown, but Genovese married the presumably grieving widow less than a fortnight after the murders.

By the mid-1930s Genovese had moved from brothelkeeping, where he was prone to sample the goods, to gambling, which he found much more financially rewarding. But this source of wealth had to be protected, and disputes arose which involved more bloodshed. The police became increasingly curious about him in relation to a particular killing, so he decided that he could lead a more trouble-free existence if he went into voluntary exile. He already had fascist contacts abroad, so he returned to his homeland, determined to ingratiate himself with the Party. Genovese found that wealth lubricated the machinery of good relations, and he arrived in the old country with a fortune estimated at around $750,000. His wife, whom he endeavoured to visit clandestinely during many of his eight years in exile, kept things going in the gambling game with the help of a retinue of associates. Every time he returned to New York, he collected vast sums to take back with him so that he could make generous benefactions to Italy's building programme. Mussolini obligingly abandoned his normal anti-Mafia stance (and didn't enquire too closely about the source of the cash), and conferred on Genovese the state's highest civilian award.

With Italy's failing fortunes in World War II, Genovese had to protect his interests. So when Italy effectively switched sides in 1943, Genovese did likewise. He now assumed the role of the American émigré who was just waiting to be liberated, and subsequently cultivated the American military by becoming an interpreter who refused all payment for his services. In time, he became so useful to them that he was given signed testimonials to attest that he was 'absolutely honest' and had rendered 'valuable assistance to the Allied Military Government', a declaration which caused some embarrassment when it was discovered that their prize patriot was, in fact, robbing them of urgent supplies of oil and foodstuffs and distributing them to the black market. Eventually, his perfidy was discovered, but no charges were officially brought against him and he was sent back to America to face the earlier charge of homicide. Back in New York, the police's problem was again one of corroboration. When a new witness was finally found to give what was now rather dated evidence, he was housed in a Brooklyn jail for his own protection. The Mafia, however, was still able to ensure his silence. One January morning in 1945, he took what he believed to be an analgesic, and was dead within minutes. Nobody knows how his medicine had been doctored, but his death threw the Prosecution's case into disarray. There were various legal moves and countermoves, but the following year Genovese was able to walk free to become a truly potent force in the American Mafia.

Because of his long absence, he could not occupy the position of the Boss of bosses, yet his authority within the organization was such that he still commanded considerable respect and was able to live in some style. In 1951 the Kefauver Committee on crime estimated that he was worth $30 million (Kefauver, 1952). Behind the scenes he beavered away at undermining the authority of the ruling dynasty headed by Frank Costello, although as far as the authorities were concerned his efforts were somewhat hampered by the very pointed allegations about his gangster affiliations and the vast wealth accumulated by his wife when she sued for divorce in 1952. Uncle Frank, as Costello was fondly known, was of a somewhat different calibre than Genovese. Ruthless when necessary, but in general less inclined to violence, he tried to emulate Luciano in his attempt to secure more cooperation between the families (Katz, 1974). An attempt was made on his life in May 1957 but the would-be assassins' bullet only grazed his skull. It was almost certainly a Genovese arranged shooting, and was part of the ongoing power struggle within the ranks. Costello took the hint, kept to the secrecy code, and wisely retired to the back benches. Another key figure – the wild card in the pack – Albert Anastasia refused to accept a supernumerary position. He wanted a bigger share of what was now a very profitable pie; at this time, thought to top $3 billion a year. Only five months after the abortive attempt on Costello's life, two rather more efficient gunmen, though probably from the same source, walked into the barbershop of the Park-Sheraton Hotel in New York where 'Big Al' was having his regular treatment, shot him at point blank range and calmly walked out again. They have never been apprehended, and one suspects that the police felt that they had performed a public service.

Anastasia's murder triggered an even more intensive crime war, and eventually precipitated the now well-known conference of Mafia heads at Apalachin in up-state New York the following month, which was fortuitously discovered by the police. The received wisdom is that at this meeting the necessity of the Anastasia killing was approved and the essentiality of unity and cooperation was reaffirmed. Carlo Gambino, a tiny inoffensive-looking man, was now recognized as head of the New York families, although considerable power was still exercised by the 'kingmaker', Vito Genovese. Gambino's reign has been described as a 'carnival of murder' (Cook, 1973: 195) in which indiscretions and suspected double-dealing were settled peremptorily, often in a most brutal manner, including the use of the newly perfected hydraulic press as a way of disposing of bodies. It continued with his 15-year conviction on narcotics charges in 1959, and did not end until his death ten years later. Some might see this era as the heyday of the Syndicate. So will it continue to survive? All the indications are that it has certainly departed from its crude, earlier forms. Its interests now are so vast, its tentacles so extensive – stretching out to many legitimate enterprises – and its ongoing rackets so lucrative, that its future must hardly be in doubt.

CHAPTER NINETEEN

Delegated Despotism: Hans Frank and the Government-General in Poland

In the summer of 1942, the Third Reich held more territory than at any other point in its short and rapacious history. Its armies in Russia had penetrated further than ever before, even further than in the heady days of the previous year when the invasion had begun. There had been a massive destruction of the Soviet air force, and the Panzer units had advanced across the Russian plains with unhindered success. True, there had been the unanticipated hold-up on the outskirts of Moscow in the winter of 1941, but the *Wehrmacht* had stood fast during those biting winter months, and now it was again on the move in a renewed summer offensive. Furthermore, the Afrika Corps under the inspired leadership of Erwin Rommel had played havoc with the Allied forces in Libya, and had now advanced to the Egyptian border. Nothing seemed able to prevent a breakthrough to the Persian Gulf with its much prized oil installations and a meeting with the German armies driving down through the Caucasus. Very soon, however, the whole situation was going to change. The Germans were about to experience their first serious reverses. But there were no hints of this as yet.

At this very time, on 22 July to be exact, Dr Hans Frank, who during the war gained the reputation of being one of the worst of the Nazi satraps and was eventually listed among the top war criminals, was at the University of Heidelberg giving a very important address. At units of SS and SD (Security Service) were following up the victorious front-line troops and carrying out 'special actions' against Jews and other undesirables, Frank was speaking to a distinguished audience on 'The Idea of Justice and the European New Order' which Germany must inaugurate with 'pacification' as a necessary preliminary. In strict secrecy, plans had been laid earlier in the year for the 'Final Solution of the Jewish problem', and in anticipation of this ultimate genocidal operation using specially designed gas chambers, the SS and SD units, formed into four Einsatzgruppen (extermination squads), were busy carrying out mass killings in the towns and villages of Russia as part of a pacification policy. One such unit, for example, Einsatzgruppe D, under the command of one-time academic Otto Ohlendorf, is known – according to Ohlendorf's later admission – to have

massacred at least 92,000 people between 1941 and 1942. Frank spoke of
the need to establish a community of right and justice for the whole
Continent by instituting a 'planned division of labour' (Herzstein, 1982:
30–31); though he did not define this precisely, it meant, in effect, the
setting up of a slave state in the East to supply the needs of the German
economy.

It is here that we see the dichotomy in Frank's own thinking. Only a
little earlier in the same month, he had given a lecture in Vienna at the
Academy of Sciences in which he outlined his utopian, yet contemporary,
ideas for a united Europe. He reminded his audience of how this had been
unsuccessfully tried before, most recently by the League of Nations, but
that this time the genius of Adolf Hitler would ensure that the dream was
realized. What was not spelled out, of course, was just how this was to be
achieved, or whether it justified an aggressive war as an essential part of
the process. He is said to have resented the extra-legal methods of the SS,
but he was obviously prepared to accept their necessity if this would bring
the new Europe into being. It was really the old problem of ends and
means all over again. On one occasion Frank is reported to have pronounced on the unusual need and sensitivity for justice in the German
'racial character'. Yet on another, he insisted that 'we must not be squeam-
ish when we hear the figure of 17,000 shot' (Fest, 1972: 315). He certainly
shared the vision of his immediate superior, the Reichsführer SS, Heinrich
Himmler, and of Hitler himself, that the New Order would be a highly
stratified system which existed primarily to serve the 'master race'.

Frank was a lawyer in a movement which had little time for lawyers.
(The Leader himself had set the tone. Hitler affected to despise the legal
profession, possibly because being a man in a hurry he didn't want to be
hindered by provisos, caveats and clauses; he had more direct means for
securing his objectives.) Having been a member of the embryonic German
Workers' party as a young student in 1919, Frank joined the SA (the
paramilitary 'Storm Troopers') in 1923 as a junior barrister and soon
became the Party's legal adviser. His ambivalence showed quite early when
he broke with the Party in 1926 and rejoined in 1927, and then threatened
another break in 1929 to pursue a legal career but was persuaded to stay
by Hitler's personal invitation to become head of the Party's legal office.
His reputation rose with success. In those early days, a number of charges
were brought against the Party and its members before it came to power
in 1933, and Frank acquitted himself very ably as its most astute defence
counsel. Once in power, his star rose still higher. In 1933 he became
Bavarian Minister of Justice and head of the Association of German
National Socialist Jurists whose numbers multiplied considerably under his
leadership. Through the Association Frank hoped to introduce totalitarian
thought and principles to a legal profession which he felt had become

imbued with insidious democratic ideas during the days of the Weimar Republic.

Relations between Hitler and Frank appear to have cooled rather once the struggle for power was virtually over. Like so many despots, Hitler cultivated people who were useful to him, and in the early days he needed Frank. But once established, despots can largely dispense with strictly legal justifications; the law can be manipulated, retrospectively if needs be, to suit their requirements. This can be seen in what has come to be graphically known as the Night of the Long Knives in June 1934. Frank raised some objections to the liquidation of leaders of the SA, particularly Hitler's old colleague, Ernst Röhm. This was a joint enterprise between the SS and high officials of the German Army, ostensibly to preserve the unity of the state. The SA was seen as a growing threat to both, a suspicion that was not helped by Röhm's imprudent and bombastic insistence that the revolution was not yet over, and that the SA would carry it through. The murders were unquestionably extra-legal, but afterwards they were found 'necessary' in order to protect the state from an SA takeover, although no certain evidence of a coup actually exists.

Again, the inner contradictions were present. Time and time again throughout his career, Frank never seemed to be quite at one with himself. Or, at least, his legal training seemed to intrude on his ideological commitment. In his 'Guiding Principles for German Judges' (1936) he insisted that a 'judge has no right of review over the decisions of the Führer'. Yet in the same statement he adds that in order to fulfil his task, a 'judge must be independent' and not bound to follow instructions (quoted by Fest, 1972: 322). Later, in 1938, he published a small book in which he praised the Nazi seizure of power as 'the greatest revolution in world history', yet he also reiterated the basic right of each people 'to shape its state institutions in a way that suits it for its existence' (quoted by Weinreich, 1946: 38).

By 1939, Frank was obviously again *persona grata* with the Führer because when war broke out he was given a key position in the administration of the conquered territory of Poland. Hitler's Polish campaign had lasted less than a month, and by prearrangement with the Soviets the Germans had occupied the western part of Poland only. This contained about 75 per cent of the Polish population and was then divided into territory mainly peopled by Volksdeutsche and considered to be part of the Greater German Reich and a rump state known as the Government-General which was intended to function as a 'service state' for the Reich. It also acted as a repository for those who were considered as *untermenschen*, especially Jews and undesirable 'sub-humans' such as Slavs. It was from this state-within-a-state that people were consigned to the death camps, and it was here that Hans Frank took up his new duties.

The Government-General had its own officials, army staff and security services. Its administration was vitiated by jealousies and irritating bureaucratic wrangling that did not exactly make for efficiency. Frank set up his HQ in the one-time royal palace at Cracow, and here he ruled with all the extravagance and ceremonial of an early potentate, the master of all he surveyed. His rule was sometimes beneficial – even occasionally magnanimous – but more often callous and insensitive; not always deliberately cruel but often indifferent to the fate of his subjects. As one commentator puts it, he 'was a man who wanted to project "Nietzschean" hardness without yielding to spasms of bourgeois conscience' (Herzstein, 1982: 29). As a vassal of the Führer he was mandated to carry out Hitler's Eastern policies, which consisted mainly of getting rid of all those who might prove to be a nuisance to the regime – leaders, intellectuals, and so on – and extracting as much wealth from the territory as possible in the interests of the German state. Germany was still at war, so all this had to be done quickly and effectively and, characteristically, without any undue consideration for human life.

Without doubt, the formation of the Government-General was a measure to solve the 'Jewish question'. Early in 1940, Walter Buch, supreme judge of the Nazi Party and therefore one of the highest dignitaries in the land – and a colleague of Frank's – wrote that the whole purpose of the Party (and by implication the war against Poland) was that 'one day the German people might start its struggle for liberation against its Jewish oppressors'. Victory, he suggested, would only be attained when Hitler destroyed the 'Jewish sub-man's' corrosive influence on other people (quoted by Weinreich, 1946: 89). So the order was given in October 1939 that ghettos were to be established for the Jewish population in the main cities of Poland, although Frank seems to have been unable to implement this in Warsaw until October 1940. In this way, the Germans neatly contained the Jewish community (about 30 per cent of the Warsaw population) in preparation for more radical measures, although the whole process was presented to the outside world and to the Jews themselves as a form of communal autonomy. The same year, Frank inaugurated the Institute for German Work in the East at the University of Cracow. It was attended by a host of dignitaries from the *Wehrmacht* and the SS, and was portrayed as a 'spiritual bulwark of Germandom' in the East. It had more than a veneer of academia. It was suitably staffed, and to underline its credibility it published two journals and a periodical. However, the underlying anti-Semitic purpose of the journals is betrayed in such articles as 'The Jewish Question in the Government-General as a Population Problem', written by a racial expert with the strangely Jewish-sounding name of Dr Peter-Heinz Seraphim, in turn a professor at three German universities and the author of definitive works on the Jews of Eastern

Europe which had been financed by the Reich Treasury. At least Seraphim had the good sense and scholarship to qualify the racial factor, and was prepared to argue that anti-Semitism in Eastern Europe was preponderantly the result of conflicting economic interests, mixed with emotional and sometimes religious-moral rejection. But having witnessed scenes of massacre in the Ukraine in 1941, he seems only to have been concerned about the 'manner' of the executions, and invited his readers to have some sympathy for the psychological stress suffered by the executioners.

Another expert on Jewish affairs, Dr Fritz Arlt, who had pioneered the card-indexing of whole city populations, and was also interested in the 'final struggle in history ... against the Jews', emphasized the demographic aspects of the problem. As for Poland, he recommended 'seasonal migration, permanent resettlement or physical extermination to reduce population density'; mass murder was thus to become a means to economic rationalization (Burleigh, 1988: 216). It is clear, therefore, that the primary function of the Government-General was that of containment and exploitation. All dissident and heterodox ideas and factions had to be crushed. As Dr Werner Best, himself a lawyer and a high SS official, expressed it, 'any attempt to gain recognition for, or even to uphold, different political ideas will be ruthlessly dealt with as the symptom of a disease which threatens the healthy unit of the indivisible national organism' (quoted by Hohne, 1972: 170). Frank too wanted to impose National Socialist policy on those within his jurisdiction but was loathe to let the SS police have untrammelled authority in his 'province', and in 1942 made a sustained attack on police practices, which did not exactly endear him to his superiors. But, again, it is difficult to know whether this was occasioned by increased sensitivity towards the subject peoples or whether it was simply a matter of pique that SS officials were encroaching upon his special preserves. So many of his actions hardly suggest that he suffered from bouts of moral rectitude, but rather that he was annoyed that his authority was being questioned. After all, it was Frank, the ultra-Nazi, who wanted to divest the legal code of its more liberal provisions, and had declared that now that the Nazis had established the Government-General they would never give it up. He admitted quite openly that this would 'cost the lives of several thousand Poles primarily from the intellectual upper class' (quoted by Hohne, 1972: 293). Indeed, in a government session in December 1941, Frank expressed the desire that eventually his domain would be free of Jews. The problem was how could they otherwise be accommodated? And added that Berlin had said, 'Why bother? Liquidate them ... [therefore] we must take measures that will somehow result in [their] extermination' (quoted by Broszat in Koch, 1985: 407–08).

Such policies were given the gloss of academic respectability by university tutors who were thoroughly imbued with pseudo-Darwinian eugenicism. Professor Albert Brackmann, for example, a professional historian, was anxious to underpin Nazi practices with some of his specialized knowledge about 'peoples of the East'. In a paper presented in September 1939, as the conquest of Poland had more-or-less reached its completion, he put forward his proposals for securing the 'German East'. He recommended that Germany maintain a large settlement area which would serve the German people exclusively. Others must not be admitted otherwise it would result in the bastardization – and, therefore, weakening – of the Germanic peoples. The introduction of Polish people in particular, he argued, would result in a dilution of the 'blood'; indeed, he felt that reparations should be made by the defeated Poles in atonement for the sacrifice made by German troops in the course of their campaign. Moreover, Germans did not want to be polluted by Polish 'cultural incapability'; it was 'racial hybridisation' that had brought about the ruin of the great peoples of the past. So all Jews, gypsies and their 'hybrids' would be required to leave immediately, as these, for the most part, were 'totally useless' (Burleigh, 1988: 167 ff.). It will surprise no one to learn that Brackmann was informed that the Führer had been thinking along similar lines for some time.

Frank was not altogether in accord with Brackmann's ideas. He was not opposed to the possibility of 'Germanisation'. Thus his ambivalence can again be seen in his contradictory attitudes towards German-Polish relations. He was keen, for example, to introduce the right cultural elements into his 'realm', presumably for both his staff and any native converts, although the 'curriculum' mainly served to promote anti-Semitism and to enhance German cultural achievements. He therefore welcomed overtures from PuSte (*Publikationsstelle*), an academic research organization that specialized in studies of German-Polish issues and opened a branch in Cracow in January 1940. There were even plans for a special German institute, perhaps to merge with the existing university, and a number of eminent academics joined in these discussions. In a speech in May 1940, Frank confidently predicted that what was German would remain German – after all, Germans were the bearers of civilization.

Despite the fact that Hitler had insisted that the Government-General did not require an elaborate administration, an army of some 400 bureaucrats was brought in to run the many administrative districts set up by the conquerors. The liquidation of large numbers of the Polish intelligentsia by the 'special actions' of the SS did not make the task of running the country any easier. By 1944, the number of officials had increased enormously, and still the 'state' was something of an organizational shambles. This was partly because most of them did not speak the language and partly because Frank's civil administration was counterbalanced, as we have seen, by the presence of the SS and SD, and even further complicated by the pressure of *Wehrmacht* units under their own commander. Foremost though among the German importees were the self-styled experts in ethnic questions, such as Professor Friedrich Lenz of the Institute of Racial Hygiene who claimed to have discovered fine variations in racial categories which could then be applied to the Jewish-Slavic problem. Fritz Arlt, whom we have already encountered, who had studied anthropology and sociology at Leipzig, and had the rather unique qualification of gaining his doctorate for a psycho-racial study of women in Icelandic sagas, is fairly typical of this breed of academics. It was he who had categorically stated in an article that Jews were 'different in spirit, belief, character and behaviour' and that there was 'no bridge [for them] to the community of non-Jews' (quoted by Burleigh, *ibid.*: 215). In November 1939, he was recruited by the Government-General to take charge of its demographic section which dealt with such matters as 'welfare' and 'resettlement'. Ironically – and tragically – the experts were not always sure exactly who was a Jew and who was not. When the question of a community of Karaite Jews in Lithuania – a people of somewhat Asian appearance – came up for discussion, the SS took no chances. Their policy was, when in doubt, exterminate. The policy of the experts towards the other subjects of 'lesser value' in the Government-General, was that their education should be severely restricted to element-ary number and the ability to write their names. After their leaders had been killed, the racial identity of the remainder was to be extinguished, and they would spend their days in unremitting manual toil for the Reich.

The part of Poland that had been annexed from Germany in 1919 and which had now reverted to the Reich by virtue of conquest, was denuded of many of its inhabitants, a proportion of whom found their way to the Government-General, a contingency to which Frank raised fruitless objec-tions. In theory, these lands were earmarked for German settlers, but the numbers that arrived proved disappointing. And even these dwindled to a mere trickle when the tide of war turned after the defeat at Stalingrad early in 1943, and the Germans were on the retreat. By the summer of 1943, industry had still not been able to absorb some 25 per cent of them, and as a new culture area it certainly did not prove to be an effective buffer-zone against the advancing Russians.

The worsening war situation only exacerbated the frictions that arose in the actual running of the Government-General, particularly between Frank and the SS chief, Friedrich Krueger. These were such that the SS sent a damning report to Berlin on Frank's administration, but by this time Hitler had rather more to worry about than the purported incompetence of one of his vassals (Reitlinger, 1986: 133). The SS actually did have something to complain about. Frank lived in lavish style, and was not above a little peculation on the side; indeed, he did not make that much of a secret of his confiscations. Frank liked to live well. As a man of culture, he liked to surround himself with good furniture, expensive paintings, and so on. Valuable artefacts were plundered from other Polish institutes to adorn his and other top officials' residences, and he was not alone in this by any means. In 1942, his friend and colleague Dr Carl Lasch, first President of the German Academy of Law, was convicted on similar charges and shot without trial by the Gestapo (Reitlinger, *ibid.*: 225). Frank protested in a series of lectures given at German universities, and the Berlin hierarchy was so incensed that Frank was divested of his legal offices. He was allowed to remain as head of the Government-General, however, as Hitler regarded this as a particularly unpleasant office. Unpleasant it may have been, but it allowed Frank to live in luxury. Libraries were looted, and research laboratories divested of equipment which eventually found its way to German universities. The homes of Polish aristocrats were ravaged, and furniture, tapestries, china and so forth were taken to enhance the impression that Frank & Co were a kind of latter-day Venetian nobility.

The ruling hierarchy of the Government-General, comprising as it did SS representatives as well as economists, lawyers, and so on, did not all have the agonized heart searchings of Hans Frank. Not that *he* had the most tender sensitivities. On one occasion not long after he took over the office, he was asked by a journalist what was the difference between his Government-General and the German Protectorate in Czechoslovakia. He replied that in the Protectorate one might read on a poster that on any particular day seven Czechs had been shot, but that the Polish forests could not produce enough paper for posters announcing Polish executions (Burleigh, 1988: 255). He made clear that productive labour was the key issue in such a primitive economy, and that anyone who tried to obstruct German intentions would be pitilessly exterminated. As far as the Jews were concerned, the Government-General gave them asylum in its city ghettos while they awaited transit to the East, where the vast majority was murdered. While in the Government-General, Jews became the subjects of considerable research, which appears to have been hopelessly biased from the beginning with investigations setting out to confirm the researchers' own distorted pre-judgments. While awaiting 'resettlement', they were also required to work for their masters, usually existing on pathetic rations which Frank gradually reduced. He laconically commented that during the winter months 'the rate of deaths will doubtless increase, but then this war will bring about the total annihilation of the Jews' (Graber, 1980: 168). He stated clearly that, 'It is purely incidental if we condemn 1–2 million Jews to starve to death. We naturally hope that this can be avoided by speeding up the anti-Jewish measures' (Krausnick and Broszat, 1970: 120). One of Frank's experts was equally open in his view that if the Jews did not work satisfactorily, they effectively pronounced judgments on themselves; they no longer had any justification for their existence. The consensus of Nazi opinion was that Poland would be much better off without them. So the deportations accelerated in numbers and frequency.

The poor wretches did not have that far to go. Many of the extermination camps were clearly set up within the Government-General's sphere of authority. In January 1942, a delegation from the euthanasia programme appeared and within six months three camps had been established. It was a tribute to German organization, but an indictment of the accommodating bias of German scholarship vis-à-vis the official ideology. Such policies and practices were in keeping with Frank's original brief. Hitler's broad directive had been that 'all men capable of leadership in Poland must be liquidated', and added that there was no need to burden the Reich with this' (Graber, 1980: 148). More camps were set up, and ultimately the Frank administration, with all its inefficiencies (and personal reservations), was responsible for the deportation of some 2.5 million Jews, most of whom did not survive. Little wonder that Frank, recalling the events of a meeting in January 1943, said to his audience that there had been a lot of talk about anti-Jewish measures and he wanted to remind them that 'all of us here want to remember that we are on Roosevelt's war crimes list. I have the honour of being at the top of the list. We are all accomplices in a world historical sense' (quoted by Bower, 1983: 64–65). Yet the same man could set up conferences on astronomy, award a Copernicus prize (Copernicus having been suitably 'germanized'), and then allow himself to ruminate philosophically – and publicly – on Hitler – the man who had 'saved the human race from hopelessness in the face of infinity'.

Frank has the well-deserved reputation of being a fanatical Nazi and a ruthless administrator, yet his career is marked by strange ambiguities. His on-going rivalry with Reichsführer Himmler and the SS over their brutal campaign against Polish peasants caused him considerable disquiet. He wanted a coherent Eastern policy which, as things turned out, was never destined to exist. He felt that theirs was a disastrous course of action which made nonsense of any possible Polish state; it merely drove those who might have been won over into the arms of the partisans. He was sure that certain Polish elements – though not Jews – could be successfully assimilated within the Greater German Reich under the control of a German upper class. But many of them had fled into the forests, and others were forced into the Government-General, all of which played havoc with Frank's economic arrangements. Not that he was plagued by moral considerations; he seems mainly to have been concerned to preserve his own status and authority. The SS, however, knew far too much about his illegal 'trading' activities, especially in furs, and he was eventually forced to back down in the face of SS pressure, even to the point of supporting Himmler's demand to have General Blascowitz of the *Wehrmacht* transferred because the general protested against SS brutalities. This succeeded because the SS had Berlin's blessing for their ruthless Eastern 'policies' (see Martin Broszat in Koch, 1985).

But, in his own way, Frank was no coward. He took full advantage of his eminence as a lecturer to launch an unprecedented attack on the SS from the rostrums of many famous German universities. To Party notables he preached his message of lost legality. 'Without law ... no German Reich is conceivable ... A people cannot be ruled by force'. Or again, 'I shall continue to assert ... that it would be bad if the Police State were to be presented as the ideal of National Socialism'. On the other hand, he could also insist that 'in no circumstances can a State be endangered by being humane' (quoted by Hohne, 1972: 296–97). As we have seen, Frank was stripped of his ministerial offices for his outspokenness, but allowed to stay on in his old capacity in the Government-General. And there he vegetated in uncomfortable luxury, still dreaming of full reinstatement in what had in reality become a realm of the damned for rulers and subjects alike.

Another 'old comrade' who had been relegated to the margins of authority was Alfred Rosenberg, one of the principal idealogues of the Party. As the war reached a critical stage for the Reich in 1942–43, Rosenberg found that his ideas for the settlement of the 'reoccupied territories' were no longer in great demand. The much-vaunted summer offensive in Russia had effectively failed, and the German armies were faced with a catastrophic defeat at Stalingrad. Rommel and his Afrika Corps were on the retreat in the Western Desert, and, to compound matters, in late 1942 the British and the Americans had landed a combined force in North Africa to cut off his escape. Add to this the beginning of the mass bombing raids on Germany itself, and one can understand the growing impatience with the irrelevancies of the petulant memo-war that Rosenberg was conducting in order to get his colleagues to think more philosophically about the Reich's future policies. At just this time, Rosenberg, possibly in collaboration with others, came up with the idea of an anti-Jewish Congress to which he would invite other notables among Germany's diminishing stock of friends who shared this common European 'ideal'. Finally his persistence paid off. Several months after its inception Hitler gave the go-ahead for what could be no more than a showy propaganda exercise, and preparatory meetings were held in February 1944. One of the first items to be considered was the venue. And what better place for a Congress than the seat of Eastern territories' scholarship, Cracow in the Government-General?

Frank was enthusiastic about the project. And just to demonstrate the tenuous grasp that some of the Nazi idealogues had upon reality, Frank was able to argue that: 'The time for such an anti-Jewish demonstration is particularly advantageous because it underscores at this juncture of the war the unbroken fighting will of Germany' (Weinreich, 1946: 219). He thought that Cracow was a particularly fit place for the Congress because the 'Government-General previously was the domain of Eastern Jewry and the Jewish power-reservoir for poisoning all of Europe' (Weinreich, *ibid.*: 223). Representatives from several departments gathered in much-bombed Berlin to work out the details. Just when the Reich was anticipating the Allied invasion of Europe, working committees were formed, topics were agreed, a list of guests was compiled, and the date was set for July. The Foreign Ministry asked all German embassies and legations to submit lists of possible participants, and it was anticipated that some 450 invitations would be sent out, including some to friendly neutrals such as Sweden. The programme was to consist of newsreels and anti-Jewish films, and addresses, mostly by prominent academics, on such topics as 'The Jew in the Economic Life of Nations' and 'The Parasitic Qualities of the Jews'. It was also to include talks by the renegade Englishman John Amery on 'Jewish Influence in the English Ruling Stratum'; and (because the Nazis were anxious for Islamic support) the Grand Mufti of Jerusalem on 'Palestine, a World Political Pivot of the Jewish Drive for Power'. Frank – generous to a fault – even arranged for the setting up of a brothel for the delectation of the delegates. The women, who needless to say were not to be Poles or Ukrainians, were the responsibility of high Nazi officials who were now reduced to pimping for the Party (see Herzstein, 1982: 73).

The Second Front, the Allied assault on German-occupied France, began before the Congress could take place, so it was called off, but only after some pressure from the Reich Chancellery. The initiators, Rosenberg and Frank, finally gave in with obvious reluctance. It is perhaps typical of idealogues that in desperate situations their eschatological hopes become more pronounced. They still dream dreams and see visions. They find it difficult to believe that what they are witnessing is the end of their aspirations. They cannot accept that this is really the finale. Even within weeks of the war being ultimately lost, some of them held out millennial longings for some kind of miraculous revival (note Berlin's delight at the death of Roosevelt only days before the end of the war). Even Hitler – at many levels, the supreme realist – was moving around phantom armies on his map table almost to the day of his suicide (see O'Donnell, 1979).

When Frank was finally taken into custody by the Allies, he handed over his portfolio of diaries in 38 volumes which detailed every day of his governorship. These confirm that he was a man riddled with doubts and contradictions. At one point sentimental, at another cruel; by turn, trying to ameliorate the brutalities of the SS and then trying (feigning?) to beat them at their own game. He wanted to curry favour with Hitler whose confidence he had largely lost, while also being prepared to make highly contentious speeches. Fundamentally, his aims for the province were different from those advocated by Hitler, who saw Poland merely as a booty state. It was all becoming too much for him, and he actually submitted his resignation 14 times, though without success. But to most the insecurity never showed. He just went on 'enjoying' his trade. In one memorandum he noted that 'power and the certainty of being able to use force without any resistance are the sweetest and most noxious poisons that can be introduced into a government. In the long run this position is absolutely lethal' (quoted by Fest, 1972: 326).

Perhaps Fest is close to the truth when he says that Frank did not have any convictions, only moods. And yet towards the end of his life (he was hanged as a war criminal in 1946), he professed a religious conversion and seems genuinely to have reflected on his own guilt, admitting that he had liked Hitler's ideas though not his methods, which he felt he should have rejected. But the longing was still there: 'as I prepare to say farewell to this earth in order to follow the Führer ... I am seized by the most profound melancholy when I recall this tremendous setting out of a whole great self-confident nation ... why, why was it all lost, why did it fade away, why is it all gone, destroyed? I am seized by uncomprehending horror at the senselessness of destiny' (Fest, *ibid.*: 330). One is constrained to ask what real hope is there for those, like Frank, who cannot see. Nazism was a cancer, and in the end a cancer kills itself.

Summary

To paraphrase the old axiom, some people are born despots, some achieve despotic status, and others have despotism thrust upon them. This is rather simplistic, but it does accord very generally with the facts. If for the moment we confine our examples to Imperial Rome, Nero would fit in our first category, as would a later emperor, Heliogabalus. Both were born into situations of internecine in-fighting. Intrigue and betrayal were commonplace in the Imperial family. And although emperors were there to serve the nation, they actually enjoyed so much wealth and power that many of them can be unambiguously regarded as despots. Augustus (Octavian), the founder of the Imperial House, comes into the second category. From his youth, he too had lethal tendencies, but in his case they were tempered in such a way that he created an almost respectable kind of despotism in later life. Indeed, his form of despotism was tinged with a kind of puritanism. He posed as a *primus inter pares*, but no one was left in any doubt as to who was really in charge. Claudius is a particularly good example of the third category. He probably did not want to rule, and certainly did not anticipate it. But when the Praetorians 'elected' him after the assassination of his nephew, Caligula, he settled down to the task with true despotic relish, setting a textbook model for his step-son, Nero, who probably conspired in his murder.

As a very general rule, we can say with Max Weber that all states are instruments of domination (Bendix, 1960). After all, politics is all about the acquisition, retention, and extension of power, by force if necessary. This is just as true of tribal societies as modern societies, as we saw with the Zulu Matabele tribes. However, this would have to be qualified in the case of those very small-scale societies where power tends not to be exercised in an oppressive way because, as Malinowski pointed out, such societies comprise a complex of interrelated kinship ties and age groups. In such cases, 'people feel related to each other in myth if not in reality' (Ribbens, 1979: 186–87). Myth and religion usually legitimize political relationships, and in more developed tribal societies they may well validate the superiority of one group in relation to another.

In complex pre-industrial societies, this was taken a stage further. Differential authority was much more related to social strata than lineage and age groups, and the ruler's power was not uncommonly legitimized by purported links with the state gods. In ancient Egypt and Imperial China, where it was believed that in some sense the rulers were the progeny of divine beings, their power became theoretically – and often actually – unquestionable. There were thus few checks on autocratic power because the ruler's control extended to every facet of state organization, so much so, in fact, that in ancient Egypt it could be said that 'law proceeds from the mouth of the Pharaoh'. On the other hand, it is difficult to go along with Karl Wittfogel's economic reductionism and his insistence that power is primarily based on the control of scarce resources; it is a thesis that can be qualified in many ways, not least because there are so many exceptions to the 'rule' (see Andreski, 1964). As a thesis, it is 'appealing in its simplicity' but tends to understate the importance of other factors that contribute to a society's continuance and viability (Sjoberg, 1965: 117).

Despots were not usually known for the consideration they gave to their subjects. Even in complex pre-industrial systems, such as certain Greek states (notably Athens and some of its allies) where there was a claim to operate within a broad democratic framework, it is arguable that the reins of government were still largely in the hands of the aristocracy. Various groups were excluded from the franchise, particularly resident aliens, women and, inevitably, slaves. But we know there were inconsistencies. In matters of polity, the practice in these states was probably frequently divorced from the theory. In more recent autocracies such as that of the Perons in Argentina, some attempt was usually made to give the impression of public participation and voters' wishes were taken into account, even if it was only to hold somewhat suspect elections to confirm the ruler in office. Modern autocrats thrive on mass support, and some, such as Castro, go out of their way to court popularity with the masses, even if this is not always successful.

Broadly speaking, despotism arises during periods of social unrest and political turmoil, or perhaps when, for some reason or another, the existing political system is in the process of dissolution. The aim of the despot may be initially to restore order to the system, as in the case of Dionysios in Syracuse, or to re-establish some kind of unity among warring factions, as we found with Timur and the Tartar tribes. He would not, however, usually try to restore the status quo, because, typically, despots – such as Napoleon – have their own special political goals that they wish to pursue. Often, they are men with a singular vision, in which case there may be an attempt to impose new and radical patterns of political organization on the existing system, as with Lenin and Stalin. This may require monopolization of political decision-making without being bound by traditional norms or recognized social elites. Indeed, it may well require the forcible suppression of existing factions and interests which are seen as a possible threat to the new order. Alternatively, where the despot is a conqueror, it often pays to recognize the customary mores and cultural patterns of the subject states. It can be politically advantageous to exploit such patterns for administrative and control purposes. Historically, a little syncretism often comes in useful. In some instances, accommodation can be reached at the religious level where similarities between the gods can be conveniently identified, a strategy that worked well in Ptolemaic Egypt. However, it should be borne in mind that religion does not always function as a buttress for despotic power. To cite Egypt again, some earlier Pharaohs found themselves at loggerheads with the priesthoods; in this way religious sanctuaries constituted a counterweight to autocratic rule. Rapprochement was certainly the practice (always within limits, of course) of the great expansionist empires such as Persia and Rome. All despotic rulers have to find allies or cultivate certain groups within their own society or sometimes even among subject peoples, and it often paid (as with Cesare Borgia) to play one group off against another. In exceptional instances, this is not done; the new regime is so ideologically motivated that everything must be subordinated to its interests, which may require the virtual enslavement or even extermination of selected groups and peoples. This would apply to modern despots such as Hitler and Pol Pot (in 1970s Kampuchea). Not infrequently, of course, mass killings take place not for any discernible ideological reasons but simply out of fear and revenge (Idi Amin), as a form of punishment (Athenians and Spartans), to consolidate power (Alexander the Great, Stalin, Saddam Hussein), or perhaps for the sheet pleasure of killing (Mutesa).

All despots need to forge instruments of power and to mobilize the various resources necessary for the realization of their aims. Ultimately, they need supporters, those who either share their ideals or who seek their own advantage as servants of the ruler and are thus prepared to implement his policies. This may be done by cultivating already well-placed people in the traditional hierarchy or by some kind of populist appeal to the masses over the heads of the aristocracy. Perhaps, quite commonly, it means introducing a whole new echelon of ministers/councillors/advisers from among those who already helped to secure the despot in power. Frequently, it is some combination of these because the ruler normally wants to ensure some continuity of tradition, and needs the know-how of the established bureaucracy to administer the various organs of government. In this way, what may begin as charismatic leadership may eventually become transmuted into a legal-rational regime which gives at least the gloss of legitimization to the despot's policies and practices.

In the despot's highly centralized administration, there will necessarily be a paucity of public political roles and a general reduction of political activity. There will also be a weakening of hereditary structures and a clear system of social differentiation. These status distinctions between the ruler(s) and the ruled will inevitably be reflected in the distribution of rights, as well as goods and services. His main objectives will be:

1. To maintain his position against possible opponents, and be able to recruit the necessary support when he is threatened by some external power(s).

2. To further his aims and policies by mobilizing the requisite resources of manpower and wealth through confiscation, tribute or taxation. In practice, this often means the accumulation of riches and lands at the expense of vulnerable neighbouring states. Though military expansionism also involves yet further regulation and control which can gradually undermine the ruler's authority.

3. To introduce or support the appropriate ideology with which to motivate his subjects and justify his actions. This need not be a cynical or contrived exercise foisted on the masses as a convenient political fiction. There is good evidence that in actual cases it has been a *believed* ideology which has to be 'realized' (Nazi racism and the Holocaust).

Fundamental to despotism in its totalitarian guise is a particular theory of the state; a collectivist – almost tribal – theory that demands that the interests of the state must always come first. In one form, it can be seen in the writings of Plato, who had a deep aversion to the radical democracy of Athens. He believed that the majority in its collective will can exert a pressure as great as that of any despot. He was very conscious of the phenomenon known as the tyranny of the majority, but recognized that it was often under the influence of persuasive demagogues. This view is almost diametrically opposite to that of Rousseau who argued that the 'natural man', as an individual, may well be totalitarian in his thinking but that this irrationality becomes tempered in the mass. The 'general will' thus becomes the basis of the social contract (Klapp, 1973: 139). But again, as we have seen, in cataclysmic situations such as the French Revolution, such ideas (as Rousseau came to recognize) require serious modification. In these circumstances, democracy can show itself to be as unstable as despotism, and opponents of democracy have seen this as yet further evidence of self-styled leaders pandering to the debased tastes of an uneducated mob.

It could be argued that certain forms of autocracy can be justified in special social conditions, such as crises of some kind. In the Roman Republic it was constitutional to give a consul the 'imperium' in a wartime emergency, usually for six months. But possessing power is a heady experience and towards the end of the Republic this expedient was abused; those with the Senate's imperium, such as Pompey and Caesar, became military dynasts. And Rome is by no means the only example of this.

The abuse of power begs the question – just as relevant today – whether we should trust those who presume to set themselves up as our leaders. By what right do they put themselves forward as candidates for power? And is it really so easy, even in a democratic society, to institute the necessary curbs on nepotism, peculation, and the general abuse of privilege? It is still probably true that a high percentage of those who become politicians – for which there is no formal training – do so for some personal advantage.

We began our study with an attempt to define our terms, and it is this problem of definition which vitiates any discussion of autocratic rule. As our study has shown, this takes a great variety of forms. First of all, we can probably dispense with the term 'absolutism', as in Absolute Monarch. It is true that some rulers, such as the Ashanti kings, enjoyed 'eminent domain' whereby it was believed that they owned *all* the land and its produce, at least in theory. Absolutism was also the term used about some European monarchs in the eighteenth century, but we know that not only was their rule not absolute, it is doubtful if *any* ruler has absolute power to do exactly what he pleases in any imaginable situation without taking into consideration at least some other parties. Autocracy, therefore, probably remains the best general term that covers most contingencies. It subsumes the term despotism which has been used rather broadly in this study. But then it was convenient to identify a particular kind of autocracy. Many rulers have been, and are, autocratic, but are they despots? What features in particular characterize despotic rule? What makes it different? All despots are rulers, but not all rulers are despots although they may act despotically from time to time, either capriciously or as part of a calculated political programme.

There is a common tendency to identify despotism with elaborate rituals that reinforce a sense of separateness between the ruler and his subjects. Thus, in earlier anthropological and historical writings we find references to 'ritual isolation', especially in systems based on the notion of divine kingship. In some pre-Columbian societies, for instance, the ruler ate alone; physical contact was forbidden to all but a few intimates. In some societies, a ruler's feet were not allowed to touch the ground, or he might only speak to others through a curtain because his gaze was considered dangerous (Lenski, 1966: 157 ff.). In yet other societies, notably Imperial China and ancient Persia, subjects – even dignitaries – were required to prostrate themselves before the monarch and not look at him at all during an interview. Rulers too had the usual paraphernalia of distinctive regalia to signify their office; courts and courtiers with a clearly defined protocol; and a collection of high-sounding titles that proclaimed their greatness and achievements. Witness those of the Egyptian pharaohs or the emperors of China who claimed a mandate to rule the earth, although, needless to say, its peoples were quite unaware of it. Rulers also often had a motley collection of wives and concubines, and either rudimentary or developed bureaucracies to administer the kingdom for them, usually including military commanders, chief ministers and, not uncommonly, a royal executioner. In certain cases, the despotic nature of their rule can be seen most clearly in relation to the accession and death. In the Mogul empire, for example, a new ruler came to power after having liquidated his brothers who were regarded as potential rivals; this was thought to be one way of ensuring a strong monarchy. Sometimes the death of a ruler was attended by mass human sacrifices, normally of wives and attendants who were required to serve him in the next life (see Murdock, 1959).

Autocracy, then, implies the lack of any customary rules or legal limitations on the authority of the autocrat, or, indeed, any restrictions on his rule by institutional groups such as ministers and priests to whom he may be thought to be accountable. An autocrat may be described as totalitarian but, as we have seen, this implies a special kind of polity which involves the systematic control of all social life in the interests of the state. How then is despotism different? In truth, the line is very fine. The key factor is not only that there are no effective limitations to the rule of the despot, but that there are no effective curbs on his *will*. It is the *arbitrary nature of despotic rule*, which so often results in cruelties and injustices, that tends to mark it out from simple autocracy. The whims of the despot may not always be given completely free rein though, if they are, it is not usually for very long. Greek tyrannies, as we noted, rarely lasted more than two generations. But the final sanction, especially for very capricious despots, is the coup d'état, or, failing that, assassination, or – as in the case of Caligula – both.

Bibliography

Adams R. *Social Change in Latin America Today*, Random House, New York, 1960.

Aldred C. *Egypt to the End of the Old Kingdom*, Thames & Hudson, London, 1974.

Alexander J. *Catherine the Great: Life and Legend*, OUP, Oxford, 1989.

Allsop K. *The Bootleggers*, Hutchinson, London, 1962.

Andreski S. *Elements of Comparative Sociology*, Weidenfeld & Nicolson, London, 1964.

Andrew C. and Gordievsky O. *KGB The Inside Story*, Hodder & Stoughton, London, 1990.

Andrewes A. *The Greek Tyrants*, Hutchinson, London, 1966.

Anglo S. *Machiavelli*, Paladin, London, 1969.

Arendt H. *The Origins of Totalitarianism*, Meridian, New York, 1958.

Ashe R. *Two Kings of Uganda*, Cass, London, 1970.

Austin M. 'Greek Tyrants and Persians 546–479', *Classical Quarterly* **40** (ii), 289–306, 1990.

Bakhash S. *The Reign of the Ayatollahs: Islam and the Islamic Revolution*, Tauris, London, 1985.

Beloff M. *The Age of Absolutism 1660–1815*, Arrow Books, London, 1963.

Bendix R. *Max Weber: an Intellectual Portrait*, Heinemann, London, 1960.

Boak A. and Sinnigen W. *A History of Rome* (5th Edition), Macmillan, New York, 1965.

Bohannan P. *African Outline*, Penguin, Harmondsworth, 1964.

Bosworth A. *Conquest and Empire*, CUP, Cambridge, 1988.

Bower T. *Blind Eye to Murder*, Paladin, London, 1983.

Bowle J. *A History of Europe*, Heinemann, London, 1980.

Bowman A. *Egypt after the Pharaohs*, British Museum Publications, London, 1986.

Bradford S. *Cesare Borgia*, Futura Books, London, 1981.

Bresheeth H. and Yuval-Davis N. (eds), *The Gulf War and the New World Order*, Zed Books, London, 1991.

Bruce G. *Eva Peron*, Heron Books, Geneva, 1972.

Bulloch H. and Morris H. *Saddam's War*, Faber & Faber, London, 1991.

Bullock A. *Hitler and Stalin: Parallel Lives*, Harper & Row, London, 1992.

Burckhardt J. *The Civilization of the Renaissance in Italy*, Harper & Row, New York, 1958.

Burleigh M. *Germany Turns Eastwards*, CUP, Cambridge, 1988.

Burn A. *Alexander the Great and the Middle East* (Revised Edition), Pelican, Harmondsworth, 1973.

Bury J. and Meiggs R. *A History of Greece* (Revised Edition), Macmillan, London, 1978.

Bwengye F. *The Agony of Uganda: from Idi Amin to Obote*, Regency Press, London, 1985.

CARDRI, *Saddam's Iraq*, Zed Books, London, 1989.

Carew-Hunt R. *The Theory and Practice of Communism*, Bles, London, 1962.

Carlton E. *Ideology and Social Order*, RKP, London, 1977.

Carlton E. *War and Ideology*, Routledge, London, 1990.

Carlton E. *Occupation: the Policies and Practices of Military Conquerors*, Routledge, London, 1992.

Carlton E. *Massacres: an Historical Perspective*, Scolar Press, Aldershot, 1994.

Cartwright F. and Biddiss M. *Disease and History*, Dorset Press, New York, 1991.

Chamberlain E. *Cesare Borgia*, International Textbooks, London, 1969.

Chambers J. *The Devil's Horsemen*, Weidenfeld & Nicolson, London, 1979.

Charques R. *A Short History of Russia*, English University Press, London, 1959.

Chirovsky Fr. N. *An Introduction to Russian History*, Vision Press, London, 1967.

Cobban A. *A History of Modern France 1715–1799*, Vol. 1, Penguin, Harmondsworth, 1963.

Cobban A. *A History of Modern France 1799–1871*, Vol. 2, Penguin, Harmondsworth, 1965.

Cohan A. *Theories of Revolution*, Nelson, London, 1975.

Conquest R. *Inside Stalin's Secret Police: NKVD Politics 1936–39*, Macmillan, London, 1985.

Conquest R. *The Great Terror: A Reassessment*, Hutchinson, London, 1990.

Cook F. *Mafia*, Coronet, London, 1973.

Cottrell L. *The Tiger of Ch'in*, Pan, London, 1964.

Covensky M. *The Ancient Near Eastern Tradition*, Harper & Row, New York, 1966.

Cronin V. *Napoleon*, Penguin, Harmondsworth, 1976.

Crooke W. *Islam in India*, OUP, Oxford, 1921.

Darwish A. and Alexander G. *Unholy Babylon*, Gollancz, London, 1991.

David R. The Egyptian Pharaohs, Elsevoir-Phaidon, Lausanne, 1975.

David R. *The Ancient Egyptians*, RKP, London, 1982.

Davies J. 'Toward a Theory of Revolution', *American Sociological Review*, 27, no. 1, February 1962.

Dawson R. *Imperial China*, Hutchinson, London, 1972.

Deacon R. *The French Secret Service*, Grafton Books, London, 1990.

Deaux K. and Wrightsman L. *Social Psychology in the 80s*, Brooks/Cole, Monterey, CA, 1984.

Dekmejian R. H. *Islam in Revolution: Fundamentalism in the Arab World*, Syracuse University Press, Syracuse, NY, 1985.

Eberhard W. *A History of China*, RKP, London, 1950.

Edwards I. *The Pyramids of Egypt*, Michael Joseph, London, 1972.

Eisenstadt S. 'The Wittfogel Thesis' in *Journal of Asian Studies*, 1957–58, 435–46.

Eisenstadt S. *The Decline of Empires*, Prentice-Hall, Englewood Cliffs, NJ, 1967.

Eisenstadt S. *The Political Systems of Empires*, Free Press, New York, 1969.

Elton G. *England under the Tudors*, Methuen, London, 1955.

Elton G. *Henry VIII*, The Historical Association, London, 1962.

Fairbank J. (ed.) *Chinese Thought and Institutions*, University of Chicago Press, Chicago, 1957.

Fakhry A. *The Pyramids*, University of Chicago Press, Chicago, 1974.

Fallers L. *Bantu Bureaucracy*, Chicago University Press, Chicago, 1965.

Feiling K. *A History of England*, Macmillan, London, 1966.

Fest J. *The Face of the Third Reich*, Pelican, Harmondsworth, 1972.

Fiedler I. *A Theory of Leadership Effectiveness*, McGraw-Hill, New York, 1967.

Finley M. *A History of Sicily*, Chatto & Windus, London, 1968.

Franzero C. *The Life and Times of Cleopatra*, Alvin Redman, London, 1967.

Friedrich C. and Brzezinski Z. *Totalitarian Dictatorship and Autocracy*, Praeger, New York, 1965.

Fryer J. *The Great Wall of China*, New English Library, London, 1975.

Gardiner A. *Egypt of the Pharaohs*, OUP, London, 1961.

Gernet J. *A History of Chinese Civilization*, CUP, Cambridge, 1982.

Gibb C. 'Leadership' in Lindzey G. and Aronson E. (eds), *Handbook of Social Psychology*, Vol. 4, Addison-Wesley, Reading, MA, 1969.

Gibb H. *Mohammedanism*, OUP, Oxford, 1969.

Gilbert M. *The Holocaust*, Collins, London, 1986.

Graber G. *History of the SS*, Mayflower Books, London, 1980.

Grant M. *Nero*, Weidenfeld & Nicolson, London, 1970.

Grant M. *Cleopatra*, Panther, London, 1974.

Grant M. *From Alexander to Cleopatra*, Weidenfeld & Nicholson, London, 1982.

Green P. *Alexander the Great*, Weidenfeld & Nicolson, London, 1970.

Green P. *Alexander of Macedon*, University of California Press, Berkeley, 1991.

Greig I. *Subversion*, Stacey, London, 1973.

Grey I. *Catherine the Great: Autocrat and Empress of all Russia*, Hodder & Stoughton, London, 1961.

Griffin M. *Nero: The End of a Dynasty*, Batsford, London, 1984.

Guisso R., Pagani C. and Miller D. *The First Emperor of China*, Sidgwick & Jackson, London, 1989.

Gutteridge W. *The Military in African Politics*, Methuen, London, 1969.

Hatifi A. *Timur-nama*, Madras University Press, Madras, 1958.

Haywood R. *The Ancient World*, McKay, New York, 1971.

Hennessy A. 'Fascism and Populism in Latin America' in Walter Laquer, *Fascism*, Pelican, Harmondsworth, 1979.

Herodotus, *The Histories* (trans. A. de Selincourt), Penguin, Harmondsworth, 1972.

Herzstein R. *When Nazi Dreams Come True*, Abacus, London, 1982.

Hibbert C. *The Rise and Fall of the House of Medici*, Penguin, Harmondsworth, 1979.

Hibbert C. *Africa Explored*, Allen Lane, London, 1982.

Hibbert C. *The French Revolution*, Penguin, Harmondsworth, 1986.

Hiro D. *Inside the Middle East*, RKP, London, 1982.

Hiro D. *Islamic Fundamentalism*, Paladin, London, 1988.

Hoffer E. *The True Believer*, Mentor, New York, 1960.

Hohne H. *The Order of the Death's Head*, Pan Books, London, 1972.

Hookham H. *Tamburlane the Conqueror*, Hodder & Stoughton, London, 1962.

International Commission of Jurists, *Violations of Human Rights and the Rule of Law in Uganda*, Geneva, 1974.

International Commission of Jurists, *Uganda and Human Rights: Reports to the United Nations*, Geneva, 1977.

Ives E. *Faction in Tudor England*, The Historical Assocation, London, 1979.

Jeffrey L. *Archaic Greece*, Benn, London, 1978.

Johnson H. *Sociology: a Systematic Introduction*, RKP, London, 1964.

Johnson P. *A History of the Modern World 1917–1980s*, Weidenfeld & Nicolson, London, 1983.

Kamau J. and Cameron A. *Lust to Kill*, Corgi Books, London, 1979.

Kamil J. *The Ancient Egyptians*, David & Charles, Newton Abbot, 1976.

Katz L. *Uncle Frank*, W. H. Allen, London, 1974.

Kefauver E. *Crime in America*, Gollancz, London, 1952.

Klapp O. *Models of Social Order*, Mayfield Publishing, Palo Alto, CA, 1973.

Kobler J. *Capone*, Coronet, London, 1974.

Koch H. (ed.) *Aspects of the Third Reich*, Macmillan, London, 1985.

Kochan L. *The Making of Modern Russia*, Penguin, Harmondsworth, 1967.

Koestler A. *Darkness at Noon* (trans. D. Hardy), Jonathan Cape, London, 1941.

Krausnick H. and Broszat M. *Anatomy of the SS State*, Paladin, London, 1970.

Kuper L. *Genocide*, Pelican, Harmondsworth, 1981.

Kyemba H. *State of Blood*, Transworld Publishers, London, 1977.

Lane-Fox R. *Alexander the Great*, Futura, London, 1973.

Lapiere R. *A Theory of Social Control*, McGraw-Hill, New York, 1954.

Laqueur W. (ed.) *Fascism*, Penguin, Harmondsworth, 1979.

Latey M. *Tyranny*, Pelican, Harmondsworth, 1972.

Lenski G. *Power and Privilege*, McGraw-Hill, New York, 1966.

Levy R. *The Social Structure of Islam*, CUP, Cambridge, 1971.

Lewis B. *The Arabs in History*, Arrow Books, London, 1958.

Lieuwen E. *Arms and Politics in Latin America*, Praeger, New York, 1960.

Llewellyn A. *The Tyrant from Below*, McDonald & Evans, London, 1957.

Llewellyn B. *China's Courts and Concubines*, Allen & Unwin, London, 1956.

Loewe M. *Everyday Life in Early Imperial China*, Batsford, London, 1968.

Maas P. *The Valachi Papers*, Panther, London, 1970.

Machiavelli N. *The Prince* (trans. L. Ricci), (Revised Edition), OUP, London, 1935.

Mack Smith D. *Mussolini's Roman Empire*, Peregrine, Harmondsworth, 1979.

McNeal R. *Stalin: Man and Ruler*, Macmillan, London, 1989.

Macrae D. Critique of the Oriental Despotism in Man, June 1959.

de Madariaga I. *Catherine the Great*, Yale University Press, New Haven, CT, 1993.

Mallett M. *The Borgias: the Rise and Fall of a Renaissance Dynasty*, Paladin, London, 1969.

Manz B. *The Rise and Rule of Tamburlaine*, CUP, Cambridge, 1989.

Medvedev R. *On Stalin and Stalinism*, OUP, Oxford, 1979.

Mendelssohn K. *The Riddle of the Pyramids*, Thames & Hudson, London, 1974.

Milgram S. *Obedience to Authority*, Harper & Row, New York, 1974.

Mitchell R. *The Society of Muslim Brothers*, OUP, Oxford, 1969.

Mitford N. *The Sun King*, Hamish Hamilton, London, 1966.

Moore B. *Social Origins of Dictatorship and Democracy*, Penguin, Harmondsworth, 1969.

Moorehead A. *The White Nile*, Hamish Hamilton, London, 1962.

Mortimer E. *Faith and Power: the Politics of Islam*, CUP, Cambridge, 1982.

Mousnier R. *Louis XIV*, The Historical Association, London, 1974.

Murdock G. *Africa: its Peoples and their Cultural History*, McGraw-Hill, New York, 1959.

Nicholle D. *The Age of Tamerlane*, Osprey Publishing, London, 1990.

Nilsson M. *Imperial Rome*, Schocken, New York, 1962.

O'Donnell P. *The Berlin Bunker*, Dent, London, 1979.

Oldenbourg Z. *Catherine the Great*, Heinemann, London, 1965.

Oliver R. and Fage J. *A Short History of Africa*, Penguin, Harmondsworth, 1969.

Petrov V. and Petrov E. *Empire of Fear*, Deutsch, London, 1956.

Plaidy J. *A Triptych of Poisoners*, Robert Hale, London, 1958.

Plamenatz J. *Man and Society*, Longmans, London, 1963.

Polybius, *The Rise of the Roman Empire* (trans. I. Scott-Kilvert), Penguin, Harmondsworth, 1979.

Reitlinger G. *The SS – The Alibi of a Nation*, Arms & Armour Press, London, 1986.

Revill J. *World History* (2nd Edition), Longmans, London, 1962.

Ribbens G. *Patterns of Behaviour*, Edward Arnold, London, 1979.

Rodzinski W. *A History of China*, Vols. I & II, OUP, Oxford, 1979/1983.

Rodzinski W. *The Walled Kingdom*, Fontana, London, 1984.

Roscoe J. *The Baganda*, Cass, London, 1965.

Rowe J. Introduction in Ashe R. *Two Kings of Uganda*, Cass, London, 1970.

Sagan E. *Cannibalism: Human Aggression and Cultural Form*, Harper & Row, New York, 1974.

Sagan E. *At the Dawn of Tyranny*, Faber & Faber, London, 1985.

Scarisbrick J. *Henry VIII*, Eyre & Spottiswoode, London, 1968.

Schott I. *Dictators*, Magpie Books, London, 1992.

Seligman C. *Races of Africa* (3rd Edition), OUP, London, 1959.

Service E. *Profiles in Ethnology* (3rd Edition), Harper & Row, New York, 1978.

Short M. *Crime Inc*, Thames-Methuen, London, 1986.

Shorter A. *The Egyptian Gods*, RKP, London, (Reprt.) 1978.

Sigmund P. (ed.), *The Ideologies of Developing Nations*, Praeger, New York, 1967.

Silvert K. *Expectant Peoples: Nationalism and Development*, Random House, New York, 1963.

Sjoberg G. *The Preindustrial City*, Free Press, New York, 1965.

Smith G. *Ghosts of Kampala*, Weidenfeld & Nicolson, London, 1980.

Smith L. B. *Henry VIII: the Mask of Royalty*, Jonathan Cape, London, 1971.

Sondern F. *The Mafia*, Panther, London, 1961.

Spencer A. *Death in Ancient Egypt*, Pelican, Harmondsworth, 1982.

Starkey D. *The Reign of Henry VIII*, George Phillip, London, 1985.

Steindorf G. and Seele K. *When Egypt Ruled the East*, University of Chicago Press, Chicago, 1957.

Stoessinger J. *Why Nations Go to War*, St. Martin's Press, New York, 1993.

Sudic D. *Cult Heroes*, Deutsch, London, 1989.

Suedfeld P. and Rank A. 'Revolutionary Leaders', *Journal of Personality and Social Psychology*, 1976, 34, 169–78.

Suetonius, *The Twelve Caesars* (trans. R. Graves), Penguin, Harmondsworth, 1957.

Sullivan M. *The Arts of China*, Sphere, London, 1973.

Szule T. *Twilight of the Tyrants*, Holt, New York, 1959.

Tacitus, *Annals of Imperial Rome* (trans. M. Grant), Penguin, Harmondsworth, 1959.

Tarn Sir W. and Griffith G. *Hellenistic Civilization* (3rd Edition), Methuen, London, 1952.

Thucydides, *The Peloponnesian War* (trans. M. Grant), Penguin, Harmondsworth, 1972.

Tocqueville Alexis de *The Ancien Regime and the French Revolution* (trans. Stuart Gilbert), Fontana, Glasgow, 1966.

Tomasek R. (ed.) *Latin American Politics*, Anchor Books, New York, 1970.

Tompkins P. *Secrets of the Great Pyramid*, Allen Lane, Harmondsworth, 1973.

Ullman R. 'Human Rights and Economic Power: the United States versus Idi Amin', *Foreign Affairs* 56, April 1978, 529–43.

Wach J. *Sociology of Religion*, Kegan Paul, New York, 1945.

Walbank F. *The Hellenistic World*, Fontana, Glasgow, 1981.

Warmington B. H. *Nero: Reality and Legend*, Chatto & Windus, London, 1981.

Weinreich M. *Hitler's Professors*, Yiddish Scientific Institution, New York, 1946.

Weiss J. *The Fascist Tradition*, Harper & Row, New York, 1967.

Wheaton E. *Prelude to Calamity*, Gollancz, London, 1969.

Wilson J. *The Culture of Ancient Egypt*, University of Chicago Press, Chicago, 1956.

Wittfogel K. *Oriental Despotism*, Yale University Press, New Haven, 1957.

Worsley P. *The Trumpet Shall Sound*, Paladin, London, 1970.

Woodward E. *A History of England*, Methuen, London, 1970.

Wright D. *Revolution and the Terror in France 1789–1795*, Longman, London, 1974.

Wrightsman L. 'The Social Psychology of U.S. Presidential Effectiveness' quoted in Deaux and Wrightsman (1984), q.v., 402–03.

Yong Yap and Cotterell A. *The Early Civilization of China*, Weidenfeld & Nicolson, London, 1975.

Index